PUTIN IN HIS OWN WORDS

Compiled and translated in part by Daniel Sochor, BA
(Russian Studies), JD

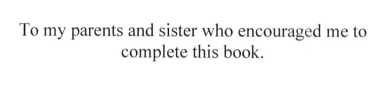

To my parents and sister who encouraged me to complete this book.

CONTENTS

There is always hope when people are forced to listen to both sides; it is when they attend only to one that errors harden into prejudices.

John Stuart Mill, *On Liberty*

Chapter 1

INTERNATIONAL RELATIONS

Of course, it can be a pleasing and even profitable task to portray oneself as the defender of civilisation against the new barbarians. The only thing is that Russia has no intention of attacking anyone. This is all quite absurd. ...

Another mythical and imaginary problem is what I can only call the hysteria the USA has whipped up over supposed Russian meddling in the American presidential election. The United States has plenty of genuinely urgent problems, it would seem, from the colossal public debt to the increase in firearms violence and cases of arbitrary action by the police.

You would think that the election debates would concentrate on these and other unresolved problems, but the elites have nothing with which to reassure society, it seems, and therefore attempt to distract public attention by pointing instead to supposed Russian hackers, spies, agents of influence and so forth. I have to ask myself and ask you too: Does anyone seriously imagine that Russia can somehow influence the American people's choice? America is not some kind of 'banana republic', after all, but is a great power. Do correct me if I am wrong. ...

Friends and colleagues, I would like to have such a propaganda machine here in Russia, but regrettably, this is not the case. We have not even global mass media outlets of the likes of CNN, BBC and others. We simply do not have this kind of capability yet.

As for the claim that the fringe and populists have defeated the sensible, sober and responsible minority – we are not talking about populists or anything like that but about ordinary people, ordinary citizens who are losing trust in the ruling class. That is the problem. By the way, with the political agenda already eviscerated as it is, and with elections ceasing to be an instrument for change but consisting instead of nothing but scandals

and digging up dirt – who gave someone a pinch, who sleeps with whom, if you'll excuse me. This just goes beyond all boundaries.
...

We do not know what Mr Trump would do if he wins, and we do not know what Ms Clinton would do, what would go ahead or not go ahead. Overall then, it does not really matter to us who wins. Of course, we can only welcome public words about a willingness to normalise relations between our two countries. ...

As for Mr Trump, he has chosen his method of reaching voters' hearts. Yes, he behaves extravagantly, of course, we all see this. But I think there is some sense in his actions. I say this because in my view he represents the interests of the sizeable part of American society that is tired of the elites that have been in power for decades now. ...

Meeting of the Valdai International Discussion Club October 27, 2016 Sochi

Bells are tolling for those who have been killed in Aleppo. Bells should also be tolling for those now losing their lives in Mosul and its vicinity. The operation in Mosul is getting underway now. As far as I know, the terrorists have already shot more than 200 people in the hope of stopping the offensive on the town. Let's not forget this. And in Afghanistan? Whole wedding parties of 120 people were wiped out with a single airstrike. A single strike! Have we forgotten this? And what about what's happening in Yemen? Let the bells toll for all of these innocent victims. I agree with you here.

We keep hearing Aleppo, Aleppo, Aleppo. But what is the issue here? Do we leave the nest of terrorists in place there, or do we squeeze them out, doing our best to minimise and avoid civilian casualties? If it is better to not go in at all, then the offensive against Mosul shouldn't go ahead at all either. Let's just leave everything as it is. Let's leave Raqqa alone too. Our partners keep saying, "We need to take back Raqqa and eliminate the nest of terrorists there". But there are civilians in Raqqa too. So, should we not fight the terrorists at all? And when they take hostages in towns, should we just leave them be? Look at Israel's example. Israel never steps back but always fights to the end, and this is how it survives. There is no alternative. We need to fight. If we keep retreating, we will always lose.

Meeting of the Valdai International Discussion Club October 27, 2016 Sochi

It is another terrorist group, Jabhat al-Nusra, that controls the situation in Aleppo. This group was always considered a wing of Al Qaeda and is included in the UN's list of terrorist organisations. What we find particularly depressing and hard to understand is that our partners, especially the Americans, are always finding a way to try to exclude this group from the list of terrorist organisations. Let me tell you why. It seems to us as though our partners are always repeating the same mistake. They want to use these terrorist organisations' and radicals' combat potential to pursue their own political aims, in this case, to combat President Assad and his government, and do not understand that they cannot simply stall them [the rebels] and get them to live by civilised rules after they have tasted victory over someone.

We have reached repeated agreements with the Americans that they will differentiate between Jabhat al-Nusra and its like and the so-called healthy opposition forces, including in Aleppo. They have agreed that this is necessary. What's more, we have even agreed on concrete deadlines, but nothing is done from one month to the next.

We recently reached a ceasefire agreement, a D-day agreement, as our American friends said. I insisted that they first of all resolve the matter of separating Jabhat al-Nusra and other terrorists from the healthy opposition forces and only then declare the ceasefire.

But the Americans insisted that we first need to declare a ceasefire and then they will take care of separating the terrorists from the non-terrorists. Finally, we agreed to make concessions, agreed to their terms, and on September 12 declared a day of silence and cessation of hostilities. On September 16, American aircraft launched a strike against Syrian army forces that killed 80 people.

At this same moment, immediately after the airstrike, ISIS launched an offensive in this very same place. Our American colleagues told us that this airstrike was made by error. This error cost the lives of 80 people and, also just coincidence, perhaps, ISIS took the offensive immediately afterwards. At the same time, lower down the ranks, at the operations level, one of the American military service personnel said quite frankly that they spent several days preparing this strike. How could they make an error if they were several days in preparation? This is how our ceasefire agreement ended up broken. Who broke the agreement? Was it us? No. …

Look, everyone is talking about humanitarian access in Aleppo. Everyone is trying to convince us that we should do this. But they do not need to convince us, because we believe it too, we believe that a humanitarian convoy should be sent there. But how can this be accomplished? There is only one road the convoys can take, with militants on one side of the road and the Syrian army on the other side. We know about the provocation, the attack on one of the convoys, and we know for certain that the attack was delivered by a terrorist group.

We have suggested that the militants and the Syrian army both pull away from the road, providing safe transit for the humanitarian convoys. Everyone agrees, and the idea has even been put on paper, and then nothing happens; none of our partners are doing anything. They either do not want to or cannot pull the militants back, I do not know which.

An exotic proposal has been made – I am going to surprise you and your audience. It has been proposed that our armed units, Russian military personnel, be deployed on the road to ensure transit safety. The Russian military, who are courageous and decisive people, have said they would do it. But I told them that this could only be done jointly with the US, and ordered them to make the proposal. We have proposed this, and they [the Americans] promptly refused. They do not want to deploy their troops there, but they also do not want to pull these opposition groups back, who are really terrorists. What can we do in this situation? ...

We should be busy not with political rhetoric, but with looking for solutions to the situation, including in Syria. What solutions are there? There is only one solution – to convince all parties to the conflict to take the road of political settlement. I reached an agreement with President Assad and he has accepted to take the road of adopting a new constitution and holding elections on the basis of this constitution. But we have not succeeded in convincing anyone else to take this road.

If the people do not vote for President Assad, there will be a democratic change of power, but without the help of armed intervention from outside and under strict international control, under UN supervision. I do not understand who could find this proposal unacceptable. It is a democratic solution to the question of power in the country. We remain optimistic though and hope that we will finish by persuading our colleagues and partners that this is the only possible solution to the problem.

Answers to questions from French journalists from TF1 TV channel October 12, 2016 Kovrov

A while back, about a decade ago, Russia was never mentioned, they said there was nothing to talk about with regard to Russia because it was a third-rate regional power that was of no interest. Today, the number one problem in the entire [US] election campaign is Russia. It is the main talking point. ... We try not to talk about this, but they always whisper this to us in the course of every election campaign ... They keep whispering into our left ear and then into our right ear: Pay no attention to this, all of this will pass and we will be friends again. This is wrong. It is wrong to use Russia as a bargaining chip in internal political struggles and damage interstate relations. ...

What are we witnessing? Some hackers published information about the unseemly conduct of Ms Clinton's campaign headquarters – supporting one candidate for the party nomination at the expense of the other. Hysterical accusations that this is in Russia's interests were made. But there is nothing in Russia's interests there. They freak out about it to distract the attention of the American people from the importance of what was published by the hackers. And the important thing is that public opinion is being manipulated, but nobody talks about it. Everyone is talking about who did it, but is it so important who did it? What is important is the content of this information.

Russia Calling! Investment Forum October 12, 2016 Moscow

The French foreign minister left Moscow for Washington and the following day he and Mr Kerry accused Russia of every sin imaginable; no one talked to us or discussed anything with us, and they threw this resolution at the Security Council, clearly expecting our veto. Why? Not for the resolution to be adopted – they submitted it knowing our position and without even discussing our proposals with us – but for it to be vetoed. Why? To escalate the situation and unleash anti-Russian hysteria in the controlled media, in fact deceiving their people and their citizens. I am referring now not only to France but also to many European countries and the United States. To all appearances, this is especially valuable in the context of an election campaign.

Russia Calling! Investment Forum October 12, 2016 Moscow

As you know, we do not welcome hackers and their actions, but it was thanks to them that we learned that people who took part in the Olympic Games and were outwardly perfectly healthy were actually taking prohibited substances that gave them and give them clear advantages in sports competition.

Meeting with Russia's summer sports Paralympic team September 19, 2016 The Kremlin, Moscow

[Journalist]: If I had to look at the West and to sum up where they think, their side of the argument would be that … you want to expand Russia's zone of influences, in some case geographically, but also the very least to control the countries on your border. And on the moment, the main area of nervousness on that is the Baltics — Estonia, Lithuania, Latvia. You talked about trust, would you be able to say something that would give them reassurance on that count?

Vladimir Putin: Look, I believe that all sensible people who are involved in real politics understand that references to threats posed by Russia to, let us say, the Baltic States are absolute nonsense. Do you think we are going to start a war with NATO? How many people are there in the NATO countries? About 600 million, right? Russia's population is 146 million. Yes, we are the largest nuclear power. But do you really think we are going to use nuclear weapons to take over the Baltics? Nonsense! That's the first thing, but not the most important one.

The most important thing is that we have a vast political experience, and we are convinced that you cannot do anything against the will of the people. Nothing can be done against the will of the people! However, it seems that some of our partners fail to understand this. Thinking of Crimea, they choose not to notice that the will of the Crimean people, 70 percent of which are ethnic Russians and the rest speak Russian as their native language, was to join Russia. They prefer to ignore this. In one place, in Kosovo, the will of the people can be honoured, but here – it cannot. All of this is about political games. ... As for influence, well, we do want Russia to have stronger and more tangible influence, but we want it to be absolutely peaceful and positive. What we have in mind is economic and humanitarian influence, which implies developing equal cooperation with our neighbours.

Interview to Bloomberg September 5, 2016 Vladivostok

Our intelligence services prevented a sabotage and reconnaissance group from the Ukrainian Defence Ministry from infiltrating Crimean territory. ... This attempt to provoke a flare-up of violence and spark a conflict is nothing other than a desire to divert public opinion at home from those who seized power in Kiev and who continue to hold it and to rob their own people in order to remain in power as long as they can and create conditions for continuing to rob their people. This was an act committed using low and base means, and it is a very dangerous game. ...

Those who support the current authorities in Kiev must decide just want they want. Do they want their clients to continue carrying out provocations of this kind, or do they want to genuinely reach a peaceful settlement? If they do want this, and I very much hope they do, it is time to finally take some real steps to put the needed pressure on the current authorities in Kiev.

Joint news conference with President of Armenia Serzh Sargsyan August 10, 2016 The Kremlin, Moscow

The referendum campaign [on whether the United Kingdom should leave the European Union] and subsequent results point to the British Government's self-assuredness and supercilious attitude to life-changing decisions in their own country and Europe in general. It will have global effects. Again, they are inevitable – both positive and negative. Needless to say, everything will settle back to normal in the mid-term. Time will tell whether there will be more pluses or minuses.

It seems to me that ordinary British citizens understand why this happened. First, nobody wants to feed and subsidise weaker economies and support other states and entire nations. This is an obvious fact. Apparently, people are displeased about security, which is being eroded by powerful migration waves. People want to be more independent.

One of the EU leaders – a former leader – told me that the ratio of binding decisions adopted by the European Parliament is higher than that made by the USSR Supreme Soviet in relation to Soviet republics. This means that the concentration of power at the top there is very high. Some like it and want to continue down this road of erasing national borders, whereas others do not like it.

Answers to media questions June 24, 2016 Tashkent

We will work with whoever is elected president. It is regrettable to see that the Russian card gets played the way it does during nearly every US election campaign, and I think that this is very counterproductive, but no matter what the campaign rhetoric, we will look not at the words, but at the deeds of whoever takes office in the White House, and we will look for ways to normalise relations of course, and set our cooperation in the economy and international security back on track.

Meeting with heads of international news agencies June 17, 2016 St Petersburg

If they treat us respectfully, if they seek compromise solutions, the way we do, then we will find a solution that will suit everyone: both ourselves and our partners. Russia should simply be treated as an equal partner. This is the only correct conclusion based on what is happening now.

Direct Line with Vladimir Putin April 14, 2016 Moscow

As for specific individuals, take the United States as an example. First Bush Sr was in power there, later on Bush Jr – all from the same family. Clinton was in power for two terms and now his wife is laying claim to this position, and the family may remain in office. What does this have to do with turnover? As the saying goes, "Husband and wife are a single devil," and they will be at the helm. I am not saying this is all bad. There are pros and cons to it.

Direct Line with Vladimir Putin April 14, 2016 Moscow

How would you comment on Barack Obama's admission that Libya was his biggest mistake?

Vladimir Putin: First, it proves once again that the incumbent US President is a man of integrity. I am not being ironical in the slightest, because it takes courage to make such confessions.

Direct Line with Vladimir Putin April 14, 2016 Moscow

Vladimir Putin: When I saw you coming off your plane today and carrying your belongings, I got a bit upset. On the one hand, this is very egalitarian, but, on the other hand, things must be looking blue in the United States if nobody can help the Secretary of State carry his suitcases. But the economy seems to be doing fine and there are no big cuts. Then I thought that you probably have in this case something that you couldn't trust anyone to carry, something precious, probably money for better bargaining on key issues.

Speaking seriously, we are really glad to see you because – this time I am not joking at all – we usually manage to find some points of contact and, relying on them, move forward towards resolving bilateral and international issues. Welcome!

US Secretary of State John Kerry: Mr President, thank you. When we have a private moment, I'll show you what's in my briefcase. And I think you'll be surprised, pleasantly.

Meeting With US Secretary of State John Kerry March 24, 2016 The Kremlin, Russia

President al-Assad has made many mistakes in the course of the Syrian conflict. However, don't we all realise full well that this conflict would never have escalated to such a degree if it had not been supported from abroad through supplying money, weapons and fighters? Tragically, it is civilians who suffer in such conflicts.

Interview to German newspaper Bild Part 2 January 12, 2016 Sochi

We did everything wrong from the outset. We did not overcome Europe's division: 25 years ago the Berlin Wall fell, but Europe's division was not overcome, invisible walls simply moved to the East. This created the foundation for mutual reproaches, misunderstanding, and crises in the future.

Interview to German newspaper Bild Part 1 January 11, 2016 Sochi

Despite all the attempts (you and your colleagues have been making) to upset our relations using mass media and anti-Russia rhetoric, I believe that you have failed to do this to the extent that you wanted to. Of course, I do not mean you personally. I refer to the media in general, including German ones. In Germany, the media are under a strong foreign influence, first and foremost from the other side of the Atlantic.

Interview to German newspaper Bild Part 1 January 11, 2016 Sochi

If someone is not happy with our stance, they could find a better option than declaring us an enemy every time. Would not it be better to listen to us, to critically reflect on what we say, to agree to something and to look for a common solution?

Interview to German newspaper Bild Part 1 January 11, 2016 Sochi

You asked me if I was a friend or not. The relations between states are a little different from those between individuals. I am no friend, bride, or groom; I am the President of the Russian Federation. That is 146 million people! These people have their own interests, and I must protect those interests. We are ready to do this in a non-confrontational manner, to look for compromise but, of course, based on international law, which must be understood uniformly by all.

Interview to German newspaper Bild Part 1 January 11, 2016 Sochi

Journalist: What do you think of Donald Trump?

Vladimir Putin: He's a very bright person, and talented, without any doubt. But it's not our business to determine his qualities – that's up to the American voters. But we see today that he's the absolute leader in the presidential race. He says that he wants to move to a different level of relations, to a more solid, deeper level of relations with Russia. How can we not welcome this? Of course we welcome this.

Comment following annual news conference December 17, 2015 Moscow

Why are some people who suffer from certain diseases since childhood allowed to take some drugs whereas others who do not suffer from the same diseases since childhood are prohibited from taking them? If an athlete has to take medicines for health reasons, he should take part in Paralympic rather than Olympic sports.

Vladimir Putin's annual news conference December 17, 2015 Moscow

Some time ago, they invaded Iraq and destroyed that country (for good or bad is beside the point). The void set in. Then, elements tied to the oil trading emerged. This situation has been building up over the years. It is a business, a huge trafficking operation run on an industrial scale. Of course, they needed a military force to protect smuggling operations and illegal exports. It is great to be able to cite the Islamic factor and slogans to that effect in order to attract cannon fodder. Instead, the recruits are being manipulated in a game based on economic interests. They started urging people to join this movement. I think that is how ISIS came about. Next, they needed to protect delivery routes. We began attacking their convoys. Now, we can see that they are splitting up with five, six, ten, fifteen trucks hitting the roads after dark. However, another flow, the bulk of the truck fleet, is headed for Iraq, and across Iraq through Iraqi Kurdistan. In one place there – I will ask the Defence Ministry to show this picture – we spotted 11,000 oil trucks. Just think of it – 11,000 oil trucks in one place. Unbelievable.

Vladimir Putin's annual news conference December 17, 2015 Moscow

We did not have such missiles, but now we do – a 1,500-kilometre-range Kalibr sea-based missile and aircraft-carried Kh-101 missile with a 4,500-kilometre range. So why would we need a base there [in Syria]? Should we need to reach somebody, we can do so without a base.

Vladimir Putin's annual news conference December 17, 2015 Moscow

[Question]: As a follow-up to your allegations that there are no Russian servicemen in Donbass, Captain Yerofeyev and Sergeant Alexandrov, Third Brigade, the city of Togliatti, send their regards to you. Are you going to exchange them for Sentsov, Savchenko, Afanasyev, Kolchenko, and Klykh?

Vladimir Putin: Regarding exchanges. We've never said there are no people there who deal with certain matters, including in the military area, but this does not mean that regular Russian troops are present there. Feel the difference.

Vladimir Putin's annual news conference December 17, 2015 Moscow

Today's loss is a result of a stab in the back delivered by terrorists' accomplices. There is no other way I can qualify what happened today. Our aircraft was shot down over Syrian territory by an air-to-air missile launched from a Turkish F-16 plane. It fell on Syrian territory, four kilometres from the Turkish border. ... We have long been recording the movement of a large amount of oil and petroleum products to Turkey from ISIS-occupied territories. This explains the significant funding the terrorists are receiving. Now they are stabbing us in the back by hitting our planes that are fighting terrorism.

Meeting with King Abdullah II of Jordan November 24, 2015 Sochi

They tell us, "You're hitting the wrong targets!" Then we say, "Tell us where we should strike, give us the targets!" But they don't give them to us. "Then tell us where we shouldn't hit." And they don't tell us that, either. How, then, can we be criticized?

You know, I don't want to sneer at this. Strangely enough, they have their own reasons for it. And one of them, I will tell you point blank, is that they are afraid to give us a list of territories not to strike, because they fear that this is exactly where we will strike, that we will deceive them. It seems they judge us based on their own notions of decency.

But I can confirm that right now (on the battlefield so to speak), we have established contacts with some (not all of course) of the uncompromising, even armed Syrian opposition groups; they themselves asked us not to strike the territories they control. We have reached these agreements and are fulfilling them.

Moreover, this part of the armed opposition believes that it is possible to begin active operations against terrorist organisations – against ISIS first of all – with our support from the air. And we are prepared to provide that support. If this happens, it will mean that President al-Assad's army on one side and the armed opposition on the other are fighting their common enemy. It seems to me that this can become a good foundation for subsequent work and a platform for political settlement.

Responses to journalists' questions following the G20 summit. November 16, 2015 Antalya

They assured us that the anti-missile defence system and its European segment were designed to defend against Iranian ballistic missiles. However, we know that the Iranian nuclear issue has been resolved, with appropriate agreements signed. Moreover, corresponding parliaments have already approved them, but work on the anti-missile defence system continues.

Therefore, references to the Iranian and North Korean nuclear missile threats are a cover-up for their true intentions, which are actually directed at neutralising the strategic nuclear potential of other nuclear states, apart from the United States and their allies, primarily that of Russia, of course, and at obtaining a decisive military supremacy with all the ensuing consequences.

We have said repeatedly that Russia would take the necessary reciprocal measures to strengthen its nuclear potential. We will also work on anti-missile defence systems as well, but at the first stage, as we have repeatedly said, we will focus also on offensive systems capable of overcoming any anti-missile defence systems.

Meeting on Armed Forces development November 10, 2015 Sochi

If one country thinks that it has created a missile defence shield that will protect it from any strikes or counter-strikes, it has its hands free to use whatever types of weapons it likes, and it is this that upsets the strategic balance.

Meeting of the Valdai International Discussion Club October 22, 2015 Sochi

We should not break down the terrorists into moderate and immoderate ones. It would be good to know the difference. Probably, in the opinion of certain experts, it is that the so-called moderate militants behead people in limited numbers or in some delicate fashion. …

Fifty years ago, I learnt one rule in the streets of Leningrad: if the fight is inevitable, be the first to strike. And I assure you, the threat of terrorist strikes against Russia has not become greater or less due to our actions in Syria. ... It is better for us to fight them there, as I already said, rather than await them here.

Meeting of the Valdai International Discussion Club October 22, 2015 Sochi

If we fear that the terrorists will do something, they will definitely do it. We must take pre-emptive action. Of course, there are risks, but let me say that these risks existed anyway, even before we began our operations in Syria. If we just stood by and let Syria get gobbled up, thousands of people running around there now with

Kalashnikovs would end up on our territory, and so we are helping President Assad fight this threat before it reaches our borders. ...

It's a well-known fact that the Americans have shut down the programme to train the Free Syrian Army. They started out with plans to train 12,000 people, then said they would train 6,000, and then they trained only 60 people, and it turned out in the end that only 4–5 people are actually out there fighting ISIS. They spent $500 million on this. They would have done better to give $500 million to us, and we would have put it to better use in terms of fighting international terrorism, that's for sure.

Interview to Vladimir Solovyov October 12, 2015 Sochi

We will start with an issue that will likely be the subject of much discussion today, namely, my request to the Federation Council on using Russia's Armed Forces beyond our country's borders. The Federation Council has examined this request and approved it.

Syria is the issue here. The only real way to fight international terrorism (and international terrorist groups are creating chaos in Syria and the territory of neighbouring countries right now) is to take the initiative and fight and destroy the terrorists in the territory that they have already captured rather than waiting for them to arrive on our soil.

We all know that thousands of people from European countries, Russia, and the post-Soviet region have joined the ranks of the so-called Islamic State, a terrorist organisation that – I want to stress again – has nothing to do with genuine Islam. There is no need to be an expert to realise that if they succeed in Syria, they will inevitably return to their own countries, and this includes Russia. ...

We have informed all of our partners about Russia's plans and actions in Syria. Let me repeat: Russia's involvement in the anti-terrorist operations in Syria is in accordance with international law and based on the official request from the President of the Syrian Arab Republic.

Meeting with Government members   September 30, 2015 Novo-Ogaryovo, Moscow Region

What do you like most about America?

Vladimir Putin: America's creative approach to solving the problems the country is faced with, its openness and open-mindedness which make it possible to unleash the potential of the people. I believe that largely due to these qualities America has made such tremendous strides in its development.

Interview to American TV channel CBS and PBS September 29, 2015 Novo-Ogaryovo, Moscow Region

There is no other way to settle the Syrian conflict other than by strengthening the existing legitimate government agencies, support them in their fight against terrorism and, of course, at the same time encourage them to start a positive dialogue with the "healthy" part of the opposition and launch political transformations.

Interview to American TV channel CBS and PBS September 29, 2015 Novo-Ogaryovo, Moscow Region

The 70th anniversary of the United Nations is a good occasion to both take stock of history and talk about our common future. In 1945, the countries that defeated Nazism joined their efforts to lay a solid foundation for the postwar world order. Let me remind you that key decisions on the principles defining interaction between states, as well as the decision to establish the UN, were made in our country, at the Yalta Conference of the leaders of the anti-Hitler coalition. ...

We should all remember the lessons of the past. For example, we remember examples from our Soviet past, when the Soviet Union exported social experiments, pushing for changes in other countries for ideological reasons, and this often led to tragic consequences and caused degradation instead of progress.

It seems, however, that instead of learning from other people's mistakes, some prefer to repeat them and continue to export revolutions, only now these are "democratic" revolutions. Just look at the situation in the Middle East and Northern Africa already mentioned by the previous speaker. Of course, political and social problems have been piling up for a long time in this region, and people there wanted change. But what was the actual outcome? Instead of bringing about reforms, aggressive intervention rashly destroyed government institutions and the local way of life. Instead of democracy and progress, there is now violence, poverty, social disasters and total disregard for human rights, including even the right to life.

I'm urged to ask those who created this situation: do you at least realize now what you've done? But I'm afraid that this question will remain unanswered, because they have never abandoned their policy, which is based on arrogance, exceptionalism and impunity.

A power vacuum in some countries in the Middle East and Northern Africa obviously resulted in the emergence of areas of anarchy, which were quickly filled with extremists and terrorists. The so-called Islamic State has tens of thousands of militants fighting for it, including former Iraqi soldiers who were left on the street after the 2003 invasion. Many recruits come from Libya whose statehood was destroyed as a result of a gross violation of UN Security Council Resolution 1973. And now radical groups are joined by members of the so-called "moderate" Syrian opposition backed by the West. They get weapons and training, and then they defect and join the so-called Islamic State. ...

Gentlemen, the people you are dealing with are cruel but they are not dumb. They are as smart as you are. So, it's a big question: who's playing whom here? The recent incident where the most "moderate" opposition group handed over their weapons to terrorists is a vivid example of that.

We consider that any attempts to flirt with terrorists, let alone arm them, are short-sighted and extremely dangerous. This may make the global terrorist threat much worse, spreading it to new regions around the globe, especially since there are fighters from many different countries, including European ones, gaining combat experience with Islamic State. Unfortunately, Russia is no exception.

Now that those thugs have tasted blood, we can't allow them to return home and continue with their criminal activities. Nobody wants that, right?

Russia has consistently opposed terrorism in all its forms. Today, we provide military-technical assistance to Iraq, Syria and other regional countries fighting terrorist groups. We think it's a big mistake to refuse to cooperate with the Syrian authorities and government forces who valiantly fight terrorists on the ground.

We should finally admit that President Assad's government forces and the Kurdish militia are the only forces really fighting terrorists in Syria. Yes, we are aware of all the problems and conflicts in the region, but we definitely have to consider the actual situation on the ground. ...

What we actually propose is to be guided by common values and common interests rather than by ambitions. Relying on international law, we must join efforts to address the problems that all of us are facing, and create a genuinely broad international coalition against terrorism. Similar to the anti-Hitler coalition, it could unite a broad range of parties willing to stand firm against those who, just like the Nazis, sow evil and hatred of humankind. And of course, Muslim nations should play a key role in such a coalition, since Islamic State not only poses a direct threat to them, but also tarnishes one of the greatest world religions with its atrocities.

70th session of the UN General Assembly September 28, 2015 New York

We never forget that many people from the former Soviet Union live in Israel. This gives the relations between our countries an extra dimension.

Meeting with Prime Minister of Israel Benjamin Netanyahu September 21, 2015 Novo-Ogaryovo, Moscow Region

You know, I hear this all the time: Russia wants to be respected. Don't you? Who does not? Who wants to be humiliated? It is a strange question. As if this is some exclusive right – Russia demands respect. Does anyone like to be neglected? It is actually not about respect or the absence thereof – we want to ensure our interests without in any way harming our partners. However, we are counting on a constructive, direct and substantive dialogue. When we see an absence of dialogue or an absence of desire to talk to us, this naturally causes a certain response.

Plenary session of the 19th St Petersburg International Economic Forum June 19, 2015 St Petersburg

Our position is based on the fear that Syria could descend into the same kind of situation as what we see in Libya or in Iraq. You know, after all, that before the state authorities and Saddam Hussein himself were destroyed, there were no terrorists in Iraq. Let's not forget this. People prefer not to talk about this today, but is it really so hard to see who created the conditions for terrorism to flare up in these places? After Iraq was invaded, the old authorities were all sent fleeing or were destroyed, and Saddam was hanged. And then we ended up with the Islamic State.

Look at what is happening in Libya. It has ceased to exist as a state and is in the process of total disintegration. Even US diplomats have suffered losses there. We know the tragic events that took place there. The main issue, as we see it, is that we do not want to see Syria take this same road. This is our main motivation for supporting President Assad and his government. We think this is the right position. It would be difficult to expect us to take any other line. Moreover, I think that many would agree with our position on this issue.

I mentioned Iraq several times. We know what is going on there. The United States supports Iraq, supports, arms and trains the Iraqi army. In two or three attacks, the Islamic State captured so many weapons, more than the Iraqi army probably even has. This includes armoured vehicles and missiles, though the general public is poorly informed about all of this. This was all just recently. The Islamic State is now better armed than the Iraqi army. And this has all happened with the United States' support.

The United States supposedly withdrew from Iraq, but our special services and the information we receive from Iraq itself indicate that thousands of US service personnel are still in Iraq. The results are deplorable and tragic.

We do not want all of this to repeat itself in Syria. We call on our partners in the United States and Europe, but above all in the United States, of course, to make greater efforts to fight this absolute evil that is fundamentalism, the Islamic State and similar groups that essentially all have their roots in the well-known global terrorist organisations that have already launched repeated attacks against the United States itself. Our call is for political settlement, which should, of course, guarantee the regime's transformation, and we are ready to discuss this matter with President Assad too.

The UN just recently declared the importance of working together with President Assad to fight the Islamic State and other terrorist groups. We are ready to work with the [Syrian] President to ensure that the political transformation process can go ahead so that all people in Syria feel that they have access to the instruments of power, and in order to put an end to this armed confrontation. But we cannot achieve this from outside and through the use of force. This is the real issue.

Plenary session of the 19th St Petersburg International Economic Forum June 19, 2015 St Petersburg

For a long time, you could say for decades, we had been calmly and quietly proposing various elements of cooperation, but we were constantly pushed back until we reached a line we cannot cross.

Plenary session of the 19th St Petersburg International Economic Forum June 19, 2015 St Petersburg

US military spending is higher than that of all countries in the world taken together. The aggregate military spending of NATO countries is 10 times, note – 10 times higher than that of the Russian Federation. Russia has virtually no bases abroad. ... I invite you to publish the world map in your newspaper and to mark all the US military bases on it. You will see the difference. ... I think that only an insane person and only in a dream can imagine that Russia would suddenly attack NATO. I think some countries are simply taking advantage of people's fears with regard to Russia. They just want to play the role of front-line countries that should receive some supplementary military, economic, financial or some other aid.

Interview to the Italian newspaper Il Corriere della Sera June 6, 2015

It is time to begin implementing the Minsk Agreements. Specifically, there needs to be a constitutional reform to ensure the autonomous rights of the unrecognised republics. The Kiev authorities do not want to call it autonomy, they prefer different terms, such as decentralisation. Our European partners, those very partners who wrote the corresponding clause in the Minsk Agreements, explained what should be understood as decentralisation. It gives them the right to speak their language, to have their own cultural identity and engage in cross-border trade – nothing special, nothing beyond the civilised understanding of ethnic minorities' rights in any European country. ... And if somebody wants these territories to remain part of Ukraine, they should prove to those people that their lives would be better, more comfortable and safer within a unified state; that they would be able to provide for themselves and ensure their children's future within this state. But it is impossible to convince these people by means of weapons. These issues, issues of this kind can only be resolved by peaceful means.

Interview to the Italian newspaper Il Corriere della Sera June 6, 2015

It was not Russia who soured these relations. We have always advocated maintaining normal relations with all states, both in the East and in the West. The main condition for restoring normal relations is respect for Russia and its interests.

Direct Line with Vladimir Putin April 16, 2015

The world is moving along the integration path, including Latin America and North America – Canada, the United States and Mexico – as well as Europe. And this process is under way in Asia as well. Yet we are being accused of trying to revive the empire.

Direct Line with Vladimir Putin April 16, 2015

Superpowers that have laid claim to exceptionalism and see themselves as the only centre of power in the world do not need allies. What they need are vassals.

Direct Line with Vladimir Putin April 16, 2015

After World War II, we tried to impose our own development model on many Eastern European countries, and we did so by force. This has to be admitted. There is nothing good about this and we are feeling the consequences now. Incidentally, this is more or less what the Americans are doing today, as they try to impose their model on practically the entire world, and they will fail as well.

Direct Line with Vladimir Putin April 16, 2015

[On Ukraine] What happened? People simply got sick and tired of poverty, stealing and the impudence of the authorities, their relentless greed and corruption, from oligarchs who climbed to power.

Direct Line with Vladimir Putin April 16, 2015

As for how long we will have to endure the sanctions, I would put the question differently. This should not be about enduring anything – we must benefit from the situation with the sanctions to reach new development frontiers. Otherwise we probably would not have done it. This goes for import substitution policies, which we are now forced to implement. We will move in this direction, and I hope that these efforts will foster the development of the high-tech sectors of the economy with higher growth rates than previously seen.

Direct Line with Vladimir Putin April 16, 2015

Crimea has always been and remains Russian, as well as Ukrainian, Crimean-Tatar, Greek (after all, there are Greeks living there) and German – and it will be home to all those peoples. As for state affiliation, the people living in Crimea made their choice; it should be treated with respect, and Russia cannot do otherwise.

Interview with VGTRK February 23, 2015 The Kremlin, Moscow

I do not want to give any advice, but still – the current leadership of a large European nation such as Ukraine should first return the country to normal life: fix the economy, the social sector, its relations with the southeast region of the country in a civilised manner, and ensure the lawful rights and interests of the people living in Donbass. If the Minsk agreements are implemented, I am certain this will be done.

Interview with VGTRK February 23, 2015 The Kremlin, Moscow

Clearly, no one has ever succeeded in scaring, suppressing or isolating Russia and never will. Such attempts have been made regularly, over the centuries, as I have said publicly on numerous occasions, and in the 20th century it happened several times: in the 1920s, the 1940s and later. It did not work then and it will not work now. Meanwhile, we have to be prepared to experience certain difficulties and always rebuff any threats to our sovereignty, stability and the unity of our society.

Gala reception marking Security Agency Worker's Day   December 20, 2014
The Kremlin, Moscow

Russia will always act consistently to protect its interests and sovereignty and will strive to strengthen international stability and support equal security for all countries and peoples. At the same time, the situation in the world around us is not becoming any simpler. You all know about the USA's plans to build a missile defence system. NATO has stepped up its activity too, including in Europe, especially in Eastern Europe. In this respect, I want to say that our military doctrine nevertheless remains unchanged and is exclusively defensive in nature, as you know. But we will defend our country's security firmly and consistently.

Speaking this year and before this audience, I have to say a few words about the events in Crimea of course. I want to thank once again the heads of our Armed Forces and all of the personnel involved for their precise, restrained, and carefully weighed action and for their courage and professionalism during the events there. You assuredly protected Crimea's residents from great tragedy, from bloodshed and humanitarian disaster, and made it possible for them to express their free will as citizens in the referendum that took place.

Expanded meeting of the Defence Ministry Board   December 19, 2014
Moscow

Together with the qualitative development of the armed forces, it is also becoming more prestigious to serve in the army. This year, there are six people competing for every one place in some of the

Defence Ministry academies. The number of contract servicemen has increased by more than 75,000 people. There is now real competition for the right to serve on contract in the armed forces as privates and sergeants. Most of the people applying are well-trained and motivated. More than two thirds of contract servicemen in 2014 have higher or vocational education.

Expanded meeting of the Defence Ministry Board   December 19, 2014 Moscow

Didn't they tell us after the fall of the Berlin Wall that NATO would not expand eastwards? However, the expansion started immediately. There were two waves of expansion. Is that not a wall? True, it is a virtual wall, but it was coming up. What about the anti-missile defence system next to our borders? Is that not a wall?

You see, nobody has ever stopped. This is the main issue of current international relations. Our partners never stopped. They decided they were the winners, they were an empire, while all the others were their vassals, and they needed to put the squeeze on them. I said the same in my Address [to the Federal Assembly]. This is the problem. They never stopped building walls, despite all our attempts at working together without any dividing lines in Europe and the world at large.

I believe that our tough stand on certain critical situations, including that in the Ukraine, should send a message to our partners that the best thing to do is to stop building walls and to start building a common humanitarian space of security and economic freedom.

News conference of Vladimir Putin December 18, 2014 Moscow

All those who are following their heart and are fulfilling their duty by voluntarily taking part in hostilities, including in southeast Ukraine, are not mercenaries, since they are not paid for what they do.

News conference of Vladimir Putin December 18, 2014 Moscow

Mr President, are the current economic developments the price we have to pay for Crimea? Maybe the time has come to acknowledge it?

Vladimir Putin: No. This is not the price we have to pay for Crimea... This is actually the price we have to pay for our natural aspiration to preserve ourselves as a nation, as a civilisation, as a state. And here is why. ... After the fall of the Berlin Wall and the breakup of the Soviet Union, Russia opened itself to our partners. What did we see? A direct and fully-fledged support of terrorism in North Caucasus. They directly supported terrorism, you understand? Is that what partners usually do? ...

Sometimes I think that maybe it would be best if our bear just sat still. Maybe he should stop chasing pigs and boars around the taiga and start picking berries and eating honey. Maybe then he will be left alone. But no, he won't be! Because someone will always try to chain him up. As soon as he's chained they will tear out his teeth and claws. In this analogy, I am referring to the power of nuclear deterrence. As soon as – God forbid – it happens and they no longer need the bear, the taiga will be taken over.

We have heard it even from high-level officials that it is unfair that the whole of Siberia with its immense resources belongs to Russia in its entirety. Why exactly is it unfair? So it is fair to snatch Texas from Mexico but it is unfair that we are working on our own land – no, we have to share. And then, when all the teeth and claws are torn out, the bear will be of no use at all. Perhaps they'll stuff it and that's all.

So, it is not about Crimea but about us protecting our independence, our sovereignty and our right to exist. That is what we should all realise.

News conference of Vladimir Putin December 18, 2014 Moscow

You may be aware of the agreement between the opposition and the Ukrainian government of 21 February. The agreement was signed by the three foreign ministers of Germany, Poland and France as guarantors of the agreement. Do you follow me? We had talks with the leaders of the United States, who kept telling us, "Yanukovych should not use force no matter what." He didn't and what he got was a coup.

We are now being told, "What could we do? The situation got out of control, which is called an excessive act in criminal law." I beg to differ. If that's an excessive act, then what were you supposed to say, even if you weren't able to stop these radicals who broke into the presidential administration and took over the Government building? You should have told them as follows, "We do want to see you in Europe, we do want you to sign and ratify the association agreement, you are indeed part of the European family, but if you act this way, you will never be part of Europe, and we will never support you. Go back to the agreement of 21 February, form a national unity government and start working together." I'm sure that if that was their position, there would be no civil war in Ukraine with its many casualties.

News conference of Vladimir Putin December 18, 2014 Moscow

You said that Russia, to a certain extent, contributed to the tension that we are now seeing in the world. Russia did contribute but only insofar as it is more and more firmly protecting its national interests. We are not attacking in the political sense of the word. We are not attacking anyone. We are only protecting our interests. Our Western partners – and especially our US partners – are displeased with us for doing exactly that, not because we are allowing security-related activity that provokes tension.

Let me explain. You are talking about our aircraft, including strategic aviation operations. Do you know that in the early 1990s, Russia completely stopped strategic aviation flights in remote surveillance areas as the Soviet Union previously did? We completely stopped, while flights of US strategic aircraft carrying nuclear weapons continued. Why? Against whom? Who was threatened? So we didn't make flights for many years and only a couple of years ago we resumed them. So are we really the ones doing the provoking?

So, in fact, we only have two bases outside Russia, and both are in areas where terrorist activity is high. One is in Kyrgyzstan, and was deployed there upon request of the Kyrgyz authorities, President Akayev, after it was raided by Afghan militants. The other is in Tajikistan, which also borders on Afghanistan. I would guess you are interested in peace and stability there too. Our presence is justified and clearly understandable. Now, US bases are scattered around the globe – and you're telling me Russia is behaving aggressively? Do you have any common sense at all? What are US armed forces doing in Europe, also with tactical nuclear weapons? What are they doing there?

Listen, Russia has increased its military spending for 2015, if I am not mistaken, it is around 50 billion in dollar equivalent. The Pentagon's budget is ten times that amount, $575 billion, I think, as recently approved by Congress. And you're telling me we are pursuing an aggressive policy? Is there any common sense in this?

Are we moving our forces to the borders of the United States or other countries? Who is moving NATO bases and other military infrastructure towards us? We aren't. Is anyone listening to us? Is anyone engaging in some dialogue with us about it? No. No dialogue at all. All we hear is "that's none of your business. Every country has the right to choose its way to ensure its own security." All right, but we have the right to do so too. Why can't we?

Finally, the ABM system – something I mentioned in my Address to the Federal Assembly. Who was it that withdrew unilaterally from the ABM Treaty, one of the cornerstones of the global security system? Was it Russia? No, it wasn't. The United States did this, unilaterally. They are creating threats for us, they are deploying their strategic missile defence components not just in Alaska, but in Europe as well – in Romania and Poland, very close to us. And you're telling me we are pursuing an aggressive policy?

News conference of Vladimir Putin December 18, 2014 Moscow

Mr Putin, you were recently in Turkey on an official visit... But it's odd: after you left, European bureaucrats rushed off to Turkey... By all appearances, they wanted to convince Turkey to join the sanctions against Russia. Could you comment on this?

Vladimir Putin: ... I had no doubt about this. While on a visit there, I told Mr Erdogan: "Perhaps we'd better not say certain things in public right now. Why tease the geese? They'll come rushing in tomorrow."

News conference of Vladimir Putin December 18, 2014 Moscow

Regarding this idea that Russia is coming under pressure from all sides, you are exaggerating somewhat there. No one is pressuring us, they are trying to, yes, but not from all sides. Their arms are not long enough to reach us from all sides even if they'd like to. It's true though what Alexander Solzhenitsyn said, I cannot remember his exact words, but he said it was time to stand up for Russia because otherwise they'd squeeze us out once and for all. That was roughly what he said. Of course we, like anyone who considers themselves a Russian and a patriot, must take an objective look at what is happening out there and choose the appropriate response, or at the very least formulate our own position on the situation. That is for sure.

Meeting with members of the Council for Civil Society and Human Rights and federal and regional human rights commissioners December 5, 2014 The Kremlin, Moscow

The policy of containment was not invented yesterday. It has been carried out against our country for many years, always, for decades, if not centuries. In short, whenever someone thinks that Russia has become too strong or independent, these tools are quickly put into use. However, talking to Russia from a position of force is an exercise in futility, even when it was faced with domestic hardships, as in the 1990s and early 2000s. ...

Despite our unprecedented openness back then and our willingness to cooperate in all, even the most sensitive issues, despite the fact that we considered – and all of you are aware of this and remember it – our former adversaries as close friends and even allies, the support for separatism in Russia from across the pond, including information, political and financial support and support provided by the special services – was absolutely obvious and left no doubt that they would gladly let Russia follow the Yugoslav scenario of disintegration and dismemberment, with all the tragic fallout for the people of Russia. It didn't work. We didn't allow that to happen. Just as it did not work for Hitler with his people-hating ideas, who set out to destroy Russia and push us back beyond the Urals. Everyone should remember how it ended.

Presidential Address to the Federal Assembly December 4, 2014 The Kremlin, Moscow

Since 2002, after the US unilaterally pulled out of the ABM Treaty, which was absolutely a cornerstone of international security, a strategic balance of forces and stability, the US has been working relentlessly to create a global missile defence system, including in Europe. This poses a threat not only to Russia, but to the world as a whole – precisely due to the possible disruption of this strategic balance of forces.

I believe that this is bad for the US as well, because it creates the dangerous illusion of invulnerability. It strengthens the striving for unilateral, often, as we can see, ill-considered decisions and additional risks. ... We have no intention of becoming involved in a costly arms race, but at the same time we will reliably and dependably guarantee our country's defence under the new conditions. There are absolutely no doubts about this.

Presidential Address to the Federal Assembly December 4, 2014 The Kremlin, Moscow

Take a look at our millennium-long history. As soon as we rise, some other nations immediately feel the urge to push Russia aside, to put it "where it belongs," to slow it down. How old is the theory of deterrence? We tend to think it dates back to the Soviet era though it is centuries old. But we shouldn't fan any passions over it on our side because that is how the world functions. It is a battle for geopolitical interests and, consequently, for the nation's significance, as well as the ability to generate a new economy, to resolve social problems, and to improve living standards. ... The US achieved a certain position after World War II. Why do I say this? The struggle for geopolitical interests leads to the situation when a country either becomes stronger, resolving its financial, defence, economic and subsequently social issues more effectively, or slides into the category of third- or fifth-rate countries, losing the possibility of safeguarding the interests of its people.

Interview to TASS News Agency November 24, 2014

Vladimir Putin: Shale gas production is becoming unprofitable. Perhaps, the Saudis especially want to 'kill' their rivals...

Andrei Vandenko: But would it be better for us, if a neighbour's horse died?

Vladimir Putin: It depends on the neighbour, his horse and how he used it.

Interview to TASS News Agency November 24, 2014

Andrei Vandenko: Have you gauged them this time? The consequences of the actions taken on Crimea and what will follow.

Vladimir Putin: Yes. It was a strategic decision.

Andrei Vandenko: Good. All is well that ends well.

Vladimir Putin: You are quite right. I believe it will be precisely this way. Because we are stronger.

Andrei Vandenko: Stronger than whom?

Vladimir Putin: Everybody. Because we are right. The strength is in the truth. When a Russian feels he is right, he is invincible. I am saying this with absolute sincerity, not for the sake of just saying. If we knew we had done something bad and were unfair, then everything would be hanging by a thread. When you lack the inner certainty that what you do is right, this always causes some inner hesitations, and these are dangerous. In this particular case I have none.

Interview to TASS News Agency November 24, 2014

It is very clear that what we are dealing with here are the geopolitical interests of a particular country or group of countries. It is a big question even whether the interests of these countries' elites are in keeping with those of their peoples. I have often debated these issues with my colleagues and we will yet discuss them further. In the end, just as the market sets national currencies' exchange rates, I am sure that life will organise everything in normal fashion and we will certainly move on. No one wants to raise the level of tension in the world, believe me. No one in the USA needs this either, not the general public anyway, the ordinary people, and so everything will sort itself out in the end.

I think that more people here like America and Americans than dislike them. But the majority of our people take a negative view of the US establishment's policies. No one can deny though that America is a great power, a powerful country, and the Americans are a talented and successful people. There is plenty that we can learn from them.

Russian Popular Front's Action Forum November 18, 2014 Moscow

The world is full of contradictions today. We need to be frank in asking each other if we have a reliable safety net in place. Sadly, there is no guarantee and no certainty that the current system of global and regional security is able to protect us from upheavals. This system has become seriously weakened, fragmented and deformed. The international and regional political, economic, and cultural cooperation organisations are also going through difficult times.

Yes, many of the mechanisms we have for ensuring the world order were created quite a long time ago now, including and above all in the period immediately following World War II. Let me stress that the solidity of the system created back then rested not only on the balance of power and the rights of the victor countries, but on the fact that this system's 'founding fathers' had respect for each other, did not try to put the squeeze on others, but attempted to reach agreements. The main thing is that this system needs to develop, and despite its various shortcomings, needs to at least be capable of keeping the world's current problems within certain limits and of regulating the intensity of the natural competition between countries.

It is my conviction that we could not take this mechanism of checks and balances that we built over the last decades, sometimes with such effort and difficulty, and simply tear it apart without building anything in its place. Otherwise we would be left with no instruments other than brute force. What we needed to do was to carry out a rational reconstruction and adapt it to the new realities in the system of international relations. But the United States, having declared itself the winner of the Cold War, saw no need for this. Instead of establishing a new balance of power, essential for maintaining order and stability, they took steps that threw the system into sharp and deep imbalance.

The Cold War ended, but it did not end with the signing of a peace treaty with clear and transparent agreements on respecting existing rules or creating new rules and standards. This created the impression that the so-called 'victors' in the Cold War had decided to pressure events and reshape the world to suit their own needs and interests. If the existing system of international relations, international law and the checks and balances in place got in the way of these aims, this system was declared worthless, outdated and in need of immediate demolition. Pardon the analogy, but this is the way nouveaux riche behave when they suddenly end up with a great fortune, in this case, in the shape of world leadership and domination. Instead of managing their wealth wisely, for their own benefit too of course, I think they have committed many follies.

We have entered a period of differing interpretations and deliberate silences in world politics. International law has been forced to retreat over and over by the onslaught of legal nihilism. Objectivity and justice have been sacrificed on the altar of political expediency. Arbitrary interpretations and biased assessments have replaced legal norms. At the same time, total control of the global mass media has made it possible when desired to portray white as black and black as white.

In a situation where you had domination by one country and its allies, or its satellites rather, the search for global solutions often turned into an attempt to impose their own universal recipes. This group's ambitions grew so big that they started presenting the policies they put together in their corridors of power as the view of the entire international community. But this is not the case. The very notion of 'national sovereignty' became a relative value for most countries. In essence, what was being proposed was the formula: the greater the loyalty towards the world's sole power centre, the greater this or that ruling regime's legitimacy. ...

The measures taken against those who refuse to submit are well-known and have been tried and tested many times. They include use of force, economic and propaganda pressure, meddling in domestic affairs, and appeals to a kind of 'supra-legal' legitimacy when they need to justify illegal intervention in this or that conflict or toppling inconvenient regimes. Of late, we have increasing evidence too that outright blackmail has been used with regard to a number of leaders. It is not for nothing that 'big brother' is spending billions of dollars on keeping the whole world, including its own closest allies, under surveillance.

Let's ask ourselves, how comfortable are we with this, how safe are we, how happy living in this world, and how fair and rational has it become? Maybe, we have no real reasons to worry, argue and ask awkward questions? Maybe the United States' exceptional position and the way they are carrying out their leadership really is a blessing for us all, and their meddling in events all around the world is bringing peace, prosperity, progress, growth and democracy, and we should maybe just relax and enjoy it all? Let me say that this is not the case, absolutely not the case.

A unilateral diktat and imposing one's own models produces the opposite result. Instead of settling conflicts it leads to their escalation, instead of sovereign and stable states we see the growing spread of chaos, and instead of democracy there is support for a very dubious public ranging from open neo-fascists to Islamic radicals.

Why do they support such people? They do this because they decide to use them as instruments along the way in achieving their goals but then burn their fingers and recoil. I never cease to be amazed by the way that our partners just keep stepping on the same rake, as we say here in Russia, that is to say, make the same mistake over and over.

They once sponsored Islamic extremist movements to fight the Soviet Union. Those groups got their battle experience in Afghanistan and later gave birth to the Taliban and Al-Qaeda. The West if not supported, at least closed its eyes, and, I would say, gave information, political and financial support to international terrorists' invasion of Russia (we have not forgotten this) and the Central Asian region's countries. Only after horrific terrorist attacks were committed on US soil itself did the United States wake up to the common threat of terrorism. Let me remind you that we were the first country to support the American people back then, the first to react as friends and partners to the terrible tragedy of September 11.

During my conversations with American and European leaders, I always spoke of the need to fight terrorism together, as a challenge on a global scale. We cannot resign ourselves to and accept this threat, cannot cut it into separate pieces using double standards. Our partners expressed agreement, but a little time passed and we ended up back where we started. First there was the military operation in Iraq, then in Libya, which got pushed to the brink of falling apart. Why was Libya pushed into this situation? Today it is a country in danger of breaking apart and has become a training ground for terrorists.

Only the current Egyptian leadership's determination and wisdom saved this key Arab country from chaos and having extremists run rampant. In Syria, as in the past, the United States and its allies started directly financing and arming rebels and allowing them to fill their ranks with mercenaries from various countries. Let me ask where do these rebels get their money, arms and military specialists? Where does all this come from? How did the notorious ISIL manage to become such a powerful group, essentially a real armed force?

As for financing sources, today, the money is coming not just from drugs, production of which has increased not just by a few percentage points but many-fold, since the international coalition forces have been present in Afghanistan. You are aware of this. The terrorists are getting money from selling oil too. Oil is produced in territory controlled by the terrorists, who sell it at dumping prices, produce it and transport it. But someone buys this oil, resells it, and makes a profit from it, not thinking about the fact that they are thus financing terrorists who could come sooner or later to their own soil and sow destruction in their own countries.

Where do they get new recruits? In Iraq, after Saddam Hussein was toppled, the state's institutions, including the army, were left in ruins. We said back then, be very, very careful. You are driving people out into the street, and what will they do there? Don't forget (rightly or not) that they were in the leadership of a large regional power, and what are you now turning them into?

What was the result? Tens of thousands of soldiers, officers and former Baath Party activists were turned out into the streets and today have joined the rebels' ranks. Perhaps this is what explains why the Islamic State group has turned out to be so effective? In military terms, it is acting very effectively and has some very professional people. Russia warned repeatedly about the dangers of unilateral military actions, intervening in sovereign states' affairs, and flirting with extremists and radicals. We insisted on having the groups fighting the central Syrian government, above all the Islamic State, included on the lists of terrorist organisations. But did we see any results? We appealed in vain.

We sometimes get the impression that our colleagues and friends are constantly fighting the consequences of their own policies, throw all their effort into addressing the risks they themselves have created, and pay an ever-greater price.

Colleagues, this period of unipolar domination has convincingly demonstrated that having only one power centre does not make global processes more manageable. On the contrary, this kind of unstable construction has shown its inability to fight the real threats such as regional conflicts, terrorism, drug trafficking, religious fanaticism, chauvinism and neo-Nazism. At the same time, it has opened the road wide for inflated national pride, manipulating public opinion and letting the strong bully and suppress the weak.

Essentially, the unipolar world is simply a means of justifying dictatorship over people and countries. The unipolar world turned out too uncomfortable, heavy and unmanageable a burden even for the self-proclaimed leader. Comments along this line were made here just before and I fully agree with this. This is why we see attempts at this new historic stage to recreate a semblance of a quasi-bipolar world as a convenient model for perpetuating American leadership. It does not matter who takes the place of the centre of evil in American propaganda, the USSR's old place as the main adversary. It could be Iran, as a country seeking to acquire nuclear technology, China, as the world's biggest economy, or Russia, as a nuclear superpower.

Today, we are seeing new efforts to fragment the world, draw new dividing lines, put together coalitions not built for something but directed against someone, anyone, create the image of an enemy as was the case during the Cold War years, and obtain the right to this leadership, or diktat if you wish. The situation was presented this way during the Cold War. We all understand this and know this. The United States always told its allies: "We have a common enemy, a terrible foe, the centre of evil, and we are defending you, our allies, from this foe, and so we have the right to order you around, force you to sacrifice your political and economic interests and pay your share of the costs for this collective defence, but we will be the ones in charge of it all of course." In short, we see today attempts in a new and changing world to reproduce the familiar models of global management, and all this so as to guarantee their exceptional position and reap political and economic dividends.

Meeting of the Valdai International Discussion Club October 24, 2014 Sochi

What happened in Crimea? First, there was this anti-state overthrow in Kiev. Whatever anyone may say, I find this obvious – there was an armed seizure of power. In many parts of the world, people welcomed this, not realising what this could lead to, while in some regions people were frightened that power was seized by extremists, by nationalists and right-wingers including neo-Nazis. People feared for their future and for their families and reacted accordingly. In Crimea, people held a referendum.

I would like to draw your attention to this. It was not by chance that we in Russia stated that there was a referendum. The decision to hold the referendum was made by the legitimate authority of Crimea – its Parliament, elected a few years ago under Ukrainian law prior to all these grave events. This legitimate body of authority declared a referendum, and then based on its results, they adopted a declaration of independence, just as Kosovo did, and turned to the Russian Federation with a request to accept Crimea into the Russian state.

You know, whatever anyone may say and no matter how hard they try to dig something up, this would be very difficult, considering the language of the United Nations court ruling, which clearly states (as applied to the Kosovo precedent) that the decision on self-determination does not require the approval of the supreme authority of a country.

Meeting of the Valdai International Discussion Club October 24, 2014 Sochi

I spoke with one of my former colleagues in Eastern Europe. He told me proudly, "Yesterday, I appointed a Chief of Staff." I was very surprised. "Oh yeah? Why is this an achievement?" "What do you mean? It has been many years since we've appointed a Defence Minister or Chief of Staff without approval from the US ambassador." I was so surprised that I said, "Wow. Why is that?" And he said, "That's just how it is. They said that if we want to join the EU, we first need to join NATO. And this is what's necessary to join NATO. We need to have military discipline." I asked him, "Listen, why have you sold your sovereignty? What is the volume of investments into your nation?" I will not tell you the volume, because it will immediately become evident which nation I am talking about. It is minimal! I said, "Listen, are you crazy? Why did you do this?" He replied, "Well, that's just how it's turned out."

But this cannot continue forever. Everyone must understand that, including our American friends and partners. It is impossible to keep humiliating one's partners forever in such a way. That kind of relationship breaks down; I know this, I've been here a long time. You can draw them in now and force them to do some things, but this cannot continue forever, and certainly not in Asia – especially not in Asia. There are countries there that truly – there are few such nations in the world – that really command their sovereignty. They treasure it and won't let anybody near it.

Meeting of the Valdai International Discussion Club October 24, 2014 Sochi

You know, the mentality here in Russia, and in Ukraine, is different from Europe. Here if a man invites a woman to a restaurant, he will pay the bill, while you would normally go Dutch, when everybody pays for themselves. However, this is a different situation. The European Union has chosen association with Ukraine and undertook certain commitments. Why don't you help Ukraine and issue it a bridge loan for a month, only for one month?

Meeting of the Valdai International Discussion Club October 24, 2014 Sochi

The South Stream project cannot be implemented unilaterally. This is just like love: it can only be happy if there are two people in this wonderful process and both want to develop their relations. Same here: we cannot unilaterally build a pipeline system worth billions of dollars if our partners are still considering whether they need to implement this project or not.

Press statement following Russian-Serbian talks and answers to journalists' questions October 16, 2014 Belgrade

Seventy years ago, our nations joined forces to defeat the criminal ideology of hatred for humanity, which threatened the very existence of our civilization. And today it is also important that people in different countries and on different continents remember what terrible consequences may result from the belief in one's exceptionality, attempts to achieve dubious geopolitical goals, no matter by what means, and disregard for basic norms of law and morality. We must do everything in our power to prevent such tragedies in the future.

Regrettably, in some European countries the Nazi virus "vaccine" created at the Nuremberg Tribunal is losing its effect. This is clearly demonstrated by open manifestations of neo-Nazism that have already become commonplace in Latvia and other Baltic states. The situation in Ukraine, where nationalists and other radical groups provoked an anti-constitutional coup d'état in February, causes particular concern in this respect.

Today, it is our shared duty to combat the glorification of Nazism. We must firmly oppose the attempts to revise the results of WWII and consistently combat any forms and manifestations of racism, xenophobia, aggressive nationalism and chauvinism.

Interview to Politika newspaper October 15, 2014

I can't help but think the seditious thought that no one actually cares about Ukraine itself. They are just using Ukraine as an instrument to shake up international relations. Ukraine is being used as an instrument and has been made hostage to the desire of some players on the international stage to revive NATO say, not so much even as a military organisation, but as a key instrument in US foreign policy, in order for the US to consolidate its satellites and scare them with a threat from abroad. But if this is the case, this is a real shame because it means that Ukraine has essentially become hostage to another's interests. I do not see anything good in this practice.

Answers to journalists' questions September 12, 2014 Dushanbe

As for the [sanctions] lists, I welcome this resolution by the European Union. The less our officials and heads of major companies go abroad and work on pressing matters instead, the better. The same is true of State Duma deputies, who need to communicate more frequently with their voters, rather than tanning somewhere at foreign resorts.

Answers to journalists' questions September 12, 2014 Dushanbe

As you know, the United States unilaterally withdrew from the ABM Treaty a few years ago and is now busy building a missile defence system. We have not seen any progress in the negotiations in this area so far. What's more, they are building missile defence systems in Europe and in Alaska, in other words, close to our borders. They are working on the theory of the so-called prompt global strike, and there are other things that are cause for concern too.

The militarisation of outer space is also continuing. The use of conventional strategic weapons is being considered, and so on and so forth. Many new threats are emerging. Just recently, as you know, the decision was taken to beef up NATO forces in Eastern Europe. ...

The crisis in Ukraine, which was provoked and masterminded by some of our Western partners in the first place, is now being used to revive NATO. We clearly need to take all of this into consideration in planning and deciding how to guarantee our country's security.

Meeting on drafting the 2016–2025 State Armament Programme September 10, 2014 The Kremlin, Moscow

Seventy-five years ago, Soviet and Mongolian troops selflessly blocked the invaders' way forward. The unconditional victory at Khalkin-Gol had tremendous military and political significance. It pushed back militarist Japan's entry into World War II by nearly two-and-a-half years and gave great moral support to the peoples of China and Korea in their struggle against the aggressors. ... Even during what were the Soviet Union's most difficult moments in the Great Patriotic War, Japan, Nazi Germany's ally at the time, did not attack the Soviet Union, thus making it possible to redeploy troops from the Far East and Siberia to the west at the end of 1941, which played a decisive part in the battle for Moscow. In this context, let me cite a telling quote from one of the Imperial Japanese Army's senior officials. He said, "We got our basic military training at Khasan, our intermediate training at Khalkin-Gol, and we are in no hurry to receive our advanced training."

75th anniversary of the Battle of Khalkin Gol September 3, 2014 Ulan Bator

Our Western partners, with the support of fairly radically inclined and nationalist-leaning groups, carried out a coup d'état there. No matter what anyone says, we all understand what happened. There are no fools among us. We all saw the symbolic pies handed out on the Maidan. This information and political support, what does it mean?

This was a case of the United States and European countries getting fully involved in a change of power, an anti-constitutional change of power carried out by force, and the part of the country that does not accept this change is being suppressed with brute military force and the use of planes, artillery, multiple launch rocket systems and tanks. If this is what today's European values are about, then I am more than disappointed. ...

Sad as it is to say, but this reminds me of the events of World War II, when the Nazi troops surrounded our towns, in particular Leningrad – you are from St Petersburg, yes? – and fired directly on the towns and their people. On Nevsky Prospekt, as you know, you can still see the sign "Citizens! Take care: this side of the street is the most dangerous in artillery attacks."

Seliger 2014 National Youth Forum August 29, 2014 Seliger, Tver Region

The Arctic plays a very important part for us in terms of guaranteeing our security too. It is regrettably the case that the United States' attack submarines are concentrated in that area, not far from the Norwegian coast, and the missiles they carry would reach Moscow within 15–16 minutes, just to remind you.

Seliger 2014 National Youth Forum August 29, 2014 Seliger, Tver Region

What do we see today? The ideological component has gone from our relations, but the competition has not slackened a bit, often it is even fiercer than it used to be. Geopolitics have always been at the basis of the interests of any state, and remain so.

Seliger 2014 National Youth Forum August 29, 2014 Seliger, Tver Region

Russia always supports the acting authorities. We are not like some of our partners. Maybe, in this regard, they are even being more pragmatic, they are always putting their eggs into multiple baskets. Moreover (the Americans do this), even if a government somewhere is loyal to them, they always work with the opposition. Always! And they even set it against the current government a bit, so that even if that government is loyal, it will stay even more loyal, and to show that yes, we have someone else to work with. I suppose that's a pragmatic position. And I see that it was used for centuries by Britain as well.

Seliger 2014 National Youth Forum August 29, 2014 Seliger, Tver Region

I have to agree with some of the speakers that all our partners in the world should see that Russia, just as any other large, powerful, sovereign state, has different tools for ensuring its national interests, and these include the Armed Forces and military equipment. However, this is not a cure-all and we do not intend to run around the world waving a razor blade, as some people do. Nevertheless, everyone should know that we have such means available.

Meeting with members of political parties represented in the State Duma August 14, 2014

Regarding the idea of studying and applying other countries' experience, including in work with young people, we most certainly should and will do this. But there is a lot of negative experience abroad too, a lot of problems with drug addiction, often xenophobia is flourishing, and various other things, not such traditional things… You know the sort of thing I have in mind. We don't need that kind of experience. But they have positive experience too of course. We need to analyse the overall situation and take the best of what they can offer, that is without question. We also need to take the best of what our own history offers, draw on our own culture, and at the same time look at what other countries are doing too.

Meeting with members of political parties represented in the State Duma August 14, 2014

Naturally, here in Russia we always cheer for our athletes. But there are no strangers on the mat, on the tatami or in the ring. This is a lesson we have learned from sport. Of course, there are opponents in the ring, on the mat and on the tatami. But there are no enemies. Wouldn't it be wonderful if it was always like that, in life as well?

Attending combat sambo championship August 9, 2014 Sochi

Russia over many centuries supported strong and trusting relations between countries. This was the case on the eve of World War I too, when Russia did everything it could to convince Europe to find a peaceful and bloodless solution to the conflict between Serbia and Austro-Hungary. But Russia's calls went unheeded and our country had no choice but to rise to the challenge, defend a brotherly Slavic people and protect our own country and people from the foreign threat.

Russia stayed true to its duties as an ally. The Russian offensives in Prussia and Galicia upset the adversary's plans and made it possible for our allies to hold the front and defend Paris. The enemy was forced to turn its attention and direct a large part of its forces east where Russian regiments put up the fiercest possible struggle. Russia withstood the attack and was then able to launch an offensive. The Brusilov offensive became famous throughout the whole world.

But this victory was stolen from our country. It was stolen by those who called for the defeat of their homeland and army, who sowed division inside Russia and sought only power for themselves, betraying the national interests. ...

This tragedy reminds us what happens when aggression, selfishness and the unbridled ambitions of national leaders and political establishments push common sense aside, so that instead of preserving the world's most prosperous continent, Europe, they lead it towards danger. It is worth remembering this today.

Unveiling of a monument to World War I heroes August 1, 2014 Moscow

However, ever more frequently today we hear of ultimatums and sanctions. The very notion of state sovereignty is being eroded. Undesirable regimes, countries that conduct an independent policy or that simply stand in the way of somebody's interests get destabilised. Tools used for this purpose are the so-called colour revolutions, or, in simple terms – takeovers instigated and financed from the outside. ...

Undoubtedly, such methods will not work with Russia. The recipes used regarding weaker states fraught with internal conflict will not work with us. Our people, the citizens of Russia, will not let this happen and will never accept this. ...Our Armed Forces remain the most important guarantor of our sovereignty and Russia's territorial integrity. We will react appropriately and proportionately to the approach of NATO's military infrastructure toward our borders, and we will not fail to notice the expansion of global missile defence systems and increases in the reserves of strategic non-nuclear precision weaponry.

Security Council meeting July 22, 2014 The Kremlin, Moscow

Our nations play an increasingly significant role in the global political arena as well. It is thanks to Russia and China's firm stance in the UN Security Council, with support from other BRICS participants, that we were able to rally most international dialogue participants – including the European Union and the United States – and prevent a foreign invasion in Syria, achieving the elimination of Syrian chemical weapons.

Speech at BRICS Summit plenary session July 15, 2014 Fortaleza

The modern world is indeed multipolar, complex, and dynamic – this is objective reality. Any attempts to create a model of international relations where all decisions are made within a single 'pole' are ineffective, malfunction regularly, and are ultimately set to fail.

Interview given to Russian news agency ITAR-TASS July 15, 2014

We need to understand clearly that the events provoked in Ukraine are the concentrated outcome of the notorious deterrence policy. As you may know, its roots go deep into history and it is clear that unfortunately, this policy did not end with the end of the Cold War.

In Ukraine, as you may have seen, at threat were our compatriots, Russian people and people of other nationalities, their language, history, culture and legal rights, guaranteed, by the way, by European conventions. When I speak of Russians and Russian-speaking citizens I am referring to those people who consider themselves part of the broad Russian community, they may not necessarily be ethnic Russians, but they consider themselves Russian people.

What did our partners expect from us as the developments in Ukraine unfolded? We clearly had no right to abandon the residents of Crimea and Sevastopol to the mercy of nationalist and radical militants; we could not allow our access to the Black Sea to be significantly limited; we could not allow NATO forces to eventually come to the land of Crimea and Sevastopol, the land of Russian military glory, and radically change the balance of forces in the Black Sea area. This would mean giving up practically everything that Russia had fought for since the times of Peter the Great, or maybe even earlier – historians should know.

Conference of Russian ambassadors and permanent representatives   July 1, 2014 Moscow

The anti-constitutional coup in Kiev and attempts to force the Ukrainian people into an artificial choice between Europe and Russia have pushed society into division and painful internal confrontation.

Presentation of letters of credence by foreign ambassadors June 27, 2014 The Kremlin, Moscow

I want to note that Russia has always been a reliable energy supplier for European countries. At the start of this week, I visited Austria, which in 1968 became the first Western European country to sign a contract for Russian natural gas imports. For nearly 50 years now we have guaranteed stable energy exports to Europe, have honoured all our obligations, and will continue to do so.

Presentation of letters of credence by foreign ambassadors June 27, 2014 The Kremlin, Moscow

Today's generation of Russian officers show their professionalism, patriotism and valour through action. These very qualities made it possible to avoid bloodshed in Crimea and to provide conditions for a free referendum on reunification with Russia. ...

During the past years, we have been consistently modernising our Armed Forces to bring them to a modern level that would fully meet the demands of the 21st century. Clearly, only a mobile and highly efficient army and navy are capable of resolving strategic tasks, of guaranteeing Russia's security, sovereignty and national interests, and most importantly – of reliably protecting our citizens from any potential military threat. ...

You should serve as mentors for young people, teaching them in the context of true patriotism, valour and tenacity, and always bearing in mind the words of the great Suvorov, who said, "I value my soldier more than myself."

Reception in honour of graduates of military academies June 26, 2014 The Kremlin, Moscow

Unfortunately, some Western politicians make insistent calls to artificially reduce Russia's share in European energy supplies and see EU dependence on Russian gas as a threat. I do not think that there is anything to fear in this respect because this dependence is always reciprocal, and interdependence is always the basis and guarantee of stability.

Meeting with Austrian business community leaders June 24, 2014 Vienna

As you know, thankfully, we did not use the Armed Forces directly, for any combat operations. Moreover, we did not even increase the presence of our Armed Forces in Crimea above the number provided in the international agreement. And in this regard, the President of Russia did not use the right given to him by the upper chamber of parliament.

Yes, I will not deny, as I have already said, that we used our military units to guarantee the free expression of will by the people of Crimea; we blocked the activities of some Ukrainian army units so that they did not get involved in the process of expression of will, and to ensure there were no victims. But fortunately, Russia's Armed Forces were not used in Crimea for any military action. ...

Of course, we will always protect ethnic Russians in Ukraine and the part of the Ukrainian population, the Ukrainian people, who feel not just an ethnic but also a cultural connection to Russia, who feel themselves part of the greater Russian community. And in addition to monitoring this carefully, we will also respond accordingly. I hope that the armed forces will not be necessary for this.

Press statements and answers to journalists' questions following Russian-Austrian talks June 24, 2014 Vienna

First of all, we are not laying down any preliminary conditions during the talks between the authorities from Kiev and east Ukraine, mainly because Russia is not a party to this conflict. I want to stress this. ... We believe, and it is impossible to avoid it, that talks need to be launched on the future structure of Ukraine itself and on ensuring the rights, the lawful rights and interests of the people living in southeast Ukraine.

We have talked about this many times, and I simply cannot allow myself to reflect on it too much, but it is clear where the conflict originated. There was a military coup d'état, with one part of the country supporting it and the other opposing it. People in central and western Ukraine took up arms, while people in the east said, "Well, if they can take up arms, why can't we?" And they too rose in arms to protect their interests. Now they are being told, "You must disarm!" They say, "No. First, let's disarm those who took up arms first." You see, this is a never-ending circle of problems. This circle needs to be broken. And how can that be done? By launching substantive talks on how the interests of all people living in that nation will be guaranteed.

Press statements and answers to journalists' questions following Russian-Austrian talks June 24, 2014 Vienna

Our American friends are unhappy with South Stream; they were unhappy in 1962 as well, when we began the gas-for-pipelines project with Germany. And now they are unhappy with this as well. Nothing has changed; the only thing that changed is that they themselves want to supply gas to the European market. But I assure you, it will not be cheaper than Russian gas. Pipeline gas is always cheaper than liquefied gas. Shale gas needs to be extracted, it needs to be turned into liquid, transported across the ocean and then regasified. This involves a lot of money. It is certainly more expensive than our pipeline gas.

But the Americans are competitors nevertheless. This is a normal situation. And they are doing everything possible to break up this contract, the same as many decades ago. There is nothing unusual here. This is typical competition. Political means are used in this competition as well. They talk about Europe's overdependence on Russian gas. We believe that any of our partners have the right to, can and should, perhaps, create the most favourable conditions possible for themselves, maintaining contacts and contracts with many partners.

Press statements and answers to journalists' questions following Russian-Austrian talks June 24, 2014 Vienna

We will not promote Russian nationalism, and we do not intend to revive the Russian Empire. What did I mean when I said that the Soviet Union's collapse was one of the largest humanitarian – above all humanitarian – disasters of the 20th century? I meant that all the citizens of the Soviet Union lived in a single state irrespective of their ethnicity, and after its collapse 25 million Russians suddenly became foreign citizens. It was a huge humanitarian disaster. Not a political or ideological disaster, but a purely humanitarian upheaval. Families were divided; people lost their jobs and means of subsistence, and had no means to communicate with each other normally. This was the problem.

Vladimir Putin's interview with Radio Europe 1 and TF1 TV channel June 4, 2014

Vladimir Putin: The point is no one should be brought to power through an armed anti-constitutional coup, and this is especially true of the post-Soviet space where government institutions are not fully mature. When it happened some people accepted this regime and were happy about it while other people, say, in eastern and southern Ukraine just won't accept it. And it is vital to talk with those people who didn't accept this change of power instead of sending tanks there, as you said yourself, instead of firing missiles at civilians from the air and bombing non-military targets.

Question: But, Mr President, the United States and the White House claim they have evidence that Russia intervened in the conflict, sent its troops and supplied weapons. They claim they have proof. Do you believe that?

Vladimir Putin: Proof? Why don't they show it? The entire world remembers the US Secretary of State demonstrating the evidence of Iraq's weapons of mass destruction, waving around some test tube with washing powder in the UN Security Council. Eventually, the US troops invaded Iraq, Saddam Hussein was hanged and later it turned out there had never been any weapons of mass destruction in Iraq. You know, it's one thing to say things and another to actually have evidence. I will tell you again: no Russian troops…

Question (via interpreter): Are you saying the US is lying?

Vladimir Putin: Yes, it is. There are no armed forces, no Russian 'instructors' in southeastern Ukraine. And there never were any.

Vladimir Putin's interview with Radio Europe 1 and TF1 TV channel June 4, 2014

Vladimir Putin: Russian troops were in Crimea under the international treaty on the deployment of the Russian military base. It's true that Russian troops helped Crimeans hold a referendum on their (a) independence and (b) desire to join the Russian Federation. No one can prevent these people from exercising a right that is stipulated in Article 1 of the UN Charter, the right of nations to self-determination.

Question: In other words, you will not return Crimea? Crimea is Russia, is that it?

Vladimir Putin: In accordance with the expression of the will of people who live there, Crimea is part of the Russian Federation and its constituent entity. I want everyone to understand this clearly. We conducted an exclusively diplomatic and peaceful dialogue – I want to stress this – with our partners in Europe and the United States. In response to our attempts to hold such a dialogue and to negotiate an acceptable solution, they supported the anti-constitutional state coup in Ukraine, and following that we could not be sure that Ukraine would not become part of the North Atlantic military bloc. In that situation, we could not allow a historical part of the Russian territory with a predominantly ethnic Russian population to be incorporated into an international military alliance, especially because Crimeans wanted to be part of Russia. I am sorry, but we couldn't act differently.

Vladimir Putin's interview with Radio Europe 1 and TF1 TV channel June 4, 2014

Vladimir Putin: Speaking of US policy, it's clear that the United States is pursuing the most aggressive and toughest policy to defend their own interests – at least, this is how the American leaders see it – and they do it persistently.

There are basically no Russian troops abroad while US troops are everywhere. There are US military bases everywhere around the world and they are always involved in the fates of other countries even though they are thousands of kilometres away from US borders. So it is ironic that our US partners accuse us of breaching some of these rules.

Question (via interpreter): But you have taken some decisions regarding your defence budget. Are you as President taking any special decisions on security and defence now, because the general environment is more risky?

Vladimir Putin: Regarding the defence budget. I'd like to say, for reference' sake, because only the analysts know this, that the defence budget of the United States, which we talked about only yesterday, is larger than the combined military budgets of every country in the world – every country – combined. So who's pursuing an aggressive policy?

As for our [defence] budget, it has hardly grown in terms of percent of GDP, barely by one-tenth of a percent. But we want to rearm our army and navy based on modern, advanced technology, by reducing quantity and improving quality. We have a relevant rearmament programme, and it was not adopted yesterday or in response to the Ukrainian crisis. It has been our policy, which we will continue to implement.

Vladimir Putin's interview with Radio Europe 1 and TF1 TV channel June 4, 2014

Question (via interpreter): We don't quite understand why you, Vladimir Putin, the man who wants to modernise Russia, support a person who is killing his own people, who is covered in their blood. How can this be?

Vladimir Putin: I'll explain very simply and clearly, and I hope that the majority of the French people who are watching and listening to this interview will understand me. We very much fear that Syria will fall apart like Sudan. We very much fear that Syria will follow in the footsteps of Iraq or Afghanistan. This is why we would like the legal authority to remain in power in Syria, so that Russia can cooperate with Syria and with our partners in Europe and the United States to consider possible methods to change Syrian society, to modernise the regime and make it more viable and humane.

Vladimir Putin's interview with Radio Europe 1 and TF1 TV channel June 4, 2014

I make my decisions based on only one principle, and that is the interests of Russia and its people. It was the interests of our country and people that demanded that we make an adequate response to primitive and unprofessional attempts to act against our interests using force, and our partners should have taken this into consideration earlier.

As for isolation, first, we think that we are in the right in this dispute both in terms of substance and in legal terms. I have already cited the Kosovo precedent as an argument for our position. As you know, Kosovo's decision on state independence was taken by its Parliament, and in Crimea the decision on state independence was based on the national referendum that asked people if they wished to remain a part of Ukraine or join the Russian Federation. Only after the vast majority of Crimea's voters – more than 90 percent – said that they want to join the Russian Federation did the Crimean Parliament declare state independence.

Meeting with heads of leading international news agencies May 24, 2014 St Petersburg

Our ambition is to integrate within the post-Soviet space but not because we want to restore the Soviet Union or an empire but because we would like to use the competitive advantages of these states that are now independent. We have a common language for interethnic and inter-state communication, which is the Russian language. We have a common transport and energy infrastructure that we inherited from a united country. Our companies are strongly connected. There is a good level of research collaboration in science and education that could be used for success in global markets and to help our nations prosper. We are now working on an agreement to establish the Eurasian Economic Union. Please try to look at this document from within, with an expert eye, without any bias. Just analyse it. Is there anything in it about recreating an empire? There's nothing. The union's only objective is economic cooperation.

Meeting with heads of leading international news agencies May 24, 2014 St Petersburg

I think that our partners in the United States and Europe employed brutal and unlawful methods in Ukraine by prompting a government coup and thereby threatening our fundamental national interests in terms of security, as well as the economy. For this anti-constitutional coup was followed, and we clearly heard it, by calls to strip national minorities of their language rights and join NATO, which means the possible deployment of NATO troops, ballistic attack systems and missile defence capabilities. We would have found ourselves in a radically new environment, which prompted us to take certain steps, including those aimed at supporting the aspirations of the people of Crimea to join Russia. We believe that in the face of such power politics we delivered an adequate response along the same lines. I hope that it will never happen again in any other circumstances or places. ...We are adamant that Russia's position was the only right option and that Russia acted in full compliance with international law. If I'm not mistaken, Article 1, Paragraph 2 of the UN Charter stipulates that the purpose of the United Nations is to ensure nations' right to self-determination.

We vigorously oppose attempts by international players to interpret international norms exclusively to suit their own agenda based on their interests in any specific global environment. In Kosovo, they said that acknowledging the right of a nation to self-determination was the right way to go, while in Crimea they turned everything upside down and started talking about territorial integrity, which is also mentioned in the UN Charter. We must find a way to reach common ground by agreeing to act in one way or the other and refraining from saying that white is black and black is white. We are calling for restoring the primacy of international law in global affairs.

Meeting with heads of leading international news agencies May 24, 2014 St Petersburg

As for the flag planted on the Arctic seabed, this was not a government move. It was rather an emotional act. I don't see it as anything that far out of the ordinary. Americans once landed on the Moon and planted the US flag there. We haven't quarrelled with them over that and never imagined they would claim ownership of the Moon. Fortunately, our space cooperation with the United States is thriving.

Meeting with heads of leading international news agencies May 24, 2014 St Petersburg

We intend to gradually increase the share of settlements in our national currencies, rubles and yuans, and to form integrated investment and banking institutions. Such a network would provide funding to major global projects in infrastructure, mineral deposit production and processing, machine and aircraft engineering, and knowledge-intensive production. We are also moving towards building a strategic Russian-Chinese energy alliance that would serve as the main framework for guaranteeing the energy security of the entire Asia-Pacific region.

St Petersburg International Economic Forum May 23, 2014 St Petersburg

Ukraine was supposed to sign an association agreement with the EU. Using absolutely modern diplomatic tools, we proved that the proposed document is at least inconsistent with Russian interests since the Russian and the Ukrainian economies are closely intertwined. ... They told us to mind our own business. Excuse me, I don't want to hurt anyone's feelings, but it's been a while since I heard anything that snobbish. They just slammed the door in our face telling us to mind our own business.

Well, then, if it is none of our business, we tried to convince our Ukrainian partners to take a look at the possible outcome. President Yanukovych decided to postpone the signing and hold additional talks. What came next? A coup d'état. No matter what you choose to call it, a revolution or something else. It's a coup d'état with the use of violence and militant forces.

St Petersburg International Economic Forum May 23, 2014 St Petersburg

[Journalist]: President Obama has accused you, as you know, of untruths when it comes to supporting some of the separatist groups in Ukraine...

Vladimir Putin: Who made him a judge? He's not a judge. Why doesn't he get a job in the judicial system then and work there?

St Petersburg International Economic Forum May 23, 2014 St Petersburg

[Journalist]: In 2009, we were all very excited to see the reset in relations with the United States. Today that reset lies in tatters. What went wrong?

Vladimir Putin: You know, it is the result of unilateral action. Some of the United States' allies agree to play by the "either you're with us or against us" rule. First, the US goes ahead and does something and then uses these allies to create a coalition to put a good face on things. Russia doesn't work that way. Agreements must be made well in advance, in strict compliance with international law and with consideration for each other's interests. Only in this case can we promise a reliable partnership.

St Petersburg International Economic Forum May 23, 2014 St Petersburg

First, we did not ruin this relationship. Second, despite the tension and perhaps diametrically opposed approaches to some critical situations, we still continue this collaboration. ... We are not going to isolate ourselves, but we can't make people like us. Still, we hope that common sense and an understanding of their own interests will encourage our partners in Europe and the United States to continue working with Russia.

St Petersburg International Economic Forum May 23, 2014 St Petersburg

Speaking of Snowden, I said it before many times. Technically, we have nothing to do with this. He happened to end up in Russia due, in my opinion, to the lack of professionalism of the US officials that tried to apprehend him. I know because I used to work for the security services.

Why did they have to scare the entire world? If they were willing to force planes with presidents on board to land, they could have forced the plane with Mr Snowden to land anywhere. They scared the whole world. The plane arrived in our transit area and then nobody wanted to accept it.

If the US security services had not scared everyone, the plane would have taken off and flown to any country. They would have forced it to land and Snowden would be sitting in a zindan or some other prison. But they scared everyone and he stayed in our transit area. What were we supposed to do? Russia is not a country that extradites fighters for human rights. (Applause)

Thank you for this response. It's true, I'm not being ironic. Mr Snowden believes he is fighting for human rights and he has devoted his life to this. He is very young. I don't know how he is going to live. I'm not kidding. How is he going to live? For now, he is in Russia. But then what? He chose this fate himself, you see? We only gave him asylum. He is not our agent. He did not give away any secrets, although the rascal really should have given us something – we gave him asylum after all. But he won't tell us anything. He uses channels that only he knows of and makes statements when he thinks it's necessary, and that's it.

St Petersburg International Economic Forum May 23, 2014 St Petersburg

Returning to Ukraine, you know what the problem is? For us it is an issue of vital importance while the US only dealt with Ukraine superficially. I was personally involved and many of the top officials present in this auditorium were personally involved, because it is vitally important to us. I don't think it is for the States.

But in the long run, we should rebuild mutual trust and be attentive to each other's interests. I'm not just saying that. You know it yourself if you specialise in international affairs. It is in the news every day. We constantly expressed concern over the enlargement of NATO but our concerns were ignored. They just said, "Every nation has the right to choose how best to protect itself."

Of course, every nation has the right. Why don't we have the right to evaluate events from the standpoint of our security? There are many ways to protect yourself. For example, the United States could have just signed a bilateral treaty on friendship and collaboration, including military collaboration. How is this treaty different from a country's accession to NATO? There is no fundamental difference. The only responsibility they can impose on the alliance members is to contribute money to the joint military budget, which they don't do anyway. Do you know that the spending of the alliance members is far less than that of the United States? The US always pushes them but with little success.

The same is happening with the missile defence system. They keep saying it is not directed against us. President Medvedev, who did very much to advance relations with the United States (it was his initiative after all), said: "Well, let's sign some document, even a trifling legal document saying this is not directed against us. Just write on this paper what you are saying verbally." No, they refused pointblank. So, what kind of dialogue is that? Just generalities. If we have the guts to talk with each other openly and honestly and to consider each other's lawful interests, our relations will certainly change for the better. But I'm an optimist and I'm still confident that the situation in Ukraine will settle down in some way and we'll find the strength to normalise our relations.

St Petersburg International Economic Forum May 23, 2014 St Petersburg

While our trade with the United States is $27.8 billion, it is $440 billion with Europe. The difference is huge, as we can see. I even suspect that our American friends (and they are smart guys, aren't they?) pushed for sanctions to gain some competitive advantages in trade and economic ties with Europe.

St Petersburg International Economic Forum May 23, 2014 St Petersburg

A tragedy would have occurred far worse than what we are currently witnessing in certain cities of Ukraine, in Odessa, where unarmed people were forced inside a building and burned alive. Almost 50 people perished in flames and another 50 went missing. Where are they? They were actually also killed. We prevented this from happening in Crimea, and I think that it was the right thing to do.

Meeting with participants in the CEO Global Summit May 23, 2014 St Petersburg

But I must give your Government colleagues their due and say that they drank quite a bit of our blood during the negotiations. The Chinese are very serious negotiators.

Meeting with Vice President of China Li Yuanchao May 23, 2014 St Petersburg

When Yanukovych signed the agreement on February 21, which was guaranteed by three European foreign ministers from Poland, France and Germany, he believed that this agreement would be honoured. Under it, Yanukovych pledged not to use the army or other armed force against protesters and to pull the Interior Ministry units, including the Berkut, out of Kiev, while the opposition was to withdraw from the occupied administrative buildings, dismantle the barricades and disarm its fighters. Yanukovych agreed to hold early parliamentary elections, to return to the 2004 constitution and to hold presidential elections in December 2014. Had they wanted it, he would have agreed to hold presidential elections in a month or a month and a half, because he was ready to agree to anything. But as soon as he left Kiev and pulled the Interior Ministry units out of the city, the opposition renewed its attacks, seizing the presidential administration building, among other government buildings and accomplishing a coup d'état in the full and classical meaning of the word. No one can say why they did it, why they acted so unprofessionally and unwisely, and why they pushed the country towards the current situation. There is no answer.

Direct Line with Vladimir Putin April 17, 2014 Moscow

Vladimir Putin: Here's an interesting question from Albina. She's six years old and her question is about Russian-US relations. Just wait, you'll like it. "Do you think President Obama would save you if you were drowning?"

I sure hope this doesn't happen, but you know that there are personal relationships as well as relations between governments. I can't say that I have a special personal relationship with the US President, but I think he is a decent man and brave enough. So, I think he definitely would.

Direct Line with Vladimir Putin April 17, 2014 Moscow

The United States is a major global player and at a certain point it seemed to think that it was the only leader and a unipolar system was established. Now we can see that it is not the case and everything in the world is interrelated. If they try to punish someone like misbehaving children or to stand them in the corner on a sack of peas or do something to hurt them, eventually they will bite the hand that feeds them. Sooner or later, they will realise this.

Direct Line with Vladimir Putin April 17, 2014 Moscow

We want our relations to be good, but we simply cannot afford to have someone always presume that we will give up our interests and step aside all the time in exchange for someone agreeing to be friendly with us. For being allowed to sit next to someone, we must make concessions here and there and turn a blind eye to certain things. This is impossible. In the end, we have reached a point beyond which we cannot retreat.

Direct Line with Vladimir Putin April 17, 2014 Moscow

Kirill Kleymenov: Mr President, you remember the story with a button that Ms Clinton gave to Mr Lavrov as a gift? The "reset" inscription on the button was mistranslated into Russian as "overload" rather than "reset." An overload is what eventually happened.

Vladimir Putin: You know, it didn't happen just now because of Crimea. I think it happened much earlier, just after the events in Libya. Dmitry Medvedev, who was Russia's President at the time, supported our western partners and upheld the resolution on Libya. This was about a ban on flights of the Libyan government's air force. The actual result was air bombing, the overthrow of Gaddafi, his murder and the murder of the US ambassador, and the collapse of the country. This is where mistrust comes from.

Direct Line with Vladimir Putin April 17, 2014 Moscow

As for our relations with Europe and western countries, I have mentioned before that this is an issue of trust. In fact, you also spoke about it. You know, this is very important, this is a vital issue – trust on both the personal and intergovernmental level.

You know what came to my mind? The current Secretary General of NATO, Mr Rasmussen, used to be Prime Minister of Denmark, a wonderful country with wonderful people. We have excellent relations with Denmark, at least that has been the case so far, and I hope it will remain so in the future. When Mr Rasmussen was

Prime Minister, he once asked me to hold an unplanned meeting. I agreed and we met.

It later turned out that he had recorded our conversation and then published it. I could not believe my eyes and ears. Sounds unbelievable, right? He explained that he recorded our conversation for history. All right, I'm flattered, but even if it was for history, shouldn't he have at least warned me or asked my permission to publish those talks? How can we speak of trust after something like that?

Direct Line with Vladimir Putin April 17, 2014 Moscow

[Question]: Are there any plans regarding the annexation of Alaska? We would be very happy to see that happen. Thank you. Pensioner Faina Ivanovna.

Kirill Kleymenov: That's a popular joke, Mr Putin. They call Alaska "Ice Krim" in jest.

Vladimir Putin: Yes, I'm aware of that. Faina Ivanovna, why do you need Alaska? By the way, Alaska was sold sometime in the 19th century. Louisiana was sold to the United States by the French at about the same time. Thousands of square kilometres were sold for $7.2 million, although in gold. We can calculate the equivalent amount, but it was definitely inexpensive. Russia is a northern country with 70% of its territory located in the north and the far north. Alaska is not located in the southern hemisphere, either, is it? It's cold out there as well. Let's not get worked up about it, all right?

Direct Line with Vladimir Putin April 17, 2014 Moscow

Ukraine is a long-suffering land; it's a very complicated community and a long-suffering one in the direct sense of the word. Nationalism and even neo-Nazism are experiencing a resurgence in western Ukraine. But you know well the history of this territory and its people. Some of these territories were part of

Czechoslovakia, some of Hungary, some of Austro-Hungary and some of Poland, where they were never full-fledged citizens. You know, something has always been growing in their heart of hearts. Some people seem to believe that it is this circumstance – because these territories were former possessions of several present-day EU countries – that imbues them with some special European substance. That they were second-rate citizens in those states seems to have been forgotten, but this still lurks in their historical memory, under the crust, deep down in their hearts, see? It's where their nationalism comes from, I think.

Central, eastern and southeastern Ukraine is another matter. I've just mentioned this area, New Russia, which has intertwined its roots with those of the Russian state. The local people have a somewhat different mentality. They found themselves part of present-day Ukraine, which had been pieced together in the Soviet period. Of course, it is difficult for them to establish proper relations and to understand each other. But we should help them to do so as much as we can.

Direct Line with Vladimir Putin April 17, 2014 Moscow

Whoever really does care about Ukraine and the Ukrainian people should make their contribution to preventing the country's economy from going bankrupt. This will take more than handing out pies at the Maidan.

Meeting with Security Council members April 11, 2014 Novo-Ogaryovo, Moscow Region

In short, we have every reason to assume that the infamous policy of containment, led in the 18th, 19th and 20th centuries, continues today. They are constantly trying to sweep us into a corner because we have an independent position, because we maintain it and because we call things like they are and do not engage in hypocrisy. But there is a limit to everything. And with Ukraine, our western partners have crossed the line, behaving crudely, irresponsibly and unprofessionally.

After all, they were fully aware that there are millions of Russians living in Ukraine and in Crimea. They must have really lacked political instinct and common sense not to foresee all the consequences of their actions. Russia found itself in a position it could not retreat from. If you compress the spring all the way to its limit, it will snap back hard. You must always remember this.

Today, it is imperative to end this hysteria, to refute the rhetoric of the cold war and to accept the obvious fact: Russia is an independent, active participant in international affairs; like other countries, it has its own national interests that need to be taken into account and respected.

At the same time, we are grateful to all those who understood our actions in Crimea; we are grateful to the people of China, whose leaders have always considered the situation in Ukraine and Crimea taking into account the full historical and political context, and greatly appreciate India's reserve and objectivity.

Today, I would like to address the people of the United States of America, the people who, since the foundation of their nation and adoption of the Declaration of Independence, have been proud to hold freedom above all else. Isn't the desire of Crimea's residents to freely choose their fate such a value? Please understand us.

Address by President of the Russian Federation March 18, 2014 The Kremlin, Moscow

In my opinion, this revolutionary situation has been brewing for a long time, since the first days of Ukraine's independence. The ordinary Ukrainian citizen, the ordinary guy suffered during the rule of Nicholas II, during the reign of Kuchma, and Yushchenko, and Yanukovych. Nothing or almost nothing has changed for the better. Corruption has reached dimensions that are unheard of here in Russia. Accumulation of wealth and social stratification – problems that are also acute in this country – are much worse in Ukraine, radically worse. Out there, they are beyond anything we can imagine. Generally, people wanted change, but one should not support illegal change. ...

What is our biggest concern? We see the rampage of reactionary forces, nationalist and anti-Semitic forces going on in certain parts of Ukraine, including Kiev. I am sure you, members of the media, saw how one of the governors was chained and handcuffed to something and they poured water over him, in the cold of winter. After that, by the way, he was locked up in a cellar and tortured. What is all this about? Is this democracy? Is this some manifestation of democracy? He was actually only recently appointed to this position, in December, I believe. Even if we accept that they are all corrupt there, he had barely had time to steal anything. ...

It is not the first time our Western partners are doing this in Ukraine. I sometimes get the feeling that somewhere across that huge puddle, in America, people sit in a lab and conduct experiments, as if with rats, without actually understanding the consequences of what they are doing. ... Did our partners in the West and those who call themselves the government in Kiev now not foresee that events would take this turn? I said to them over and over: Why are you whipping the country into a frenzy like this? What are you doing? But they keep on pushing forward. Of course people in the eastern part of the country realise that they have been left out of the decision-making process. ...

You have to understand that this kind of chaos is the worst possible thing for countries with a shaky economy and unstable political system. In this kind of situation you never know what kind of people events will bring to the fore. Just recall, for example, the role that (Ernst) Roehm's storm troopers played during Hitler's rise to power. Later, these storm troopers were liquidated, but they played their part in bringing Hitler to power. Events can take all kinds of unexpected turns.

Vladimir Putin answered journalists' questions on the situation in Ukraine March 4, 2014 Novo-Ogaryovo, Moscow Region

You know there are always some points of coincidence and points of difference between large states; they differ in their approach to the resolution of certain issues. I would like to stress here that during any sharp turns in world history Russia and the USA have always been together, I mean the First and Second World Wars. In other words, we could argue, and we continue to do so on some matters, but when the situation is extraordinary, we always join efforts.

Interview to Russian and foreign media January 19, 2014

Question: Could you please clarify if these $15 billion are the price for Ukraine's rejection of the EU association agreement? How much would you be willing to pay to...

Vladimir Putin: Right, the discussion is getting serious. Well, how much do you need?

News conference of Vladimir Putin December 19, 2013 Moscow

We are not indifferent to the status of our compatriots. And incidentally, we are constantly raising these issues as they apply to our compatriots' status in several EU nations, particularly in the Baltic states, which still have the entirely uncivilised concept of a "non-citizen." This term refers to someone who is neither a citizen, nor a foreigner, nor a stateless person – indeed, it is completely unclear who this kind of individual is, deprived of political and human rights and freedoms. And for some reason, our colleagues in the European Union tolerate this and consider this to be normal. We believe it is not normal, and we will continue fighting for equal rights. This is true for all states. But it does not at all mean we are going to brandish our swords and bring in the troops. That is simply nonsense; there is nothing like this now and never will be.

News conference of Vladimir Putin December 19, 2013 Moscow

I believe we should not follow the path of blindly copying what other countries are doing. We should understand what is going on there, analyse the situation, find the best practices and implement them in our country.

News conference of Vladimir Putin December 19, 2013 Moscow

You said that Russia is located between the East and the West. In fact, it is the East and West that are located to the left and right of Russia.

News conference of Vladimir Putin December 19, 2013 Moscow

Question: How do you see Russia's role in the Asia-Pacific region given China's growing influence here? And how seriously do you take competition with China in the region, in the light of the fact that you are also partners? To what extent are partnership and competition compatible here?

Vladimir Putin: Competition is the engine of progress in all fields, economic and political. So I do not see any contradiction or tragedy here; everything is normal, natural, and developing as it should. In some fields there is competition and in others cooperation. But today we have a great deal of common ground for cooperating with China, and this cooperation is proceeding in different directions.

Press statement and answers to journalists' questions following the APEC summit October 8, 2013 Bali, Indonesia

Ukraine, without a doubt, is an independent state. That is how history has unfolded. But let's not forget that today's Russian statehood has roots in the Dnieper; as we say, we have a common Dnieper baptistery. Kievan Rus started out as the foundation of the enormous future Russian state. We have common traditions, a common mentality, a common history and a common culture. We have very similar languages. In that respect, I want to repeat again, we are one people.

Meeting of the Valdai International Discussion Club   September 19, 2013
Novgorod Region

They say there is no democracy in Saudi Arabia either, and it's difficult to disagree with that. Nobody is getting ready to bomb Saudi Arabia. ... You know, we need to realise that there are probably countries and even entire regions that cannot function according to universal templates, reproducing the patterns of American or European democracy.

Apparently, those who committed the now famous military actions in Libya were also inspired by noble motives. But what was the outcome? There too they fought for democracy. And where is that democracy? The country is divided into several parts which are run by different tribes. Everybody is fighting against everybody else. Where is democracy?

Meeting of the Valdai International Discussion Club   September 19, 2013
Novgorod Region

It is extremely dangerous to encourage people to see themselves as exceptional, whatever the motivation. There are big countries and small countries, rich and poor, those with long democratic traditions and those still finding their way to democracy.

The Syrian Alternative September 12, 2013

And they are lying, of course, shamelessly. I watched the congress debates. A congressman asked Mr Kerry, "Is Al-Qaeda present there [in Syria]? I've heard they have gained momentum." He replied, "No. I can tell you earnestly, they are not." The main combat unit, the so-called Al-Nusra, is an Al-Qaeda subdivision; they know about this. It just felt unpleasant to me. After all, it is clear... We communicate with them, we assume they are decent people. But he is lying, and he knows he is lying. It is sad.

Meeting of the Council for Civil Society and Human Rights September 4, 2013
The Kremlin, Moscow

[On US control of the internet] During election campaigns, we know that our colleagues support this candidate and do not support that one. As soon as something appears online regarding a candidate they do not like – boom! They delete it immediately. It gets posted again, and boom! They remove it again. So it's very controlled.

Meeting of the Council for Civil Society and Human Rights September 4, 2013
The Kremlin, Moscow

They came to the verdict that they used chemical weapons even before the UN inspectors completed their work [in Syria]. It is just unacceptable.

Meeting of the Council for Civil Society and Human Rights September 4, 2013
The Kremlin, Moscow

They say the UN Security Council is ineffective or completely dysfunctional. But the Security Council is not there to rubberstamp decisions that are convenient for one side and serve the political interests of one of the participants in this process. If that were the case, the UN would simply need to be shut down; it would be a pointless organisation.

Meeting of the Council for Civil Society and Human Rights September 4, 2013
The Kremlin, Moscow

Vladimir Putin: You have just said that Mr Kerry believes that chemical weapons have been used by Assad's army, but the same point was used by another Secretary of State under President George W. Bush as he was trying to convince the entire international community of Iraq's possession of chemical weapons and even showed a test tube containing some white powder. All these arguments turned out to be untenable, but they were used to launch a military action, which many in the United States call a mistake today. Did we forget about that? Do we assume that new mistakes can be avoided so easily? I assure you that is not the case. Everyone remembers those facts, bears them in mind and takes them into account when making decisions.

Interview to Channel One and Associated Press news agency September 4, 2013 Novo-Ogaryovo, Moscow Region

[Journalist]: You were recorded as saying that you thought that the US State Department had an agenda to instigate unrest in Russia to try to weaken its potential rival. …

Vladimir Putin: We sometimes do get thoughts like that, I'll be frank with you, and I have told my American colleagues the same. I am not sure if it is the right thing to say this to the media, but anyway, it is obvious, so I will say this. I can hardly imagine the Ambassador of the Russian Federation to the US actively working with members of the "Occupy Wall Street" movement. I just cannot imagine such thing because the ambassador's task is to improve state-to-state relations. It is a delicate job. Given the complexity of issues, there have to be people on both sides who know how to deal with sensitive issues, who seek compromise and achieve agreements. But as we have witnessed, people from the US Embassy acted in this very fashion...

Interview to Channel One and Associated Press news agency September 4, 2013 Novo-Ogaryovo, Moscow Region

I will now tell you something I have never said before. I have dropped some hints but have never said anything like that directly. Mr Snowden first went to Hong Kong and got in touch with our diplomatic representatives. I was informed that there was such a man, an agent of the special services. I asked them what he wanted and was told that this man was fighting for human rights and the free flow of information, against violations of related human rights and law in the United States, as well as against violations of international law. I said: "So what? If he wants to stay in this country, he is welcome, provided however that he stops any kind of activities that could damage Russian-US relations. This country is not an NGO, it has its own national interests and it does not want to sever Russian-US relations." This information was communicated to him. He said: "No, I am fighting for human rights and I urge you to join me in this fight." I answered: "No, Russia will not join him, let him fight alone." And he left, just like that.

Then he took a flight to Latin America. I learned that Mr Snowden was on the way to our country two hours before his plane landed. What happened next? Information was leaked. No offence, but I think that US special services' agents along with diplomats should have acted with greater professionalism. After they learnt that he was on the way to our country on a transit flight, they put all possible destination countries under pressure, all countries in Latin American and Europe. But they could have allowed him to get to a country where his security could not be guaranteed or intercepted him along the way – they did the same, by the way, with the plane carrying the president of one Latin American country, which, to my opinion, was absolutely unacceptable, done in a rude fashion inappropriate for the United States or your European partners. That was humiliating. The United States could have done the same with respect to Snowden. What stopped them? Instead, they scared everyone; the man quickly decided to stay in Russia's transit zone and got stuck in our country. What were we to do after that? Hand him over to the United States? In this case we need to sign an agreement. You do not want to? All right, hand our criminals to us instead. You do not want that either? Good. Why would you then request extradition on a unilateral basis?

Interview to Channel One and Associated Press news agency   September 4, 2013 Novo-Ogaryovo, Moscow Region

You know, no matter what happens, and wherever Ukraine goes, anyway we shall meet sometime and somewhere. Why? Because we are one nation. And however angry the nationalists from both sides can be with my words, and there are nationalists in our country, as well as in Ukraine, this is in fact true. Because we have one Dnieper Kiev baptistery, we certainly have common historical roots and a common destiny. We have a common religion, a common faith, and we have a very similar culture, languages, traditions and state of mind, as you have said correctly. Of course, there are some peculiarities and ethnic specifics in everything. ... But nowadays it so happens that we live in different states. We should proceed from the reality; we should proceed from the fact that a great number of the Ukrainian people values its samostiynost', that is independence. One should not only accept it, but respect it.

Interview to Channel One and Associated Press news agency September 4, 2013 Novo-Ogaryovo, Moscow Region

With regard to Mr Snowden, let me repeat that he is not our agent, nor is he cooperating with us. I am telling you responsibly that he is not cooperating with us today; we are not working with him. He considers himself a human rights activist and in this regard, he is a free man. If he wants to go somewhere and someone will take him, go ahead. If he wants to stay here, there is one condition: he must stop his work aimed at harming our American partners, as strange as that sounds coming from my lips.

News conference following the working meeting of the Gas Exporting Countries Forum (GECF) summit July 1, 2013 The Kremlin, Moscow

Mr Snowden has committed no crimes in the Russian Federation, thank goodness. There is another such character – Mr Assange... Ask yourself this: should such people be extradited so that they can be imprisoned or not? In any case, I personally would prefer not to get involved in such cases. It's like shearing a piglet: there's a lot of squealing and very little wool.

News conference with President of Finland Sauli Niinistö June 25, 2013 Residence Kultaranta

What is "developed" and "developing"? Take China – is it a developed economy or not? I think that it might very well be considered developed. Although it is in China's interest to consider its economy developing, because it gives it several advantages. But the Chinese are a smart and cunning people, with a great culture. They know that it is better, as Deng Xiaoping taught, better for now not to stick one's head out.

Meeting with G20 Youth Summit participants June 20, 2013 St Petersburg

Barack Obama: And finally, we had a discussion about the fact that as the two nuclear superpowers, we have a special obligation to try to continue to reduce tensions... We also compared notes on President Putin's expertise in Judo and my declining skills in basketball. [Laughter] And we both agreed that as you get older, it takes more time to recover.

Vladimir Putin: Mr President wants to weaken me with the statement of his declining skills. [Laughter]

Meeting with US President Barack Obama June 17, 2013 Lough Erne

The country was obviously ripe for some kind of change, drastic change. The country's leadership should have realised this and started implementing the necessary reforms. It's obvious that had they done that, what we see now in Syria wouldn't have happened. That was my first point. Secondly, I said that we're not advocates of the incumbent Syrian government or the country's incumbent president, Bashar al-Assad. And one more thing – what we wouldn't want to do is get involved in the conflict among various denominations of Islam, between Sunni and Shia. This is their internal issue. We have very good relations with the Arab world, and we have good relations with Iran and other countries.

So I will tell you what we are concerned about and why we assumed our current stance. Look at the region as a whole. There's still unrest in Egypt. There's no stability in Iraq, and there's no certainty that it will stay united within its current borders in the future. There's no stability in Yemen, and Tunisia is far from peaceful. Libya is suffering from clashes between various ethnic and tribal groups. So the region as a whole finds itself in a state of, at the very least, uncertainty and conflicts. And now Syria has joined the rest.

In my opinion, this is happening because some people from the outside believe that if the region were to be brought in compliance with a certain idea – an idea that some call democracy – then peace and stability would ensue. That's not how it works. You can't ignore this region's history, traditions and religious beliefs, and you can't just interfere. Look at what happened in Libya. Whether the regime was good or bad, the living standards in the country were the highest in the region. And what do we have now? There's fighting over resources, incessant clashes between tribes, and no one knows where that might lead.

We are very concerned that if we try the same thing with Syria, the result will be similar. Is the pocket of uncertainty between Afghanistan and Pakistan not enough? No one controls that territory, except militants who set up their bases there. Is that what we want? It's very close to our borders. So this is our primary concern.

Secondly, we are concerned over the future of all ethnic and religious groups living in Syria. We want this country to have lasting peace and security, with the people's interests and rights guaranteed. So we believe that first of all the Syrian people are to be given an opportunity to decide how their state should be organized, how their lawful rights, interests and security should be ensured. When there is consensus on these issues, systemic change should take place, not vice versa, when you eliminate some forces and try to establish order, and chaos engulfs the country instead.

There's a question our Western counterparts fail to answer. One of the main armed opposition groups – specialists in Arab countries will correct me if I'm wrong – is called the Al-Nusra Front. The US State Department dubbed it a terrorist organisation connected with Al-Qaeda. The Al-Nusra itself doesn't make a secret out of it. So these are the people that will make up Syria's future government? Our Western counterparts say that it will not happen. "How will you get rid of them, then? Chase them away like flies?" I ask. "No," they say. So what is going to happen? They say they don't know.

This is no joke, though, this is very serious. I'll give you another example. On the one hand, some Western countries support some organisations that are at war with Bashar al-Assad's regime in Syria, but these same Western countries fight these same organisations in Mali. They're not just the same organisations – they are the same people. Some have left Syria and come to Mali. The West is fighting them in Mali, but once they cross the border into Syria, they get support from the West. What is the logic in all of this?

Visit to Russia Today television channel June 11, 2013 Moscow

Vladimir Putin: First, I have repeatedly voiced Russia's official stance – Iran has the right to a peaceful nuclear program and it cannot be singled out for discrimination. Second, we need to be aware that Iran is located in a very challenging region. I have told our Iranian partners about that. That's why Iranian threats made towards neighbouring countries, in particular Israel, threats that Israel can be destroyed, are absolutely unacceptable. This is counterproductive.

Oksana Boyko: This is not a proper quote of the Iranian president.

Vladimir Putin: It doesn't quite matter whether it's a proper quote or not. It means it's best to avoid a wording that could be improperly quoted or could be interpreted differently. That's why the focus on Iran does have a reason behind it. I have no doubts that Iran is compliant with the rules, simply because there is no proof of the opposite. According to the latest IAEA report, Iran has been abiding by the commitments it has taken up. True, there are some outstanding issues but with due patience and friendly attitudes, they can be resolved.

I have a great respect for Iran and a great interest in it. This is a great country indeed. You don't often hear this attribute mentioned in relation to Iran but this is true. This is a country with a great culture, a great history and a great nation. They are very proud of their country, they have their own understanding of their place both in the region and in the world, and that's something you have to respect. You have grasped the core of the problems. Iranians are very smart and cunning politicians. To a certain degree, they have exploited this confrontation with the United States.

Oksana Boyko: They are not the only ones.

Vladimir Putin: They are extremely crafty in this, and they do it to tackle their domestic political issues. When there is an external enemy, it unites the nation. But I guess the United States has been employing the same technique. After the collapse of the Soviet Union, there have been no external threats that would allow Washington to dominate in the West. There must be a threat so that the US can protect its allies from it. This position yields political and economic benefits. If everyone relies on one country for protection, then this country is entitled to some preferences. So it's very important to possess this status of a global defender to be able to resolve issues even beyond the realm of foreign policy and security issues. I think the US has been using Iran for this very purpose, that is to unite its allies in the face of a real or fake threat.

Visit to Russia Today television channel June 11, 2013 Moscow

The US is a democratic state, there's no doubt about that, and it originally developed as a democratic state. When the first settlers set foot on this continent, life forced them to forge a relationship and maintain a dialogue with each other to survive. That's why America was initially conceived as a fundamental democracy. With that in mind, we should not forget that America's development began with a large-scale ethnic cleansing, unprecedented in human history. I wouldn't like to delve so deeply into it, but you are forcing me to do it.

When Europeans arrived in America, that was the first thing they did. And you have to be honest about it. There are not so many stories like that in human history. Take the destruction of Carthage by the Roman Empire. Legend has it that Romans plowed over and sowed the city with salt so that nothing would ever grow there. Europeans didn't use salt because they used the land for agriculture but they wiped out the indigenous population. Then there was slavery, and that's something that is deeply ingrained in America. In his memoirs, US Secretary of State Colin Powell revealed how hard it was for him as a black man to break through, how hard it was to live with other people staring at him. It means this mentality has taken root in the hearts and minds of the people, and is likely to still be there.

Now take the Soviet Union. We know a lot about Stalin now. We know him as a dictator and a tyrant. But still I don't think that in the spring of 1945 Stalin would have used a nuclear bomb against Germany, if he had had one. He could have done it in 1941 or 1942 when it was a matter of life or death. But I really doubt that he would have done it in 1945 when the enemy had almost given up and had absolutely no chance to reverse the trend. I don't think he would have. Now look at the US. They dropped the bomb on Japan, a country that was a non-nuclear state and was very close to defeat.

So there are big differences between us. But it's quite natural that people with such differences are determined to find ways to understand each other better. I don't think there is an alternative. Moreover, it's not by chance that Russia and the US forged an alliance in the most critical moments of modern history – that was the case in WWI and WWII. Even if there was fierce confrontation, our countries united in the face of a common threat, which means there is something that unites us. There must be some fundamental interests that bring us together. That's something we need to focus on first. We need to be aware of our differences but focus on a positive agenda that can improve our cooperation.

Visit to Russia Today television channel June 11, 2013 Moscow

Any state pursues its national interests, and the US is no exception. What's unique here is that the collapse of the Soviet Union left America as the world's single leader. But there was a catch associated with it in that it began to view itself as an empire.

But an empire is not only about foreign policy, it's also about domestic policies. An empire cannot afford to display weakness, and any attempt to strike an agreement on equitable terms is often seen domestically as weakness. But the leadership cannot afford to display weakness due to domestic policy considerations.

I think that the current administration realises that it cannot solve the world's major issues on its own. But first, they still want to do it, and second, they can only take steps that are fit for an empire. Domestic policy considerations play a huge role. Otherwise you would be accused of weakness. In order to act otherwise you either have to win overwhelming support or there must be a change in mentality, when people understand that it's much more beneficial to look for compromises that to impose your will on everyone. But it certainly takes time to change those patterns of thinking in any country, in this case it's the US. First and foremost, this change should take place in the minds of the ruling elite in the broad sense of this phrase. I don't think that it's impossible. I think we've almost come to that point. I very much hope we will reach it soon.

Visit to Russia Today television channel June 11, 2013 Moscow

Television channels showed how members of the armed Syrian opposition take out the internal organs of their dead enemies and eat them. I hope that we will not see such negotiators at Geneva 2, otherwise it would be difficult for me to guarantee the safety of the Russian delegation. It would probably be difficult to work with people like that as well.

News conference following the Russia-EU Summit June 4, 2013 Yekaterinburg

We do not seek to worsen our relations with anyone; on the contrary, we seek to develop and deepen these relations. But we are against turning the other cheek. Russia's society, our traditions, our culture and our laws should be respected.

Answers to journalists' questions following Direct Line   April 25, 2013
Moscow

Margaret Thatcher was one of the most brilliant political figures in the modern world. I knew her personally, and she always made a strong impression.

As for her contribution, she was a pragmatic, tough and consistent politician. That approach helped the UK to recover from the recession at the time. We all know that she came under harsh criticism for some of her policies, including the budgetary restrictions and limiting trade unions' rights. But I think in an emergency, and the situation was indeed critical at the time, her actions proved to be effective. I think the British people should be grateful to her for that.

She made a significant contribution to the development of the British-Soviet and British-Russian relations, for which we will always be indebted to her and will remember her efforts with gratitude.

Press statement and answers to journalists' questions following Russian-Dutch talks April 8, 2013 Amsterdam

Hugo Chavez was a good friend of Russia. He was most definitely an internationalist by conviction, but at the same time he was proud of his Native American origins and called himself an Amerindian with pride. He loved his people.

He was courageous by nature, stuck to his principles, knew how to set the goals he considered essential, knew how to stick to them right to the end, and knew how to realise them. He showed character.

Opinions can differ over Hugo Chavez's policies. Taking his economic policies say, there is a lot you could argue about, but there is absolutely no doubt that he was trying to develop his country and refused to let the difficulties and burdens of this development effort rest solely on the shoulders of ordinary people.

He put all his strength and effort into pulling hundreds of thousands, perhaps even millions, of Venezuelans out of poverty and need.

As for international relations, I have no doubts at all about saying that he sought to build friendly relations with all countries without exception, without any exception, but he was never going to do so at the expense of his beloved Venezuela's interests, and was never going to try please everyone in every way at the expense of his own people's interests.

Chavez was without question a very talented and charismatic man, a brave man, and in his own lifetime became a symbol of Latin America's struggle for independence and true freedom. In this sense, I think that in his lifetime he joined the ranks of such outstanding sons of Latin America as Simon Bolivar, Ernesto Che Guevara, and Fidel Castro...

Vladimir Putin answered journalists' questions at the end of his trip to Vologda
March 7, 2013 Vologda

Vladimir Putin: As for Syria and other countries, I must say that we had a very active discussion and even argued on some points. I think that Mr President has come to agree with our opinion on some matters. I think that we should listen to our partners' opinions on certain aspects of this complex issue too. I got a feeling that it would be hard to resolve without a bottle of good wine, or even a bottle of vodka.

Francois Hollande: A bottle of port would probably be best.

Joint news conference with President of France Francois Hollande February 28, 2013 The Kremlin, Moscow

What concerns do our partners in the United States and their lawmakers voice? They talk about human rights in Russian prisons and places of detention. That is all well and good, but they also have plenty of problems in that area. I have already talked about this: Abu Ghraib, Guantanamo, where people are kept jailed for years without being charged. It is incomprehensible. Not only are those prisoners detained without charge, they walk around shackled, like in the Middle Ages. They legalised torture in their own country.

Can you imagine if we had anything like this here? They would have eaten us alive a long time ago. It would have been a worldwide scandal. But in their country everything is quiet. They have promised many times that they would close down Guantanamo, but it's still there. The prison is open to this day. We don't know, maybe they are still using torture there. These so-called secret CIA prisons. Who has been punished for that? And they still point out our problems. Well, thank you, we are aware of them. But it is outrageous to use this as a pretext to adopt anti-Russian laws, when our side has done nothing to warrant such a response.

News conference of Vladimir Putin December 20, 2012 Moscow

As you may know, many US states do not allow observers from international organizations to be present during elections. Do you like that? The OSCE Office for Democratic Institutions and Human Rights was told outright that they must keep a 300-metre distance or they will be arrested. And all is quiet, everyone likes it. This ODIHR wrote that the election was fine and democratic. Do you like it? I don't think so.

News conference of Vladimir Putin December 20, 2012 Moscow

I am sure that high-ranking [French] officials did not want to offend Gerard Depardieu. ... But actors, musicians, and artists are people with a special, delicate psychological makeup and, as we say in Russia, the artist is easily offended.

News conference of Vladimir Putin December 20, 2012 Moscow

If we are slapped, we must retaliate, otherwise we will always be taken advantage of.

News conference of Vladimir Putin December 20, 2012 Moscow

I am sure you have great respect for the legal system in the United States. There, just you try to put your hand in your pocket and pull something out – you'll get a bullet in the head and that'll be the end of the discussion. And the police officer will be acquitted. They have very strict laws against assault on law enforcement officers. Why do some people think that here it is allowed to tear off officers' shoulder straps, to hit a police officer in the face or try to strangle him? If we allowed this, regardless of the assailants' political views, we would ruin the law enforcement system in our country.

News conference of Vladimir Putin December 20, 2012 Moscow

The issue is that US lawmakers, having got rid of one anti-Russian, anti-Soviet act – the Jackson-Vanik amendment (and they were forced to do so for economic reasons) – decided they would pass another anti-Russian act immediately. So we understood it as US lawmakers making clear to us who's the boss here, and keeping a certain level of tension. If Magnitsky did not exist, they would have found another pretext.

News conference of Vladimir Putin December 20, 2012 Moscow

They talk about a reset [in our ties], and then they aggravate the situation themselves, without any provocation from our side. ... Mr Magnitsky died in prison and his name is now known to many. This is a tragedy, of course, and we regret it. But does nobody die in their prisons? Maybe there are even more deaths there than in our own. ... Listen, they have failed to shut Guantanamo for eight years now. They keep people there in shackles and chains without trial or investigation, like in the Middle Ages. Those who open secret prisons and use legalised torture to conduct investigations, such people are now lecturing us about some of our failings.

Meeting of the Council of Legislators   December 13, 2012   The Kremlin, Moscow

Under what conditions would Russia be willing to revise the price formula for gas sales to Ukraine?

Vladimir Putin: Do you remember the words of that book we all love so much, "Can I get the chairs in the evening and give you the money in the morning?" "Yes, but the money comes first!"

Press statements and answers to journalists' questions following meeting of the Russian-Ukrainian Interstate Commission July 12, 2012 Yalta

The USA, as we all know, is in the middle of an election campaign, and it is very tempting at such times to notch up some points by making hardline statements and playing on old ideological stereotypes and phobias that it is high time we abandoned.

Meeting with Russian ambassadors and permanent representatives in international organizations July 9, 2012 Moscow

The point is that one side wants to be fully invincible, which upsets the global balance. We believe that this is extremely dangerous. The availability of a strategic balance allowed us to avoid major global conflicts for a long time after World War Two. As soon as one side gets an illusion that it's invincible to a retaliatory strike by the other side, the number of conflicts goes up. That is not because America is an aggressive country by nature, but because it's just a fact of life.

2 March 2012 Prime Minister Vladimir Putin meets with editors-in-chief of leading foreign media outlets

Ernest Mackevicius: We are receiving thousands of calls, and many people are sending text messages. Here is one of them: "Your friend, US Senator John McCain, warned on Twitter that Muammar Gaddafi's fate could befall you. Is this just an idle threat or an actual plan of the West?

Vladimir Putin: You exaggerate greatly when you say he is my friend ... though I do know Mr McCain. I met with him once in Munich at the well-known security conference, as far as I remember. I heard these statements, of course, I read them. Well, what can I say? These statements are not addressed to me but to Russia as a whole. They want to move our country to the side, so that it won't be in the way and won't interfere in their global domination. They are still afraid of Russia's nuclear capabilities, because Russia is in their line of sight, their attention, and so it is an irritant. Also, we have our own views and we conduct an independent foreign policy, and, I hope will continue conducting it. This surely bothers someone. That's the first thing.

Second, the West is not homogenous, and we have more friends than enemies. Third, Mr McCain, as is known, fought in Vietnam. I think he has enough blood of peaceful civilians on his hands. I guess he is very fond of it and can't live without those horrible and repulsive scenes of Gaddafi's murder, with the footage of his bloody body broadcast all over the world. Is this democracy? Who did this? First, Gaddafi's convoy was bombed by drone aircraft, including US drones. Then, so-called opposition members and fighters were summoned by radio by special forces, which weren't supposed to be there, and Gaddafi was summarily executed. No one says he should have stayed – but this should have been left to the people to decide through democratic procedures. Sure, it is difficult and time-consuming, but it cannot be done in any other way.

As we know, Mr McCain was captured in Vietnam. They did not just put him in a prison camp but in a pit, where he remained for several years, and this is enough to drive anyone nuts. So there's nothing unusual about his statements.

15 December 2011   Television networks Rossiya 1, Rossiya 24, RTR-Planet and radio stations Mayak, Vesti FM, and Radio Rossii completed broadcasting the live Q&A session, A Conversation with Vladimir Putin: Continued

In the modern world the main fight is not for the mineral riches of Siberia and the Far East, attractive though they are. The main fight is for global leadership, and Russia is not going to race China to it. China has other rivals in that business, so let them settle it between themselves.

17 October 2011 Interview with Prime Minister Vladimir Putin

Integration processes are underway in North America between the United States, Canada and Mexico. The same thing is happening in Latin America and Africa. It's fine for these countries to do whatever they want, whereas in our case these critics see imperial ambitions. To these critics, to the obviously unfair ones, I say: mind your own business, deal with inflation, with the increasing government debt or with obesity – ultimately, just do something useful.

17 October 2011 Interview with Prime Minister Vladimir Putin

As for those who are trying to push Russia into a corner, they are mistaken. Russia is not a country to be pushed around.

17 October 2011 Interview with Prime Minister Vladimir Putin

It is no secret I was a KGB officer back in the Soviet era, when the country was waging a war in Afghanistan. I had a friend who served there. In fact, I had a lot of friends serving there, but this one was the senior intelligence advisor in Herat. Once, when he came home on leave, I asked, "What's the situation there like, Sasha?" Patriotic feelings were running high in those days, you know. We were convinced we were doing the right thing in Afghanistan. But here's how my friend answered: "No missile strike can go ahead without my authorisation. And every order I refuse to sign I count as a personal achievement."

I was really shocked to hear him, a fellow KGB officer, say such a thing, at that time. So I asked him to explain. And he said: "Do you have any idea of how many civilians are killed in missile strikes, whatever the motive behind them?" Sometimes, when I look at what's going on in today's world, I'm struck by how lightly decisions are taken on the use of military force in international affairs, and this despite all that preoccupation that the civilised world allegedly has about human rights.

27 April 2011 Prime Minister Vladimir Putin and Swedish Prime Minister Fredrik Reinfeldt hold joint press conference following talks

Mr Gaddafi set up a new empire, just as Napoleon in his time, when he proclaimed himself Emperor after the Revolution propelled him to the top. This comparison might not be very apt but there are some grounds for it. Libya is a monarchy – a warped and ugly one, true, but still a monarchy. Now, its inner conflicts have developed into an armed confrontation. Does this domestic conflict require intervention from outside? After all, there are many other ugly regimes in the world. ...Much has been said about a ban on flights over Libya. So far so good – but what has happened to the ban when Gaddafi's palaces are air-raided every night? They say they don't mean to kill him, but why bomb his palaces then – to get rid of mice, perhaps?

26 April 2011 Prime Minister Vladimir Putin and his Danish counterpart Lars Lokke Rasmussen address the media to summarise their talks

Peter I cut out a "window to Europe" in his time. What was his aim? Above all to promote economic activity and trade. In terms of access to external markets, they have closed the vents on us. It has become difficult to pass through transit countries. It is vital for us to have direct access to the market for our traditional goods.

20 April 2011 Prime Minister Vladimir Putin delivers a report on the government's performance in 2010 in the State Duma

We suddenly realised our Western partners had resumed active contacts with Libya. Mr Gaddafi was welcome in all European capitals, and all European leaders visited Libya. As my German friends say, Alte Liebe rostet nicht (Old love does not rust).

23 March 2011 Vladimir Putin and Boris Tadic attend a news conference on Russian-Serbian talks

A country's standing is not determined by its size today but by the welfare of its citizens above all, and this is an area where we have a lot to achieve yet.

2 December 2010 Prime Minister Vladimir Putin gives a news conference in Zurich after Russia wins the 2018 FIFA World Cup bid

China's northern regions are growing now not because of constrained conditions in the country but because the Chinese government is implementing consistent policies for the economy and for the ethnic composition of its northern territories. I think that we will eventually benefit from this, provided we choose an appropriate policy. It makes more sense to have a prosperous and flourishing neighbour than a poor and ailing one who needs permanent attention.

30 August 2010 During his trip along the new Khabarovsk-Chita highway Prime Minister Vladimir Putin replied to questions from correspondents from the Russia-24 and My Planet television channels

As everyone knows, our American partners are building a global missile-defense system, and we aren't. But missile-defense and strategic offensive weapons are closely interrelated issues. A balance of forces was what kept aggression at bay and preserved peace during the Cold War. The missile and air defense systems and offensive weapons systems contribute equally to this balance. If we do not develop a missile defence system, the risk arises that our partners will feel entirely secure and protected against our offensive weapons systems. If the balance I mentioned is disrupted, they will feel able to act with impunity, increasing the level of aggression in politics and, incidentally, in the economy. In order to maintain the balance without planning to develop a missile defence system, which is very expensive and of unclear effect, we should develop offensive strike systems. But there is a catch. In order for this balance to be maintained, if we want to exchange information, then our partners should give us information about their ballistic missile defence system and in return we would give them information about our offensive weapons.

29 December 2009 Prime Minister Vladimir Putin talks with journalists about the outcomes of his visit to the Primorye Territory

[Question]: Will Russia help the United States after its collapse?

Vladimir Putin: If this happens, there will be a lot to pay because the United States is the world's biggest power, economic power, and we have extensive links with it. It is one of our most important partners, and the global economy is very closely intertwined with the US economy. Therefore, it would be inappropriate to wish problems on any country. We would all be better off living in a prosperous world, rather than in a world of disasters.

3 December 2009 Special TV programme "Conversation with Vladimir Putin: To Be Continued"

By the way, the Soviet Union did not have the goal of dividing Germany. Even in Stalin's time, Soviet diplomacy did not pursue the goal of dividing Germany. More importantly, it acted on the assumption that Germany would be a single state, but one that was demilitarised and democratic. Incidentally, this is what happened with Austria. But our allies preferred to first announce the establishment of the Federal Republic of Germany (FRG), and that gave rise to the processes that eventually led to division.

Actually, in my view, Germany and the German people were hostages of the struggle of two superpowers and occupation forces both in the West and the East. I want to emphasise this – both in the West and the East.

8 November 2009 Vladimir Putin gave an interview for NTV Television's documentary "The Wall"

The Chinese are difficult negotiators, very difficult. I cannot think of any question which would be free from disagreement: arguing every question until they're hoarse, right up until the last minute. And sometimes the signing is simply delayed, but it is returned to later, and an agreement reached.

14 October 2009 Prime Minister Vladimir Putin answered questions from the media, concluding his official visit to the People's Republic of China

The world order created after World War I was faulty. The Treaty of Versailles not only sealed Germany's status, but placed the German people in a humiliating position. One must not humiliate nations, especially such a great nation as Germany. ...

The seeds of revenge were ingrained in the Treaty of Versailles. Okay, the victors ate alone. They failed to control themselves after World War I. But what happened after? Shortly after the Nazis came to power, in 1934 Poland signed a declaration with Germany, which was essentially also a non-aggression pact. In 1935, Britain signed a treaty with Germany, giving it more freedom of action at sea while actually denouncing this part of the Treaty of Versailles. France followed with a bilateral agreement, and in 1938, both France and Britain signed the so-called Munich agreement.

It was signed on September 29, and on September 30, Poland sent an ultimatum to Czechoslovakia. On October 1, both Germany and Poland simultaneously invaded it. Such coordination shows that the Polish leaders opened Pandora's box themselves. They let the genie out of the bottle.

But if Poland considered it acceptable to take part in the partition of Czechoslovakia, who has the moral right to complain it was treated in the same way it had treated Czechoslovakia? I am not trying to defend Soviet diplomacy in 1939, but the Soviet Union was the last to sign a non-aggression pact with Germany. ...

All in all, 55 million people were killed in World War II. The Soviet Union lost 27 million. Russia lost 70% of this number. You can look at any study to see these figures. This was the sacrifice brought by our country to the altar of a common victory.

Every nation suffered. We should not poke around in all this, promote some twisted data and stir hatred for each other. I think this is being done with a purpose. They are setting a fire and then acting as a fire brigade to receive some domestic political benefits.

I believe that the future belongs to those in our countries – and they constitute an overwhelming majority – who do not want just to live in peace but also to cooperate and be friends.

11 September 2009 Prime Minister Vladimir Putin met with members of the sixth Valdai Discussion Club

We always deal with the current authorities, and never get involved in supporting actions that could lead to any unconstitutional process on the territory of any country, especially within countries of the former USSR, because democracy in these countries is weak, their political systems are not stable, and the justice systems are quite vague. Given these conditions, stability is more important than anything.

1 September 2009 Following the talks, Prime Minister Vladimir Putin and his Polish counterpart Donald Tusk held a joint news conference

Vladimir Putin: What about our dialogue with our Belarusian partners on the supply of farm produce?

Sergei Sobyanin: I have to say that our Belarusian partners are excessively politicising the issue and have made some highly provocative statements, which of course complicate the negotiations. ...

Vladimir Putin: Provocative statements are of course unfortunate, but we shouldn't take offence. You know, in a crisis people tend to be stressed out. By the way, we should watch our words ourselves, even if we think we are right, one has to know what to say and where to say it, and we should show restraint. In politics, like in daily life, taking offence is not the best way. You know, I grew up in the Leningrad streets, and the neighbourhood kids said in such cases: "He who calls people names is himself that name."

15 June 2009 Prime Minister Vladimir Putin conducted Government Presidium meeting

Question: Mr Prime Minister, can you imagine a future where Russian security does not involve nuclear weapons?

Vladimir Putin: Of course. Why do we need nuclear weapons? Were we the ones that invented them? Have we ever used them? If those who developed the atomic bomb are ready to renounce it, just as I hope other nuclear powers – official and unofficial would be, then of course we would welcome and facilitate the process in every way possible.

10 June 2009 Prime Minister Vladimir Putin meets with German Vice Chancellor and Foreign Minister Frank-Walter Steinmeier

One ancient eastern sage said: "It is easy to love the whole world, just try to love your neighbour". If this book, at least in a small way, serves to help people in our countries know and understand each other better, and elicits goodwill between our peoples, then I would say that our aim in writing and publishing it has been achieved.

12 May 2009 Prime Minister Vladimir Putin took part in the presentation of the Japanese edition of the book "Let's Learn Judo with Vladimir Putin"

We believe that the use of force in the world arena has recently been overdone. Instead of conducting unpleasant and prolonged negotiations all too often problems are solved by crude force, and that is counterproductive.

6 April 2009 Prime Minister Vladimir Putin reported to the State Duma on the Russian Government's performance in 2008

Some people would hate to see closer relations between Russia and Europe. I think this is a very incorrect stance to take. It ignores the world development trend. That tradition has its roots in the past, and what is more, the darkest pages of the past. Our past did not only have dark times, but also much that was good. The main thing, however, is that Europe and Russia undoubtedly have a common future. We should recognize that natural interdependence, build our relations for the long term on understandable principles, and respect each other's interests. If we do so, all of Greater Europe will be prosperous and competitive in today's complicated world. I can imagine that somebody does not want Greater Europe to become more competitive, so they are poking about trying to rekindle the fears of the past.

15 January 2009   Russian Prime Minister Vladimir Putin's interview with German Television's Channel One ARD

I look at Western European media and media in North America. I am sorry to say it, but I do not find an objective assessment of events there.

8 January 2009 Russian Prime Minister Vladimir Putin met with foreign media

I have already said that supplying weapons to a conflict area is an unscrupulous and dangerous business. We certainly condemn such action.

2 October 2008 After their talks, Russian Prime Minister Vladimir Putin and Ukrainian Prime Minister Yulia Tymoshenko held a joint news conference

Question: What is your attitude to the situation in Afghanistan and do you approve of the actions of the international community in the fight against the Taliban?

Vladimir Putin: We approve of the actions of the international community in the fight against terror. But we believe that these actions are not very effective and by far not always professional. Think of the recurring air raids on the terrorist infrastructure in which many civilians have died. Or take the efforts of the international coalition in combating drug trafficking. The results are zero, indeed probably negative because the production of heroin keeps growing. It is bad in itself because the main market for Afghan heroin is Western Europe, and it is bad from the point of view of the fight against terror because the drug money is to a large extent used to finance terrorist activities.

13 September 2008 Interview granted by Prime Minister Vladimir Putin to the French newspaper Le Figaro

[On the conflict with Georgia] Of course we had to respond, how else should we have behaved? Did you expect us to wipe our "bleeding nose" and bow our head down? Do you want us to act in a way that would throw the situation in the North Caucasus and Russia totally off balance?

I can tell you more, we are aware of the creation of non-governmental organisations in some republics in the North Caucasus, which, under the pretext of our failure to defend South Ossetia, raised the question of secession from Russia. So, if we defended South Ossetia it was bad, if we had not defended it we would have been on the receiving end of another blow that would throw the Russian North Caucasus out of balance. This is the limit of impudence.

Now why did we act as we did? Because the infrastructure used to attack Tskhinvali, our peacekeepers and South Ossetia as a whole stretched far beyond Tskhinvali. I am referring to control centres, radars and arms dumps. What did you expect us to do, wield a stationery knife there?

11 September 2008 Prime Minister Vladimir Putin met with members of the Valdai International Discussion Club

It is not right to talk up the right to national self-determination in Kosovo and emphasise the principle of territorial integrity in the case of Georgia. We should at long last agree by what set of rules we are going to live. We have said it many times, we have issued warnings. We warned against Kosovo setting a precedent. But the West was adamant. Nobody wanted to listen, they forgot about international law, forgot about the UN resolutions, everything. They did as they wanted because they thought it was good for the geopolitical interests of our Western partners, above all the American partners, while the Europeans just tagged along.

11 September 2008 Prime Minister Vladimir Putin met with members of the Valdai International Discussion Club

You see, when we talk about an equal relationship, it means respecting one another. And that means recognising the other as an equal partner. And if the United States, like Western Europe... I don't mean to offend anyone, but Western Europe does not have its own foreign policy. Russia cannot and will not work in such a system of relations. ... Our American partners do not allow themselves to be challenged by anyone on the American continent. This is considered to be its holy of holies. But sending ships with missiles to within 200 kilometres of where we are – is that normal? Do you call that equality?

11 September 2008 Prime Minister Vladimir Putin met with members of the Valdai International Discussion Club

Today we have no ideological contradictions, like in the Cold War; there is no basis for a cold war. Of course, contradictions may arise. There may be competition and geopolitical interests may diverge. But there is no solid foundation for mutual hostility.

At least that is my thinking. On the contrary, we have many common problems that we can successfully tackle only by pooling our efforts. They are all well known: terrorism, non-proliferation of WMD, and infectious diseases which pose a great threat to mankind. And who knows what else may crop up.

11 September 2008 Prime Minister Vladimir Putin met with members of the Valdai International Discussion Club

Under the international agreements, the Russian peacekeepers are committed to protecting the population of South Ossetia. And now let's recall Bosnia in 1995. As we know well, the European peacekeeping contingent, represented by the Dutch troops, did not want to get involved with one of the attacking sides, and allowed it to destroy a whole village. Hundreds of people were killed or injured. The tragedy in Srebrenica is well known in Europe. Would you have wanted us to do the same? To leave and allow the Georgian troops to kill people in Tskhinvali?

29 August 2008 Russian Prime Minister Vladimir Putin interviewed by the German ARD TV channel

Roth: Another Foreign Secretary, Mr Miliband of the UK, has recently voiced his concerns over the start of the new Cold War and a new arms race. What do you think about this situation? Are we on the threshold of a new Ice Age, a new Cold War and a new arms race? What do you think?

Putin: There's this joke: Whoever is the first to cry "Stop thief" is the one who is guilty.

Roth: The British Foreign Secretary.

Putin: These are your words, not mine. Excellent. It's a pleasure talking with you. But these were your words. Speaking seriously, Russia does not want to aggravate relations with anyone. We don't want any tensions. We want a good, friendly partnership with everyone.

29 August 2008 Russian Prime Minister Vladimir Putin interviewed by the German ARD TV channel

Aren't you aware of what has been happening in Georgia in these past few years? Prime Minister Zhvania's mysterious death; the crackdown on the opposition; violent dispersal of opposition rallies; the conduct of national elections in what was almost an emergency situation. Finally, this criminal action in Ossetia, involving many human losses. And this is, certainly, a democratic country with which others should maintain dialogue, and which should be accepted into NATO, and possibly even the EU. But if another country protects its interests, simply its citizens' right to live when they have been attacked... We had 80 deaths immediately. All in all, 2,000 civilians died. And we have no right to protect them there? Or, if we protect our lives, we will be deprived of sausage? What is our choice? Between sausage and life? We choose life, Mr Roth.

Now about one more value – the freedom of the press. Look at how these events are covered by the U.S. press, this torch of democracy, and also in the European press for that matter. I was in Beijing when these events started. The city of Tskhinvali was subjected to massive shelling, Georgian troops started ground operations, there were numerous losses but nobody said a word. Your channel said nothing, the American media said nothing. There was total silence, as if nothing was happening. But when the aggressor was hit in the face, when he got his teeth knocked out, when he abandoned all his American weapons and fled as fast as he could, everyone suddenly remembered international law and the evil Russia.

29 August 2008 Russian Prime Minister Vladimir Putin interviewed by the German ARD TV channel

We must take a broader view of this conflict. ... All these state entities, each in its own time, joined the Russian Empire of their own free will. Ossetia was the first to become part of the Russian Empire in the middle of the 18th century, in 1745-1747. At that time, it was a united entity; North and South Ossetia were a single state. In 1801, if my memory serves me, Georgia itself, which was under pressure from the Ottoman Empire, voluntarily became part of the Russian Empire. Only 12 years later, in 1812, Abkhazia joined the Russian Empire. Before that it had existed as an independent state, an independent principality.

It was only in the middle of the 19th century that it was decided to incorporate South Ossetia into Tiflis Province. Within a single country, the matter was regarded as not very important. But I can assure you that subsequent years showed that Ossetians did not like it too much. However, de facto the tsar's central government put them under the jurisdiction of what is today's Georgia. When the Russian Empire collapsed after the First World War, Georgia declared its own state, while Ossetia expressed the desire to remain part of Russia. This was immediately after the events of 1917. In response Georgia conducted a punitive operation there, a very cruel one, and repeated it again in 1921.

When the Soviet Union was formed, on Stalin's orders these territories were definitively given to Georgia. As you know, Stalin was of Georgian origin. Therefore, those who insist that those territories should continue to belong to Georgia are Stalinists. They defend a decision made by Joseph Stalin. But no matter what may be happening now, and no matter by what motives the people involved in the conflict were guided, everything that we are witnessing today is, unquestionably, a tragedy. For us it is a special tragedy, because over many years of joint existence, Georgian culture – and the Georgian people have an ancient culture – has undoubtedly become part of Russia's multinational culture.

You know, for us, there is even a tinge of a civil war, although Georgia is of course an independent state; there is no doubt about it. We have never infringed on Georgia's sovereignty, and have no intention of doing so in the future. And yet, we have special spiritual links with that country and its people, considering that almost a million, or even more than a million Georgians live in this country.

28 August 2008 CNN interviews Russian Prime Minister Vladimir Putin

George told me that nobody wanted a war. We hoped that the U.S. Administration would interfere in this conflict and stop the aggressive actions of the Georgian leadership, but nothing of the kind happened. ... We are a peace-loving state, and we want to cooperate with all our neighbors and all our partners. But if someone thinks that they can come and kill us, that our place is at the cemetery, these people should think about the consequences of such a policy for themselves.

28 August 2008 CNN interviews Russian Prime Minister Vladimir Putin

What I am going to say now is only a supposition and it has to be properly verified. But I think there is food for thought. Even during the Cold War, a time of tough confrontation between the Soviet Union and the United States, we always avoided a direct clash between our civilians, not to mention military servicemen.

We have serious grounds to believe that there were U.S. citizens right in the combat zone. If that is so, if that is confirmed, this is very bad. This is very dangerous, and this is a misguided policy. But if this is the case, the said events may have a U.S. domestic politics dimension.

If my suppositions are confirmed, then there are grounds to suspect that some people in the United States deliberately provoked this conflict to aggravate the situation and create an advantage for one of the candidates in the U.S. presidential race. If this is true, this is nothing else but the abuse of administrative resources in the domestic political struggle in its worst, bloodiest form. ...

Why do you find my supposition astounding? I don't understand. There are problems in the Middle East; reconciliation has not been reached there. The situation in Afghanistan is not getting any better. Moreover, the Taliban has launched a fall offensive, and dozens of NATO servicemen are being killed. In Iraq, after the euphoria of the first victories there are problems everywhere, and the death toll has already exceeded 4,000. There are problems in the economy, as we know only too well. There are financial problems and the mortgage crisis. We are concerned about it ourselves, and want it to end as soon as possible, but it is still there.

A small victorious war would be helpful. And if it fails, the blame can be laid at our door. We can be portrayed as the enemy, and against the backdrop of this jingoism the nation can be rallied around certain political forces. I am surprised that you are astounded at what I am saying. It's as clear as day.

28 August 2008 CNN interviews Russian Prime Minister Vladimir Putin

It is a pity that some of our partners are not helping us, and are even trying to intervene. What I am talking about, for example, is the transfer of the Georgian military contingents from Iraq directly into the conflict zone using the United States' military transport planes. This will not change anything, but this is a step in the opposite direction from resolving the situation. What is surprising is not even the cynicism of such actions, because politics, as they say, is a cynical business in general. What is surprising is the level of cynicism. What surprises is the ability to swap good and bad, black and white, the slick ability to pose an aggressor as a victim of the aggression, and to make the victims responsible for its consequences.

But, of course, Saddam Hussein had to be hanged for destroying several Shiite villages. And the present Georgian leadership, who have simply wiped out ten Ossetian villages from the face of this planet, whose tanks were running over children and old men, who have burned civilians alive in sheds – these people, certainly, had to be taken under protection. If I am not mistaken, Ronald Reagan once said about a Latin American dictator: "Somoza is a bastard, but he is our bastard. And we will help him, we will protect him."

11 August 2008   Prime Minister Vladimir Putin chaired a Government Presidium meeting

France is our traditional, reliable partner. We have always talked about a strategic partnership between France and Russia. I agree with that definition. France has pursued, and I hope will continue to pursue, an independent foreign policy. I think it is part of French character, and it is hard to impose anything on the French people from the outside.

31 May 2008 Prime Minister Vladimir Putin gave an interview to the French newspaper Le Monde

[On Iran's nuclear program] In whose interests can nuclear weapons be used, in the interests of Palestine? But then Palestinians would cease to exist. We all remember what the Chernobyl tragedy was like. It is enough for the wind to change direction and it is the end.

31 May 2008 Prime Minister Vladimir Putin gave an interview to the French newspaper Le Monde

Iran is only one part of the problem. Many "threshold" countries face the choice of using nuclear energy for peaceful purposes. That means they will need enriched uranium. If they need enriched uranium and create their own closed cycle for this purpose, there will always be a suspicion that they want to enrich it further to get weapons-grade uranium. It is not easy to control. That is why we have proposed that enrichment take place in such countries which raise no suspicions, because they already possess nuclear weapons. But the countries involved in the process would have a total guarantee that they will get the necessary amount of enriched uranium and that spent nuclear fuel will be taken from them for reprocessing. Such a system can be put in place. It will be reliable and safe.

31 May 2008 Prime Minister Vladimir Putin gave an interview to the French newspaper Le Monde

The expansion of the [Nato] bloc will only create new borders in

Europe and new Berlin Walls, this time invisible walls, but equally dangerous. That limits the potential of joint effective efforts to combat common modern threats because it breeds mutual mistrust.

31 May 2008 Prime Minister Vladimir Putin gave an interview to the French newspaper Le Monde

Is it right to be an angel at home, a democrat inside your own country and a monster to the rest of the world? We are talking about democracy. What is democracy? It is rule by the people and for the people. In Ukraine all the opinion polls show that nearly 80% of the population do not want their country to join NATO. Yet our partners say that Ukraine will be a NATO member. Is it possible that all the decisions have been made in advance on behalf of the Ukrainians? Doesn't their opinion interest anyone? And you are telling me this is democracy?

31 May 2008 Prime Minister Vladimir Putin gave an interview to the French newspaper Le Monde

We consider that Kosovo's unilateral declaration of independence is unfair and unlawful. We do not accept the argument that this is simply some kind of fait accompli because this situation did not just develop on its own but received the active help of some of the players in the international community.

If arms were not supplied to the conflict zone and promises of independence not made, this situation would not have arisen. We do not understand why it is that in one part of the world people who fight for independence are called 'fighters for independence', while in another they are called 'separatists' and appeals are made to combat them. We think that a common standard should be applied in all cases.

We need to respect the provisions of international law. Only then will all countries, big and small, feel secure. Any other approach only increases tension and fuels the arms race, as small countries end up feeling that only their own defence capability and not international law will be able to protect them.

Press Conference following Talks with Prime Minister of Greece Konstantinos Karamanlis April 29, 2008 The Kremlin, Moscow

Vladimir Putin: This was my last meeting as President of Russia with George, and I would like to take this opportunity to say once again that it has always been a pleasure and has always been interesting to work with the American President. I have always valued his fine human qualities, his honesty and openness and his ability to listen. ...

George W. Bush: ... It will be our last meeting as Presidents of our country. And it's a little bit nostalgic. It's a moment where it just proves life moves on.

Press Conference following Russian-U.S. Talks April 6, 2008 Bocharov Ruchei Residence, Sochi

Regarding NATO, the Chancellor and I said today that at a time when we no longer have confrontation between two rival systems, the endless expansion of a military and political bloc seems to us not only unnecessary but also harmful and counterproductive. The impression is that attempts are being made to create an organisation that would replace the United Nations, but the international community in its entirety is hardly likely to agree to such a structure for our future international relations. I think the potential for conflict would be only set to grow.

Press Conference following Talks with Federal Chancellor of Germany Angela Merkel March 8, 2008 Novo-Ogaryovo

[Journalist]: Recently Mrs Clinton said that as a former KGB officer, by definition, you do not have a soul. How would your soul or what, Mrs Clinton suggests, replaces it, react to such a statement?

Vladimir Putin: I think that at the very least a statesman should have a head.

Transcript of Annual Big Press Conference February 14, 2008 The Kremlin, Moscow

We all know that democracy is government by the people. Our American partners are looking to deploy elements of a missile defence system in Eastern Europe, a radar station in the Czech Republic, and interceptor missiles in Poland, and these plans look like they will indeed go ahead. But who asked the Czechs and the Poles if they actually want these systems on their soil?

Transcript of Annual Big Press Conference February 14, 2008 The Kremlin, Moscow

No matter what is said during election campaigns, the fundamental interests of Russia and the United States will inevitably prompt the leadership in both countries into developing a positive dialogue as partners at the very least. ...Only by cooperating with each other can we effectively fight terrorism, strengthen the weapons of mass destruction non-proliferation regime, and combat poverty and infectious diseases.

Transcript of Annual Big Press Conference February 14, 2008 The Kremlin, Moscow

Russia's growing economic and military potential does allow us to be firmer in standing up for our national interests, both political and economic. We will never seek confrontation, but we do think it is our right to defend our interests, just as our partners do, and indeed, we can learn from them.

Transcript of Annual Big Press Conference February 14, 2008 The Kremlin, Moscow

The 'bloc' mentality should be phased out, and instead we should adopt a completely different system of international relations. A system that does not just take into account each others' interests, but also develops common rules, known as international law. And we should strictly abide by these rules. Ultimately this could provide stability in the world and protect the interests of small countries but also large ones, and even super powers like the United States.

Interview with Time Magazine December 19, 2007 Given December 12, 2007

[On raising gas prices to Ukraine] We sell gas at world prices to all our customers. Why should we sell gas at lower prices to someone? Do the Americans sell at cheaper prices? Can you walk into a shop in the USA and say, "I'm from Canada, and we Canadians are good friends of the USA, so can you sell me a Chrysler at half price?" What kind of answer would such a person get? They'd say, "Out of here, you idiot!"

Interview with Time Magazine December 19, 2007 Given December 12, 2007

There is no Soviet Union and no Warsaw Pact today, while NATO not only exists but is expanding. ...We are particularly concerned about military infrastructure coming closer to our borders. We think this is simply harmful and that it does not help to build a climate of trust in Europe and the world.

Interview with IRNA Information Agency and Iranian State Television and Radio October 16, 2007 Tehran

Frankly speaking, there are not that many countries in the world today that have the good fortune to say they are sovereign. You can count them on your fingers: China, India, Russia and a few other countries. All other countries are to a large extent dependent either on each other or on bloc leaders. This is not a very pleasant situation, but it is my deep conviction and it is true. I know that, unfortunately, in some Eastern European countries, not just the candidate for the post of defence minister but even candidates for less important posts are agreed upon with the U.S. ambassador. Is this a good thing? I do not think it is very good for either these countries or the U.S. itself because sooner or later it will provoke the same rejection that Soviet domination once provoked in these countries.

Meeting with Members of the Valdai International Discussion Club September 14, 2007 Sochi

With such substantial relations and ties in such a wide variety of areas there will always be differences somewhere. ... The question is one of what means we use and in what spirit we resolve these problems. We can take a confrontational approach and rattle our sabres, try to scare each other, or we can look for compromises and come to agreements. Our hope is that we can take the second road.

Responses to Questions from Russian Journalists September 10, 2007 Abu Dhabi

I am happy to give you the following information. In 1992, the Russian Federation unilaterally stopped sending its strategic aviation on long-range patrols. Unfortunately, not everyone has followed our example and other countries' strategic aviation continue patrols to this day. This creates certain problems for the Russian Federation in ensuring its security. In response to this situation, I have decided that Russia's strategic aviation will resume patrols on a permanent basis.

At midnight, today, August 17, 14 strategic missile-carriers, support and refuelling aircraft took off from seven air force bases in different parts of the Russian Federation and began a patrol involving a total of 20 aircraft. As from today, such patrols will be carried out on a regular basis. These patrols are strategic in nature. The aircraft involved in today's patrol will spend around 20 hours in the air, with refuelling, in coordination with the Navy. The patrols will take place above all in areas where Russian Federation shipping and economic activity is most active.

We hope that our partners will show understanding towards the resumption of patrols by Russia's strategic aviation. Our pilots have spent too long on the ground. We have strategic aviation but it spends practically no time in the air. Flights took place now and again only during large-scale military exercises, and as you know, we have held very few such exercises over the last 15 years. As I said, our pilots have spent too long on the ground. I know that they are happy to now have this chance to begin a new life and we wish them luck.

Press Statement following the Peace Mission 2007 Counterterrorism Exercises and the Shanghai Cooperation Organisation Summit August 17, 2007 General Forces Training Ground 225, Chebarkul, Chelyabinsk Region

Regarding your suggestions on correcting Russia's image, I think there is no need. ...They [the Western media] will continue blindly repeating what they've been told to say, what they've been paid to say. They are just doing their work. This is just an instrument for putting pressure on Russia.

Excerpts from Transcript of Meeting with Members of Russian Youth Organisations July 24, 2007 Zavidovo, Tver Region

What is the root of the problem that our British partners are currently making such a fuss about? A tragedy took place – the death of Litvinenko in London. The British suspect a Russian citizen – Lugovoy – and they want to extradite him to the UK. Meanwhile, thirty people wanted by our law enforcement services for committing serious and very serious crimes are hiding in London and the British have not considered for an instant handing them over to Russia.

Excerpts from Transcript of Meeting with Members of Russian Youth Organisations July 24, 2007 Zavidovo, Tver Region

A country must respect its partners. When we see respect for ourselves, we will show respect for them.

Excerpts from Transcript of Meeting with Members of Russian Youth Organisations July 24, 2007 Zavidovo, Tver Region

Vladimir Putin: ...Frankly speaking, we regret what is happening in Ukraine...

Viktor Yanukovich: ...Unfortunately, Ukraine has been going through a period of political crisis that began at the start of April. ...There are still some outstanding questions that we need to resolve, and that concern the opposition mostly. ...

Vladimir Putin: Viktor Fyodorovich, you don't have any opposition! Everyone is in power! Where's the opposition? I can't figure it out. Everyone there seems to be in power...

Beginning of Meeting with Ukrainian Prime Minister Viktor Yanukovich June 21, 2007

If we decide that in today's world the principle of a nation's right to self-determination is more important than the principle of territorial integrity, then we must apply this principle to all parts of the world and not only to regions where it suits our partners.

Press Conference following the end of the G8 Summit June 8, 2007 Heiligendamm

A missile defence system for one side and no such system for the other creates an illusion of security and increases the possibility of a nuclear conflict. ... In order to restore that balance without setting up a missile defence system we will have to create a system to overcome missile defence, and this is what we are doing now. ...Why are our American partners trying so obstinately to deploy a missile defence system in Europe...? Is it perhaps to ensure that we carry out these retaliatory measures? And to prevent a further rapprochement between Russia and Europe?

Interview with Newspaper Journalists from G8 Member Countries June 4, 2007

Let us not be hypocritical about democratic freedoms and human rights. I already said that I have a copy of Amnesty International's report including on the United States. There is probably no need to repeat this so as not to offend anyone. If you wish, I shall now report how the United States does in all this. We have an expression that is perhaps difficult to translate but it means that one can always have plenty to say about others. Amnesty International has concluded that the United States is now the principal violator of human rights and freedoms worldwide. I have the quote here, I can show you. And there is argumentation behind it.

Interview with Newspaper Journalists from G8 Member Countries   June 4, 2007

I think that after the British government allowed a significant number of criminals, thieves, and terrorists to gather in Britain they created an environment which endangers the lives and health of British citizens. And all responsibility for this lies with the British side.

Interview with Newspaper Journalists from G8 Member Countries   June 4, 2007

Der Spiegel: Mr President, former Federal Chancellor Gerhard Schroeder called you a 'pure democrat'. Do you consider yourself such?

Vladimir Putin: (laughs) Am I a 'pure democrat'? Of course I am, absolutely. But do you know what the problem is? Not even a problem but a real tragedy? The problem is that I'm all alone, the only one of my kind in the whole wide world. Just look at what's happening in North America, it's simply awful: torture, homeless people, Guantanamo, people detained without trial and investigation. Just look at what's happening in Europe: harsh treatment of demonstrators, rubber bullets and tear gas used first in one capital then in another, demonstrators killed on the streets. That's not even to mention the post-Soviet area. Only the guys in Ukraine still gave hope, but they've completely discredited themselves now and things are moving towards total tyranny there; complete violation of the Constitution and the law and so on. There has been no one to talk to since Mahatma Gandhi died.

Interview with Newspaper Journalists from G8 Member Countries June 4, 2007

If we want to place the principle of a people's right to self-determination – the principle behind the Soviet Union's policy during the time when peoples were struggling to free themselves from colonialism – above the principle of territorial integrity, this policy and this decision should be universal and should apply to all parts of the world, and at least to all parts of Europe. We are not convinced by our partners' statements to the effect that Kosovo is a unique case. There is nothing to suggest that the case of Kosovo is any different to that of South Ossetia, Abkhazia or Trans-Dniester. The Yugoslav communist empire collapsed in one case and the Soviet communist empire collapsed in the second. Both cases had their litany of war, victims, criminals and the victims of crimes. ... We are told that there is a need to hurry, but hurry where? What is taking place to make it so urgent to leap about like, excuse the expression, a flea in a lasso?

Interview with Newspaper Journalists from G8 Member Countries June 4, 2007

Saddam Hussein...was charged with carrying out reprisals against the residents of Shiite villages that resulted in the execution of around 148 people, and more in another location. Those were the kinds of figures cited, in any case. But since military operations began in Iraq, more than 3,000 Americans have been killed and the number of Iraqi civilians killed, according to various estimates, is already in the hundreds of thousands. Can we really compare these two situations?

Interview with Arab Satellite Channel Al-Jazeera February 10, 2007

I do not really understand why some of our partners are trying to return to a situation where they see themselves as cleverer and more civilised and think that they have the right to impose their standards on others. Let them go to China and try managing its more than 1.5 billion people. I doubt they would do it better than Mr Hu Jintao. The thing to remember is that standards that are imposed from outside, including in the Middle East, rather than being a product of a society's natural internal development, lead to tragic consequences, and the best example of this is Iraq.

Interview with Arab Satellite Channel Al-Jazeera February 10, 2007

NATO is not a universal organisation, as opposed to the UN. It is first and foremost a military and political alliance, military and political! Well, ensuring one's own security is the right of any sovereign state. We are not arguing against this. Of course we are not objecting to this. But why is it necessary to put military infrastructure on our borders during this expansion?

Speech and the Following Discussion at the Munich Conference on Security Policy February 10, 2007 Munich

[On Kosovo] Together we can only create certain necessary conditions and help people resolve their own problems. Create the necessary conditions and act as the guarantors of certain agreements. But we should not impose these agreements. Otherwise, we shall simply put the situation into a dead end. And if one of the participants in this difficult process feels offended or humiliated, then the problem will last for centuries. We will only create a dead end.

Speech and the Following Discussion at the Munich Conference on Security Policy February 10, 2007 Munich

If we ignore the problems and principles of countries' territorial integrity and say, "well, what's happened has happened and there's nothing that can be done about it now", if the international community does not want to do anything to restore Serbia's territorial integrity, then other peoples will also have the right to say, "well, we will also take this approach then". This applies not only to the post-Soviet area, though this is where we see the most similar situation.

Press Conference following Talks with German Chancellor Angela Merkel
January 21, 2007 Bocharov ruchei, Sochi

The problem does not lie in the relations between Georgia and
Russia. The problem lies in relations between Georgia and South
Ossetia, and between Georgia and Abkhazia. ... In the territory of
the former Soviet Union we have quite a few frozen conflicts. And
everyone I talk to says that if Russia were to desire it, then
tomorrow this could be resolved. Russia will not take this
responsibility upon herself. First and foremost it is the
responsibility of the peoples and their representatives to reach an
agreement between themselves and to find a compromise.

Joint Press Conference with Finnish Prime Minister Matti Vanhanen and
President of the European Commission Jose Manuel Barroso October 20, 2006
Lahti, Finland

I think that our colleagues' main problem is that they are not
inclined to search for compromises. They almost always insist that
we accept certain decisions that they consider optimal. But of
course this does not happen 100 percent of the time. Sometimes
we engage in joint work and in these cases, as a rule, we are able
to achieve viable results. I would very much like for this practice
to take hold in our relations with our American partners. This will
only happen in the event that they acknowledge our national
interests and take them into consideration. I repeat that we don't
intend to work against American interests, nor do we intend to
neglect our own interests in favour of our partners' interests.

Transcript of Meeting with Participants in the Third Meeting of the Valdai
Discussion Club September 9, 2006 Novo-Ogaryovo

We wanted to conclude contracts with various lobbying groups
that officially operate in Congress. You know what they told us?
And this is normal, this is in accordance with American laws. But
the people we contacted told us that State Department employees
did not support such relations with Russian partners. That is
strange. It is true that in direct dialogue with our American

117

colleagues they did not admit this. They said: "No, that can't be true, we did not do this". But this means that someone – either the representatives of the lobbies or of the State Department – is giving us the wrong information.

But such trifles prevent us from establishing a constructive dialogue. Why should this be possible for all other countries and not for Russia? We are not doing this underground, with the help of the FSB [formerly KGB] or the Foreign Intelligence Service. We are doing this openly and as it should be done with a view to engaging in a meaningful dialogue with legislators. What is wrong here? They say: "No, that is not possible". Why is it impossible? It is a trifle, a detail. It is simply evidence of how they automatically applied the presumption of the Soviet Union's guilt to Russia. This is not right, it is harmful and it bothers us.

Transcript of Meeting with Participants in the Third Meeting of the Valdai Discussion Club September 9, 2006 Novo-Ogaryovo

The Soviet Union's relations with the African continent were built on several main principles and interests. There was above all the ideological interest, the expansion of the Soviet Union's ideological influence in the world and on the African continent. There was a geopolitical interest. When it helped the peoples of Africa fight colonialism and, in the case of South Africa, fight apartheid, the Soviet Union was of course pursuing its geopolitical interests. It was expanding its zone of influence and reducing the zone of influence of its main rivals, and we should be clear about this. Today, times have changed. The Soviet Union paid a lot in its time to build up this positive political capital, and today we need to transform this into pragmatic economic relations.

Press Conference with Russian Journalists following the Official Visits to South Africa and the Kingdom of Morocco September 7, 2006 Casablanca

George W. Bush: I thought the discussion was a good discussion. It's not the first time that Vladimir and I discussed our governing philosophies. I have shared with him my desires for our country, and he shared with me his desires for his. And I talked about my desire to promote institutional change in parts of the world like Iraq where there's a free press and free religion, and I told him that a lot of people in our country would hope that Russia would do the same thing. ...

Vladimir Putin: I can tell you honestly that we certainly would not want to have the same kind of democracy that they have in Iraq.

George W. Bush: Just wait.

Press Conference Following Talks with U.S. President George W. Bush July 15, 2006 Strelna, St Petersburg

We all remember what arguments some western countries used to justify their colonial expansion into Africa and Asia. If you look back at the newspapers of those years you will see that what was said then hardly differs from what is being said now in relation to the Russian Federation. You just need to replace the civilising role and civilisation with democratisation and democracy, and it all becomes clear. We are ready to work together with all our partners on equal terms and we are attentive to well-meant criticism. We have every reason to listen to what others have to say because we are only in the process of building a modern society. But we categorically oppose the use of all levers, including arguments on the need for us to democratise our society, in order to intervene in our internal affairs. This is something we consider absolutely unacceptable.

Interview with NBC Television Channel (USA) July 12, 2006

You always seem to think that we support the countries you don't like. This is not the case. We opposed the military operation in Iraq, for example, but not because we supported Saddam Hussein. ... The same goes for North Korea. We think that we need to take decisions that will help to defuse the situation and not drive ourselves into an impasse from which we can't find an exit together. This is the difference between the way we went about resolving problems in the twentieth century and in today's world.

Back then, during the Cold War, we always acted in such a way as to cause each other harm at any price, but today we share common goals and the differences between us regard only how to go about resolving this or that problem.

Interview with NBC Television Channel (USA) July 12, 2006

A young man trusts his future bride or doesn't trust her, and if they decide to get married it's for them to work out this issue of trust. But what we are talking about are relations on a completely different level, a completely different kind of relation. I think that we need to develop a system of guarantees that can ensure security in the world and I think that we can achieve this.

Interview with NBC Television Channel (USA) July 12, 2006

But what is very important is that if everything were now as it was at the end of the 1980s, we would have far greater problems. At that time, when the Soviet Union was in Afghanistan, the West was busy raising numerous Bin Ladens, sparing no time or money in its efforts. But today the situation is entirely different. Not only do we not support the forces resisting the international coalition in Afghanistan, but we are trying to make our constructive contribution to the positive development of the situation in that country and we will continue to work in solidarity in this way.

I would like to note that for the first time in our history we have not only authorised transport aircraft to fly across our territory but have also authorised the passage of NATO railway transport taking part in the operations in Afghanistan, including for military transit.

Interview with CTV Television Channel (Canada) July 12, 2006

For fifteen years Russia has been supplying its neighbours with gas at prices that were well below market prices. For fifteen years we've been in fact helping our neighbours to the tune of three to five billion dollars per year.

We've been talking to our partners, including in Ukraine, each year about the fact that we must change to market principles. At the beginning of last year we reached this agreement with President Yushchenko. The discussion was more or less held at his initiative. Unfortunately, at the practical level we were not able to reach an adequate solution and we were forced to suspend deliveries – not to Western Europe mind you – but to Ukraine. And our Ukrainian partners perfectly understood what consequences this could have. And we did not limit the quantity of our supplies that were meant for European consumers, but our Ukrainian partners started to illegally tap into the supplies that were meant for Western Europe.

Russia has been supplying gas to Europe for more than 40 years. Despite all our internal political and economic hardships at the beginning and throughout the 1990s, there was never once any disruption to the deliveries to Western Europe.

Transcript of the Interactive Webcast with the President of Russia July 6, 2006
The Kremlin, Moscow

We respect the fundamental principles of international law, that is, the territorial integrity of countries. At the same time, of course we understand that we must respect the wishes of the population of a given territory as to how it wants to live. This is a contradiction that is visible both in life, as well as in UN documents; this contradiction has always existed. We would like, and we are going to insist on this, that such decisions be made according to common principles. So that it is not possible to act according to political expediency and the present political context and apply one approach to certain countries and regions of Europe, such as Kosovo, and a completely different one to others such as Abkhazia and South Ossetia. ...We call on all participants in the international dialogue to help us avoid this very dangerous tendency to apply double standards.

Transcript of the Interactive Webcast with the President of Russia July 6, 2006
The Kremlin, Moscow

We need to know what we would get in return. This is very easy
to understand if you just think back to childhood when you go into
the street with a sweet in your hand and another kid says: "Give it
to me". And you clutch your little fist tight around it and say:
"And what do I get then?" That is what we want to know – what
do we get in return?

Responses to Questions from Russian Journalists following the Russia-EU
Summit and Press Conference May 25, 2006 Sochi

You know, the Poles and the Russians are essentially one and the
same family. ...As is always the case with close relatives, we have
had our share of problems. I won't list them all now because we
would simply create confusion, putting forward all our claims
against each other, starting with the occupation of the Kremlin (in
the seventeenth century). We would get ourselves tangled up in all
these claims. ...There is a certain wariness in some quarters of our
respective societies with regard to each other. The politicians in
both countries are aware of this, but instead of looking to the
future in the interests of their citizens and building relations for
the future for the good of the Polish and Russian peoples, they are
always trying to raise the problems of the past in order to boost
their own prominence at home.

Transcript of the Press Conference for the Russian and Foreign Media January
31, 2006 Circular Hall, The Kremlin, Moscow

The tradition of appeasing any aggressors and extremists
following the principle of 'make agreement with anyone at any
price, if only they will leave us alone' has become firmly rooted in
European political thought. This is a dangerous way of thinking
that in practice leads to great tragedies. It is enough to remember
Chamberlain and Daladier who signed the Munich Agreement
with Hitler in 1938 and announced on their return home that they
had brought with them 'peace in our time'. But the Second World

War broke out only a year later. In this respect, the Molotov-Ribbentrop Pact was no better, but it was a necessary measure after the western countries accepted a deal with Nazi Germany.

Interview with Television Channel Nederland 1 and Newspaper NRC Handelsblad October 31, 2005

Question: As you know, two organisations, NATO and the European Union, have been increasing their membership of late and have moved eastwards in particular. In this respect, I would like to ask, do you think that Russia could ever in the future join one or both of these organisations, and if yes, then what conditions would be necessary for this to happen?

Vladimir Putin: We are actively developing our relations with both organisations, with NATO and all the more so with the European Union. Regarding NATO, ... we would need to be clear about what kind of organisation we would be joining, if this issue were on the agenda, and what tasks we would be seeking to resolve within the organisation in question.

Concerning our ability to ensure our security, our defence capability, Russia has historically always been an independent country and has always been able to ensure its defence capability through its own means. Of course, we want to and will build partnership relations with all countries and all groupings, including NATO. ... We do not see NATO as a hostile organisation and we are developing our cooperation with it. ...

Question: Could the day ever come when Russia would knock on Brussels' door and ask for membership?

Vladimir Putin: If you invite us, we would consider it. ...

Response: But you can always ask Brussels of your own initiative.

Vladimir Putin: I was taught from childhood not to ask for anything and not to regret anything.

Question: But from what you say we can conclude that you do have an interest in potentially becoming a member of the EU?

Vladimir Putin: Of course, but I must also point out that not all European countries are members of the EU. Norway, for example, which is a wealthy and self-sufficient country, is not in the EU, and I understand the Norwegian choice, just as I also understand some of the eastern European countries that want to join the EU at all cost, hoping that this will improve their economic situations and raise the living standards of their peoples, to a considerable extent through aid from the old EU members, it must be said. It would be impossible for Russia to join the EU on such principles for the objective reasons of the size of our territory, population and so on. ...

Let us first work towards making Europe a continent without borders. We always talk about human rights in the abstract, but let us take concrete steps towards at least giving people the possibility of travelling freely to each other's countries.

Interview with Television Channel Nederland 1 and Newspaper NRC Handelsblad October 31, 2005

Democracy is the form of government and society that is most effective in the modern world. No one would dispute this. But democratic institutions and principles cannot be introduced effectively to this or that territory without taking national traditions and history into account. Democracy is not a good that can simply be exported from one country to another, as it then immediately becomes a tool the former country can use to gain advantages over the latter. Genuine democracy can be established only as a result of the internal development of society itself.

Joint Press Conference with President of Egypt Hosni Mubarak April 27, 2005 Cairo

I would not like for Europe to be divided as Germany was into east and west, into first and second class people. I don't want a situation where you would have first class people able to live according to stable and democratic laws, while second class people, with figuratively-speaking dark-coloured political skin, get told by a well-intentioned gentleman in pith helmet what political course to follow. And if the ungrateful natives object, they will get punished by having bombs dropped on their heads, as in Belgrade.

Responses to Questions from Russian Journalists December 6, 2004 Ankara, Turkey

We are neighbours and we have a lot of common interests. If we unite our efforts we will win and achieve great results and successes. ...Turkey has been showing its independence in the full sense of the word, especially of late, and this is greatly increasing its recognition on the international stage. ... We must under no circumstances act as rivals, all the more so with the involvement of powers from outside the region.

Interview with the Turkish Media September 1, 2004 Sochi

When the decision was taken to deploy troops, nobody gave a thought to the economic problems of one of the world's poorest countries. Likewise, the decision-makers ignored the fact that the ethnic and tribal contradictions in Afghanistan had reached such a pitch that the country was on the brink of a civil war. ... However, whatever the rights and wrongs of that decision were, the outcome is evident. The Soviet Union became embroiled in a futile war, a war that lasted almost 10 years. And today we are duty-bound to analyse and draw lessons from the Afghan war and face the truth.

The Afghan war proved that no one has the right to interfere in the life of another country and neither communism, nor democracy, nor a market economy can be imposed by force. It is impossible to bring all this on the armour of tanks or justify it by any ideological arguments. It is a serious lesson not only for the superpowers, but for the entire international community.

It must also be recognised that the Afghan war contributed to the growth of international terrorism. To this day the world community has to discuss and coordinate positions and contribute to restoring order in that long-suffering country and seek to ensure conditions for its peaceful and economically sound development.

The Afghan war stretched human endurance to its limit. Our Afghan veterans know and remember it. They had their full share of hardship, grief, despair and adversity. They were fighting in a strange country while our own people knew practically nothing about the causes of that war or its goals or even about the courage and exploits of our soldiers. Indeed, many of those who returned from that war sometimes met with misunderstanding, indifference and even disapproval at home. And of course they wondered why.

The truth is that few people showed concern for the ruined lives of our Afghan veterans, their wounds and their mental torment. More often than not, they had to fend for themselves while political leaders had other concerns.

Speech at a Meeting to Commemorate Soldiers who Died in the Afghan War February 15, 2004 Moscow

Throughout the history of humanity, great countries and empires have always been afflicted with various problems that have only aggravated their situation. These include a feeling of being invulnerable, being convinced of their own grandeur and a sense of being able to do no wrong. This has always got in the way of countries aspiring to be empires. I certainly hope that this will not be the case with our American partners.

Excerpts from the President's Live Television and Radio Dialogue with the Nation December 18, 2003 Moscow, the Kremlin

I can tell you about the so-called Eastern Bloc from the inside. We lived in a situation of strict discipline within the bloc, because the view was that a step to the left or a step to the right was an attempt to pull free, and to jump in place was a form of provocation that brought a tough response from partners in the bloc. It was essentially the same in the Western Bloc, despite the nicer packaging and more civilised phraseology. Today there is no Eastern Bloc. The threat that perhaps came from the Soviet Union is gone because the Soviet Union itself is gone. Now there is only one bloc remaining with its internal machinery still in place...

A Speech and Answers to Questions at the APEC Business Summit October 19, 2003 Bangkok

Question: Were you disappointed that the new resolution presented by the Administration did not include a provision on the international armed forces, which you insisted on?

Vladimir Putin: Not at all. A young man can be disappointed when he finds out after the wedding that his wife's fortune is much smaller than he expected.

Interview to The New York Times October 4, 2003 Novo-Ogaryovo

President Bush: ...Vladimir and I had some very frank discussions about Iraq. I understood his position. He understood mine. Because we've got a trustworthy relationship, we're able to move beyond any disagreement over a single issue. Plus, I like him, he's a good fellow to spend quality time with.

President Vladimir Putin: Thank you, George, for your warm words.

Joint Press Conference with US President George W. Bush September 27, 2003 Camp David, Maryland, USA

Unfortunately, the American school of sovietology and the Soviet school of American studies, or rather, "the study of American imperialism", as they liked to say in Russia at the time, were for many years the hostages of politics when our countries alternated between becoming allies and bringing the world to the brink of a nuclear catastrophe.

Naturally, in these conditions, scholarly work was excessively politicised. It was not so much involved in the study of the uniqueness and diversity of American and Russian civilisations, as in finding weak points in our political systems, and looking for tools to make as many attacks as possible, and do as much damage as possible to each other. Unfortunately, the inertia of such approaches is very strong. The world has changed fundamentally and the Soviet Union is no more, but sovietology still exists.

Speech and Answers to Questions at Columbia University September 26, 2003 New York

We welcome the US activities in Central Asia. You know what our position has been since the start of the counter-terrorist operation in Afghanistan. We believe that but for resolute actions in Afghanistan the Taliban would still be running the country.

Speech and Answers to Questions at Columbia University September 26, 2003 New York

You are right that we have stockpiled more weapons than we need. It does not matter how many times over we can destroy each other. Once is enough, and we have accumulated so many weapons that even after reducing them to 1,700–2,200 warheads, as we have agreed with our American partners under the Strategic Offensive Reductions Treaty, we can wage war on all fronts and destroy any enemy many times over.

Extracts from a Transcript of the Meeting with the Finalists of the Student Essay Competition "My Home, My City, My Country" June 5, 2003 The Kremlin, Moscow

All around us are countries with highly developed economies. We need to look in the face the fact that these countries push Russia out of promising world markets when they have the chance. And their obvious economic advantages serve as fuel for their growing geopolitical ambitions.

The proliferation of nuclear weapons continues in our world today. Terrorism threatens the world and endangers the security of our citizens. Certain countries sometimes use their strong and well-armed national armies to increase their zones of strategic influence rather than fighting these evils we all face.

Can Russia have any real hope of standing up to these threats if our society is splintered into little groups and if we all busy ourselves only with the narrow interests of our particular group? And if instead of becoming a thing of the past parasitic moods are only growing? And what is helping feed these moods but a bureaucracy that instead of trying to look after and build up our national wealth often happily lets it get frittered away.

Annual Address to the Federal Assembly of the Russian Federation May 16, 2003 Marble Hall, the Kremlin, Moscow

The United Nations Charter has nothing in it that permits the UN Security Council to take decisions to change the political regime in a particular country – whether we like the regime or not.

The only task facing the international community there is to satisfy itself that Iraq has no weapons of mass destruction or to find them and force Iraq to destroy those weapons. In this connection we share the position of our American partners which is that we must do everything in order that Iraq engage in a full-fledged cooperation with the UN inspectors.

The difference of approaches lies in the following: we believe that this problem can and must be resolved by peaceful political-diplomatic means. The inspectors are working there. We trust them. They have not found anything there; at least they have not yet found anything. ... The inspectors must continue their work. ... I am convinced that unilateral actions would be a big mistake. The first main negative implication would be that a real threat of a split in the UN Security Council and in the Anti-Terrorist Coalition would arise. This could cause Iraq's disintegration with consequences for the neighbors that are hard to foresee. I think this would complicate issues of settling the Middle Eastern problem and of course it would radicalize the Islamic world, might well cause a new wave of terrorist acts, and prejudice the leadership of those Muslim countries that are guided by democratic values.

Interview Granted to France-3 Television February 9, 2003

Question: What would you advise young diplomats and all young people in Ukraine to keep them from making mistakes in the future and what is the mistake that they should guard themselves against most of all?

Vladimir Putin: You should always remember that Ukraine's strategic choice corresponds to the national interests of friendship with Russia.

Opening Remarks and Answers to Questions at a Meeting with the Teachers and Students at Taras Shevchenko Kiev National University January 28, 2003 Kiev

A bad peace is always better than a good war.

Excerpts from a Transcript of a TV and Radio Broadcast (Hotline with the President of Russia) December 19, 2002 The Kremlin, Moscow

Now there is no Warsaw Pact and the Soviet Union, which used to be the core of that bloc, no longer exists. At first glance, there is no reason for NATO to exist. So they are looking around for something to do. ... As for a "buffer zone," it is necessary if there is a hostile environment beyond that "buffer".

A Meeting with Students and Professors at Beijing University December 3, 2002 Beijing

On issues over which we differ with the United States we will of course uphold our national interests, on all issues and in all regions.

A Meeting with Students and Professors at Beijing University December 3, 2002 Beijing

We had a common state, but it went to pieces. We do not rightly know yet how to build civilised relations between ourselves on a new foundation and under new conditions. On the one hand, there are special relations and a background feeling entitling us to press for particular preferences from each other. I do not say Ukraine expects something from Russia, but Russia, too, often expects from Ukraine what it does not expect from other partners. We must get used to working in a civilised fashion by respecting each other and meeting each other halfway.

Statement to the Press and Replies to Journalists' Questions October 6, 2002
Zaporozhye

More than 20 million of our compatriots live in countries of the CIS [Community of Independent States]. Russia cannot and does not intend to refuse its responsibility over how they are getting on and to what extent their rights are respected. I would hereby like to emphasize that our position in the CIS has nothing in common with attempts to dominate or apply pressure. We don't forget for a moment in our practical policies that we are dealing with sovereign governments who in particular have the right to choose their partners in the international arena. ... The main thing is that such relationships are aimed at strengthening peace and stability and work for the peoples' good.

We don't think according to outdated categories of "zero-sum games" where the gain of one partner must surely mean a loss to another. In fact why should a greater presence of the USA in the CIS lead without fail to displacing Russia? ... In theory, it is incorrect in my view to talk about a competition for influence between Moscow and Washington among the governments of the CIS.

Interview with the Chinese Newspaper Renmin Ribao June 5, 2002

Russia always played a substantial role in world affairs, but the problem for our country was that over a long period of time a situation had developed in which Russia was on one side, and on the other – practically the rest of the world. There was also a time

131

when we spoiled relations even with our great neighbour in the East, with the People's Republic of China. And no good came out of this confrontation between Russia and the rest of the world. And most of the citizens of my country understand this very well. Russia is now returning to the family of civilised nations. And it needs nothing but that its voice be heard, that it be reckoned with, and that its national interests be considered and duly recognised.

Excerpts from a Joint Press Conference with Italian Prime Minister Silvio Berlusconi and NATO Secretary-General George Robertson May 28, 2002 Pratica di Mare air force base, Italy

I am convinced that the Russian people's attitude towards the Germans is qualitatively better that the attitude towards Germany in other parts of Europe. I have often asked myself why that is so. It seems to me I have found a very simple answer. I truly don't know whether Germans will like it: In military conflicts, Russia has never lost against Germany and Russians don't feel aggrieved. Seriously. It's true. There is not that feeling of inner hurt that accompanies a people over a long period of time and that feeds a certain hatred of Germany.

Answers to questions of Alfred Biolek during a joint interview with the Federal Chancellor of the Federal Republic of Germany Gerhard Schroeder on the program Boulevard Bio of the ARD Television Channel 9 April 2002 Weimar

America will never be Russia and Russia will never be America. But we can complement each other very well and our mutual cooperation is a key factor of world stability. We must never forget that.

Interview with the Wall Street Journal February 11, 2002

One must honestly admit that the former Soviet Union tried to dominate not only Eastern Europe, but many other parts of the world. It did little good to the Russian people and it certainly could not have elicited a positive reaction from our quasi-partners, our partners against their will. It certainly was against the will of the Poles, freedom-loving people who tolerate no diktat.

Extracts from a Joint News Conference with Polish President Alexander Kwasniewski January 16, 2002 Warsaw

Where are the roots of your thoughts about present-day Russia?

Vladimir Putin: My answer will be simple to the point of being primitive. It is economic development of the vast territories that are part of the Russian Federation and joint work with Europe and the rest of civilized humankind to develop these territories and simultaneously improve the well-being of the Russian people, and natural integration in the political, economic and defence structures of civilised nations.

From an Interview with the Polish Newspaper Gazeta Wyborcza and the Polish TVP Channel January 15, 2002

We do not support separatism in other countries and we hope that no one will support our separatists. It would be a gross error, which would plunge Europe into an endless succession of ethnic and religious conflicts.

Joint Press Conference with the British Prime Minister Tony Blair December 21, 2001 Halton, Great Britain

You know the results of rivalry. The United States created or at least did nothing to prevent the creation of the Taliban while opposing the Soviet Union. The Soviet Union also did a good many "favours" to the United States by supporting all its rivals and enemies. We forgot that sooner or later these things would get out of control.

Transcript of the Meeting with Moscow Bureau Chiefs of Leading US Media November 10, 2001 The Kremlin, Moscow

You know, Russia and the United States have a long and positive history of relations. Over the centuries Russia has traditionally felt sympathy for the United States. If we recall history, back in 1775 the English king who was actively recruiting mercenaries to fight in North America, asked Catherine the Great to send volunteers from Russia. She turned him down in a gentle but quite firm way in a personal letter. Russia was one of the few countries of the Old World to categorically oppose the division of the United States that could have resulted from the war between North and South. The United States, for its part, was probably the only great power that sympathized with Russia during the Crimean War. And there have been many other positive episodes, not to mention the Second and First World Wars when we were both allies and did much to fight the common enemy.

Interview with the American Broadcasting Company ABC November 7, 2001

Terrorists, like pernicious bacteria, quickly adapt to the organism which hosts them and behave as parasites. They use Western institutions and Western ideas of human rights and the protection of civilians but do this not to develop these ideas or defend Western values and institutions but to fight them.

Answers to Questions Following Russian-Belgium Talks October 2, 2001 Brussels

No one calls into question the great value of Europe's relations with the United States. I am just of the opinion that Europe will reinforce its reputation of a strong and truly independent centre of world politics soundly and for a long time if it succeeds in bringing together its own potential and that of Russia, including its human, territorial and natural resources and its economic, cultural and defence potential.

Speech in the Bundestag of the Federal Republic of Germany September 25, 2001 Berlin

We must not be afraid of terrorists, they should be afraid of us.

Interview with the German Magazine Focus September 19, 2001 Sochi

People all over the world, all over Europe, talk about the need for a favourable political climate in Europe, about the need to tear down old barriers in Europe. Does NATO's expansion solve this problem? It certainly does not. So why deceive ourselves? The decision simply pushes NATO's frontiers to the Russian border. The move does not create a common security space on the continent. It fails to solve the key problem. ...

Finland has made impressive use of its neutral status and its relations with the Soviet Union, and is today successfully developing its relations with Russia. We really believe that our relations with Finland can set an example for other states, the European Union included, on how to develop relations with Russia.

Statement to the Press and Answers to Questions at a News Conference with President Tarja Halonen of Finland September 3, 2001 Helsinki

We constantly hear that everybody wants to bring down some kinds of barriers and borders in Europe. We are all for it. But let us take a closer look at the implications. What does it mean to bring down borders and barriers? Let us think about it. And if it means pushing that barrier closer to the Russian border, we are not very impressed.

Excerpts from the Transcript of a Press Conference for Russian and Foreign Journalists July 18, 2001 The Kremlin, Moscow

I sometimes get the impression that members of our secret service and yours, and I think yours do it more frequently, try to use some elements in the continuing duel between the special services and thus damage the national interests both of the United States and of Russia. ... If today we permit ourselves to use some extremists to promote our national interests at the expense of others, tomorrow the same extremists may turn their weapons against us. As an example, we must determine our position with regard to the

Taliban. ... It is a known fact that there are bases for training terrorists who act not only against us, but against you too.

Conversation with Heads of Local Bureaus of Leading US Media Outlets June 18, 2001 Moscow

Nobody likes imperial ambitions. ... Everybody naturally unites against a potential imperialist.

Conversation with Heads of Local Bureaus of Leading US Media Outlets June 18, 2001 Moscow

Question: Is this a man that Americans can trust?

Vladimir Putin: ... As to whether Russia can be trusted, I am not going to answer that question. I can ask you the very same question.

George Bush: I will answer the question. I looked the man in the eye. I found him to be very straightforward and trustworthy. We had a very good dialogue. I was able to get a sense of his soul; a man deeply committed to his country and the best interests of his country.

Joint News Conference with President George Bush of the United States of America June 16, 2001 Ljubljana

Unipolarity, which we so actively and very reasonably oppose, is nothing but an attempt to monopolise international relations, an attempt to establish absolute domination in international relations. Such attempts have happened more than once in world history. World history offers many such examples. How they all ended is well known. We are absolutely convinced that there can be no monopoly on world domination in the modern world. I am sure this position is shared by an overwhelming majority of world players.

Answers to Journalists' Questions Following the Talks with Fidel Castro, Chairman of the State Council and the Council of Ministers of the Republic of Cuba December 14, 2000 Havana

Mr. Putin, how much time do you think Russia will need to implement the reforms that would make it an equal partner in international economic relations?

Vladimir Putin: One can predict more or less accurately when a child will be born, provided we know when it was conceived. And even that doesn't always work. As for the answer to your question, it depends on a number of circumstances, including the development of the world economy.

From an Interview with the Canadian CBC and CTV Channels, the Globe and Mail Newspaper and the Russian RTR Television December 14, 2000

Why hasn't Bin Laden been extradited? It is a challenge to the international community. So far neither Russia nor the world community has reacted to that threat adequately.

From an Interview with the Canadian CBC and CTV Channels, the Globe and Mail Newspaper and the Russian RTR Television December 14, 2000

The most important thing is that we know exactly who, when and how they will pay us for the gas supplies. ... And I think that now no one will have the right to say that Ukraine is stealing Russian gas like a thief by night.

Opening Remarks and Answers to Questions at a Press Conference Following a Meeting of the CIS Heads of State December 1, 2000 Minsk

In the West, unfortunately, there are still forces that live according to the laws of the Cold War. They still regard our country as the main geopolitical opponent. We have largely left that behind us, but certain circles in the West unfortunately have not.

Excerpts from a Speech at a Meeting of Top Commanders of the Russian Armed Forces November 20, 2000 Defence Ministry, Moscow

I will allow myself a historical flashback to the tragic events of 10 years ago, the disintegration of the Soviet Union. The main reason was the total self-isolation of the country. One has to admit that it was the result of an imperial policy, the wish to seal the results of World War II, to ideologise them and to dig in in Europe and the East. All this led to isolation and overstretched the resources of the state, leading to the collapse of the country.

Excerpts from a Speech at a Meeting of Top Commanders of the Russian Armed Forces November 20, 2000 Defence Ministry, Moscow

[Chechnya] should never be a source of radicalisation of our population and of getting Russia bogged down in bloody inter-regional ethnic conflicts, which is the dream of our geopolitical opponents.

Excerpts from a Speech at a Meeting of Top Commanders of the Russian Armed Forces November 20, 2000 Defence Ministry, Moscow

No one will be allowed to resolve issues with Russia from a position of strength.

Excerpts from a Speech at a Meeting of Top Commanders of the Russian Armed Forces November 20, 2000 Defence Ministry, Moscow

It is always a pleasure to talk about the problems of your neighbours. But sometimes one should take a broader look at a problem to understand that it is a common problem.

Interview with the French Newspaper Le Figaro October 26, 2000

As for your question against whom should Russia defend itself, my answer is very simple: against surprises. This, I think, is the aim of the defence policies pursued by the US, France and other states. The more predictable and fair the international order, the less states will have to spend on their security.

Interview with the French Newspaper Le Figaro October 26, 2000

Why should we be happy about Nato expanding and coming closer to our borders? Of course it is causing us concern. ... As for the expansion of the European Union, that is a completely different matter. ... We welcome this process. ... We only believe that this process must not harm our mutual relations with today's unified Europe nor with our traditional partners in eastern and central Europe.

Interview to the French Television Channels TV-1 and France-3 23 October 2000

We consider, and I am deeply convinced of this, that any attempt at hegemony harms not only the objects of the hegemony but also those who take on such a role. It is a thankless, dangerous and counter-productive task, in the first place from the point of view of national interests.

Interview to the French Television Channels TV-1 and France-3 23 October 2000

Contemporary Russia does not view anybody as an enemy nor even as an opponent. We would like, at a minimum, to have partnership relations with everybody.

Interview to the French Television Channels TV-1 and France-3 23 October 2000

If you want to live well yourself, you should also want your neighbours to live well. To give you an example: Today we are witnessing a dramatic leap in trade between Russia and China.

...As soon as things improve a bit in one country, the other country immediately benefits.

Extracts from the Transcript of a Meeting with Russian Journalists at the End of the Official Part of the Visit to the People's Republic of China July 18, 2000 Beijing

The only real choice for Russia is the choice of a strong country. A country that is strong and confident in itself. Strong not in defiance of the international community, not against other strong nations, but together with them. ... Only a strong, or effective if someone dislikes the word 'strong', an effective state and a democratic state is capable of protecting civil, political and economic freedoms, capable of creating conditions for people to lead happy lives and for our country to flourish.

Annual Address to the Federal Assembly of the Russian Federation July 8, 2000 Moscow, the Kremlin

One should not be afraid of a strong Russia. Germany and the West as a whole would have headaches if Russia were weak and unstable and barely able to play the role of a reliable and efficient partner in the economic, political and security fields.

Extracts from a Speech at a Meeting with German Businessmen June 16, 2000 Berlin

Russia is not claiming great power status. It is a great power by virtue of its huge potential, its history and culture.

Interview with the Newspaper Welt am Sonntag (Germany) June 11, 2000

Naturally, Russia views the plans of further NATO expansion as unfriendly and prejudicial to its security.

Interview with the Newspaper Welt am Sonntag (Germany) June 11, 2000

Let me remind you of a saying which has gained some currency in our country: he who does not regret the destruction of the Soviet Union has no heart, and he who wants to see it recreated in its former shape has no brain.

Transcript of a Telephone Conversation with Readers of Komsomolskaya Pravda Newspaper February 9, 2000

What we face in much of the former Soviet Union today is the problem of geopolitical change in the balance of forces, or, if you like, attempts at geopolitical change. ... If these extremist forces manage to gain a foothold in the Caucasus, and not only gain a foothold in Chechnya but several other territories, then this "contagion" could move up the Volga River and spill into other republics.

Interview with the ORT TV Channel February 7, 2000 Moscow

Of course, there are people in the West who will always criticise us and take an anti-Russian stand out of geopolitical considerations.

Interview with the RTR TV Channel January 23, 2000

Chapter 2

POLITICS AND GOVERNMENT

Vladimir Putin: The United Russia party has won the majority in the new State Duma. …

Gennady Zyuganov [leader of the Communist party]: …Will you please look into how we vote. … I was shocked, to be honest, that in Nizhny Novgorod they worked out a whole scheme. I am going to leave you a film: I must confess we planted a guy in that thievery structure that occupied everything there, and shot everything. All you have to do is watch it and instruct the special services to investigate, because a criminal gang of about 15 people has set up base there. The footage shows the whole chain, we just have to protect the guy that did the recording so they don't take revenge on him. …

Vladimir Putin: … Regarding election fraud. We just spoke about that at the meeting with the Central Election Commission. They also recorded certain violations, and will surely deal with them. At the same time, there is a general opinion that the overall election system, let me stress it, was very efficient and transparent. …

A key issue is the number of parties that can take part in the elections. … Before, they said there were not enough and that an infinite number of parties taking part in elections is a sign of democracy. Now it turns out there are too many. When we made that decision and opened the doors to a wide range of political movements, we believed it was for the better. Here is why. It was not done just for the sake of exposing every absurd policy; it was a measure to reveal the current political landscape. This way we could see how many people really did support those who shout the loudest. …

Since the lineup of political forces has become clear, this makes it possible for us to talk about optimisation now. However, again, these should be steps that do not erode the essence of democracy as an expression of the people's will. Let us think carefully and analyse the experience of the European countries, as well as the experience of countries on other continents.

For example, the United States. There are no restrictions, but there are always two parties in the arena all the same. Why does this happen? There are no limitations, but except for the two parties, we see nothing on the political Olympus. After the notorious McCarthyism period, the leftist movement was eliminated there.

Meeting with leaders of parties that gained State Duma seats following elections September 23, 2016 The Kremlin, Moscow

The situation is not easy and people feel it and they want that stability in society and the political system that we were talking about. ... This was the mood of the public in the run-up to the election and we got the results that our voters wanted.

Visiting United Russia party's campaign headquarters September 18, 2016 Moscow

[Question]: People might say there are two ways in which Russia is very difficult to rule. One is it is a very personal system, where many people vote for you rather than for a party. And the other reason is Russia is still a fairly lawless place. You have things like the murder of Boris Nemtsov which I know you condemned and you have brought people in, but the mastermind is still being sought. Is Russia a very hard place to govern at the moment?

Vladimir Putin: You know, I may assure you that it is hard to govern any country. Would you say that governing the United States is an easy task? Is it easy to address even uncomplicated matters? The Guantanamo detention camp, for example? During his first term President Obama said that he would shut it down. Yet it is still there. Why? Is it that he does not want to? Certainly he does. I am sure he does. Yet there emerge thousands of obstacles that prevent him from resolving this issue. ...

Russia is also hard to govern. Yet Russia is at a stage when its political system and market economy are being shaped. It is a complicated yet very intriguing process. ... We started building a completely new multi-party political system only in the 1990s. This is a very complex process and there are certain stages that cannot be skipped. Our citizens should get accustomed to this, feel their responsibility when they arrive at the polling stations. They should learn to question populist solutions, deliberations or candidates' mutual accusations.

Interview to Bloomberg September 5, 2016 Vladivostok

Is it worth taking part in the elections when we know that the votes will be counted in United Russia's favour anyway? Thank you.

Vladimir Putin: Well I have done nothing to earn your thanks yet. It was Stalin who once said that it is not whom people vote for that matters, but who does the counting. I hope though, that this will not be the case. ... United Russia plays a tremendously important role, but this in no way means that the party benefits from preferential treatment of any kind. If you look back to the recent gubernatorial elections in Irkutsk Region, the United Russia candidate did not make it through in the first round, did not get the required number of votes. He was short on votes by only 0.36 percent. Following your logic, it should have been a piece of cake to fiddle this figure slightly, but no one did this.

Direct Line with Vladimir Putin April 14, 2016 Moscow

Such is our mentality, especially when it comes to bureaucrats, if someone has some status, they try to squeeze maximum advantage out of it and secure an annuity.

Direct Line with Vladimir Putin April 14, 2016 Moscow

[Question]: We have all heard about the news leak, the so-called 'Panama Papers', which mention the musician Roldugin, your friend. ... I would like to take this opportunity...to ask for your comments on this matter.

Vladimir Putin: All of you here are specialists, journalists, right? You know what an information product is. Now, there has been this offshore holding controversy. Your humble servant is not there; there is nothing to talk about. However, the assignment is still there and they have to work. What did they do? They manufactured an information product. They found some of my friends and acquaintances – I will talk about them shortly – and they fiddled around and knocked something together. I saw these pictures. There are many, many people in the background – it is impossible to understand who they are, and there is a close-up photo of your humble servant in the foreground. Now, this is being promoted.

There is this friend of the Russian president, and they say he has done something, probably something corruption-related. In fact, there is no corruption involved at all. ... He is a minority shareholder in one of our companies and makes some money out of it, but not billions of dollars of course. That is nonsense. The reality is nothing of the sort. He makes a bit of money out of it. The interesting thing is that I am proud of people like Sergei Roldugin, proud to count him among my friends, and proud of him in general. He has spent nearly all of the money he has earned buying musical instruments abroad and bringing them back to Russia.

Truth and Justice regional and local media forum April 7, 2016 St Petersburg

Vladimir Putin: I know that Chechnya has been transformed over these last years. We see this with our own eyes. This is a clear fact. The transformations are not just external. Where we once saw devastation, towns and villages in ruins, we now see flourishing places, and this is no exaggeration. We see towns and villages in which people live comfortable, convenient lives. ... You have accomplished much in Chechnya, but there is still a lot to do.

You said that you are fighting unemployment, but we know what a serious problem this is, especially youth unemployment. More work needs to be done in this area, more work at the informal level too. You are good at this. I can say this quite frankly. I've said to you before that it was even something of a surprise to me that you, someone with quite different aims in life, suddenly turned into a good manager. ... What I wanted to draw to your attention is the need for closer cooperation with the federal authorities, especially on security matters. ... You and the republic's future leader will have to make every effort to ensure compliance with Russian law in all areas of life.

Ramzan Kadyrov: Mr President, thank you very much for your trust and for your assessment.

Meeting with Head of the Republic of Chechnya Ramzan Kadyrov March 25, 2016 The Kremlin, Moscow

As far as democracy is concerned, the ruling classes usually talk about freedom to pull the wool over the eyes of those whom they govern. There is nothing new about democracy in Russia. As we have already identified, democracy is the rule of the people and the influence of the people over the authorities. We have learned very well the lesson of one-party rule – that of the Communist Party (CPSU). Therefore, we made our choice long ago and we will continue developing democratic institutions in our country.

Interview to German newspaper Bild Part 2 January 12, 2016 Sochi

Finally, let's turn to the crime against Boris Nemtsov. I knew him personally and our relations had not always been bad. I never quarrelled with him but he chose this path of political competition by making personal attacks and the like. That said, I am used to this, he was not alone. However, this does not mean at all that the man should have been killed. I will never accept this. I firmly believe that this crime should be investigated and the culprits punished.

Vladimir Putin's annual news conference December 17, 2015 Moscow

[Journalist]: You have been at the helm for 15 years, and so we can say that a certain system of authority has evolved. I have a question about a very dangerous aspect of this system because we can see especially clearly now that a very dangerous second generation of the elite has grown up over this period. One of them is Rotenberg Jr, who has received the country's long-haul truckers as a present. Another is Turchak Jr, who cannot be summoned for questioning over the assault of Oleg Kashin, even though journalists continue to be beaten up in his region. There are also the children of Chaika, who have a very murky business, which should be investigated. Sorry, but I do not give a damn whether this is a paid-for reporting or not, because even rumours must be investigated. There are many more such children who are unable to revive or even preserve Russia, because they are not the elite but only a poor semblance of it.

At the same time, when journalists investigate something or public accusations are made as in the case of Prosecutor General Chaika and his team, the authorities, instead of launching an investigation, shout that the rumour is being spread by the hateful State Department or Obama, or order an inspection – for instance, how the prosecutor's office dealt with the Dozhd TV channel, which helped investigate the problem. ... Did you expect to see these results when you assumed power in 2000? Maybe the situation needs improving before it is too late?

Vladimir Putin: ... There is a famous Soviet-era joke, when an HR manager says: We are not going to promote this guy. Why? He had an incident with a fur coat. It turned out that five years ago his wife's fur coat was stolen in a theatre. Something had happened, so the guy will not be promoted, just in case. This should not be our attitude. You are right to raise this issue. No, I really mean it. This provides us with an opportunity to respond... I mean, it is our obligation to respond.

Regarding all the issues you have mentioned, especially those related to the children of high-ranking officials... Let's take for

147

example the Prosecutor General – he heads a very important institution. We have to understand did the Prosecutor General's children commit an offence or not? Did anything point to a conflict of interest in the Prosecutor General's work? Did he assist or help his children in any manner? For that we have the Presidential Control Directorate. I did not want to mention this issue, but it does not mean that we are not working on it. All the information should be carefully reviewed.

Vladimir Putin's annual news conference December 17, 2015 Moscow

The United States has a law that concerns Ukraine, but it directly mentions Russia, and this law states that the goal is democratisation of the Russian Federation. Just imagine if we were to write into Russian law that our goal is to democratise the United States...

Meeting of the Valdai International Discussion Club October 22, 2015 Sochi

Each country has its own particular features, its own traditions that find their reflection today and will find it in future. There are such traditions in Russia but it is not a question of a strong figure, although a strong figure is needed in power, it is a question of what is implied by this term. It is one thing if it is a person with dictatorial tendencies. But if it is a fair leader, who acts within the law and in the interests of a vast majority of society, who acts coherently and is guided by principles, it is a completely different matter.

Interview to American TV channel CBS and PBS September 29, 2015 Novo-Ogaryovo, Moscow Region

Of course the Government should always be criticised... Generally, criticism helps to look at things from a different perspective, which is always good.

Direct Line with Vladimir Putin April 16, 2015

We hardly ever see the courts examine cases involving large and particularly large bribes or corruption carried out by organised groups, as if there were no such cases out there.

Expanded Session of the Interior Ministry Board March 4, 2015 Moscow

This is not acceptable when ships are standing idle just drawing up the resources on which they run. The same goes for aircraft and all other systems. It is not right and not a responsible approach from the state's point of view when the new missile systems of which we are most certainly proud get delivered to the ground forces and are improperly stored. The specialists know what I am talking about.

Expanded meeting of the Defence Ministry Board   December 19, 2014 Moscow

The line that separates opposition activists from the fifth column is hard to see from the outside. What's the difference? Opposition activists may be very harsh in their criticism, but at the end of the day they are defending the interests of the motherland. And the fifth column is those who serve the interests of other countries, and who are only tools for others' political goals.

News conference of Vladimir Putin December 18, 2014 Moscow

As you know, I recently met with representatives of the human rights movement in light of Human Rights Day. They view the work of our legal system quite critically; there is nothing unusual about this, they are representatives of public organisations that react critically to any manifestations of injustice or improper execution of the law, and this does, unfortunately, happen: this happens in every country, including ours. But ultimately, you may have noticed, and I stated this earlier, I feel our legal and judicial system is one of most developed in the world – it is not without problems, of course, but ultimately, we are proud of our judicial system.

Meeting with Constitutional Court judges December 8, 2014 St Petersburg

Finally, let me say a word about the much-debated law on foreign agents. ... What was our aim when we passed this law? The aim was to prevent people abroad from using financial resources to meddle in our political life, in our internal political affairs. This was the primary objective. Why is this so important? It's so important because when internal political developments here are paid for with money from abroad, let me assure you that no matter what they say, these people are pursuing not our national interests but their own. Sometimes these interests happen to coincide, but more often than not they don't. In any case, we must decide our own future, organise our own lives and respond to our problems. We do have no shortage of problems, but it is up to us alone, here in Russia, to solve them.

Meeting with members of the Council for Civil Society and Human Rights and federal and regional human rights commissioners December 5, 2014 The Kremlin, Moscow

This is not the first time we are speaking about the need for new approaches to the activities of oversight, supervisory, and law enforcement agencies. Nevertheless, things are changing very slowly here. The presumption of guilt is still very much alive. Instead of curbing individual violations, they close the path and create problems for thousands of law-abiding, self-motivated people.

Presidential Address to the Federal Assembly December 4, 2014 The Kremlin, Moscow

You can't make everyone your ally and you shouldn't even strive to do it. On the contrary, it's good to have around some people who have doubts. But they should propose constructive solutions. If we face opponents of this type, they are very useful.

Interview to TASS News Agency November 24, 2014

No foreign country with a sense of self-respect allows the use of foreign money in internal politics. Try and do something like this in the US and you'll land in jail at once. They have far more rigid state agencies there than we do here.

Interview to TASS News Agency November 24, 2014

But this does not mean we don't have corruption. We constantly speak about it ourselves. I believe this is one of the very serious problems which we have inherited from the past when the administration at any level thought it had the right to do everything and no one could have the right to encroach on its powers and control it somehow. But then something else was added to this, which made the situation even worse. I mean the non-transparent privatisation. This was awful and this was a big mistake. We are all clever people, retrospectively. Perhaps those who made the decisions back then would have arranged things differently today. Incidentally, this was also in the 1990s when the Europeans told us that we should not listen to American experts. But we went along this road. The non-transparent privatisation made people think: well, if they let them steal billions from the state, then why can't we take away something less expensive? Why are they allowed to and we are not?

Interview to TASS News Agency November 24, 2014

A former European leader told me, "What kind of democracy is it in the USA – you cannot even consider running in an election if you don't have a billion, or even several billion dollars!" What kind of democracy is that? Besides, you elect your president using a system of electoral delegates, while we have a direct democracy. Moreover, as I have said many times already, you know that the Constitution is designed in such a way that the number of electors voting for a given candidate may be greater, while the number of people they represent is smaller. Thus, the President can be elected by a minority of voters. Is this democracy? ...

We certainly have our drawbacks. They apply to the system. Many of them clearly come from the past. There is a lot we need to change. ... We have no desire to return to our totalitarian past. This is not because we fear anything, but because this path leads to a dead end – I am certain of this, and more importantly, Russian society is sure of this.

Meeting of the Valdai International Discussion Club October 24, 2014 Sochi

Whether at the municipal or regional level however, people are looking to the authorities not for global solutions, but for solutions to their practical problems. People want to see improvement in their lives and working conditions... You need to remember that people have placed a lot of trust in you and you now need to return this trust through your effective work in office. You need to prove yourselves worthy of this trust, not ride on past achievements, but carry out the obligations placed upon you, achieve positive change and show people clear, practical results.

Meeting with newly elected regional heads September 17, 2014 The Kremlin, Moscow

I feel that the federal structure is a very important and essential component in our statehood because it allows us to better take into account the interests of all of the nation's citizens, regardless of where they live, to take into account their ethnic, historical, religious and cultural diversity. That is precisely why Russia's regions have fairly significant powers, particularly in the areas I just mentioned. Incidentally, for some reason, I don't know why, our Ukrainian partners are very afraid of federalisation. That is their choice; naturally, we will not meddle under any circumstances. There are plenty of countries in the world with a federal system of governance: Russia, the US, Brazil, Germany... The point is to give an opportunity to live a full-fledged life to people living in various territories, who have significant distinctions in the areas I mentioned. I feel that we must strengthen federalism in our nation.

Seliger 2014 National Youth Forum August 29, 2014 Seliger, Tver Region

It became clear that our development had reached a stage when rule by one party, the Communist Party in this case, did not reflect the level of our society's development and was preventing the country from moving further. This in large part was what led to the Soviet Union's collapse and to the unravelling of its economy and political system. Now we have a multiparty system. People criticise it of course and say that we have no real opposition. But I completely disagree here. We have a genuine multiparty system. We have different parties in the parliament and they compete quite intensely in election campaigns when they think they have a chance.

Seliger 2014 National Youth Forum August 29, 2014 Seliger, Tver Region

We also have the so-called non-systemic opposition, but it is also not a single whole and it features different people: people who are patriotic and people who feel differently. Regardless of how hurtful it might be to hear, perhaps, even to some of this audience, people who hold leftist views, but in the First World War, the Bolsheviks wished to see their Fatherland defeated. And while the heroic Russian soldiers and officers shed their blood on the fronts in World War I, some were shaking Russia from within and shook it to the point that Russia as a state collapsed and declared itself defeated by a country that had lost the war. It is nonsense, it is absurd, but it happened! This was a complete betrayal of national interests! We have such people in our nation today as well. Well, what can we do? Unfortunately, no nation can avoid it. But nevertheless, I feel that the basic foundations of our state's viability will never let such people into leading positions in the government.

Seliger 2014 National Youth Forum August 29, 2014 Seliger, Tver Region

Question (via interpreter): I'd like to ask you about your country, Russia. How would you describe its current political regime? Some describe it as a democracy, while others argue that Russia is so huge that it needs an iron hand. How does Vladimir Putin define the Putin regime?

Vladimir Putin: The current regime is not connected to any particular person, including the incumbent President. We have common democratic state institutions, although they reflect Russia's needs. What are they? The overwhelming majority of Russian citizens tend to rely on their traditions, their history and, if I may say so, their traditional values. I see this as the foundation and a factor of stability in the Russian state, but none of this is associated with the President as an individual. Moreover, it should be remembered that we only started introducing standard democratic institutions recently. They are still in the process of evolving.

Question (via interpreter): Can a person stand in opposition to the authorities in Russia without fear of losing his ties and reputation, without being punished?

Vladimir Putin: We have many opposition parties, and we have recently liberalised the procedure for registering political parties. We have dozens of parties that participate in municipal and regional elections.

Question (via interpreter): But is it possible to be a personal opponent of Vladimir Putin without exposing oneself to risks?

Vladimir Putin: If you listen to some of our radio stations and watch some TV shows, I assure you, you are unlikely to find anything similar to this kind of opposition in France.

Vladimir Putin's interview with Radio Europe 1 and TF1 TV channel June 4, 2014

EDWARD SNOWDEN: Zdravstvuyte. I'd like to ask you a question about the mass surveillance of online communications and the bulk collection of private records by intelligence and law enforcement services. Recently, the United States, two independent White House investigations, as well as a federal court all concluded that these programmes are ineffective in stopping terrorism. They also found that they unreasonably intrude into the private lives of ordinary citizens – individuals who have never been suspected of any wrongdoing or criminal activity; and that these kinds of programmes are not the least intrusive means available to such agencies for these investigative purposes. Now, I've seen little public discussion of Russia's own involvement in the policies of mass surveillance. So I'd like to ask you: Does Russia intercept, store, or analyse in any way the communications of millions of individuals, and do you believe that simply increasing the effectiveness of intelligence or law enforcement investigations can justify placing societies – rather than subjects – under surveillance? Thank you.

VLADIMIR PUTIN: Mr Snowden, you are a former intelligence officer, and I have worked for an intelligence agency, too. So let's talk like two professionals. To begin with, Russia has laws that strictly regulate the use of special equipment by security services, including for the tapping of private conversations and for the surveillance of online communications. They need to receive a court warrant to be able to use this equipment in each particular case. So there is no, and cannot be any, indiscriminate mass surveillance under Russian law.

Since criminals, including terrorists, use these modern communication systems for their criminal activity, security services should be able to respond accordingly and use modern equipment to combat crime, including terrorism. Yes, we do this, but not on such a large scale and not arbitrarily. Hopefully – I hope very much – we will never act in this manner. Besides, we do not have such technical capabilities and funds as the United States. But the main thing is that, happily, our security services are strictly controlled by the state and society and their operation is strictly regulated by law.

Direct Line with Vladimir Putin April 17, 2014 Moscow

Only a small group of people are involved in writing laws, while millions are working on ways to evade them. Therefore, we need to weigh our every step, every word, and every comma.

Meeting of the Agency for Strategic Initiatives Supervisory Board April 8, 2014 Novo-Ogaryovo, Moscow Region

I want to stress the point that we must make a clear distinction between lawful opposition activity, which is part of any democratic country's life, and extremism, which is built on hatred, inciting ethnic, interethnic and social strife, and denial of the laws and the Constitution. We must make a clear distinction between civilised opposition to the authorities, and serving foreign interests to the detriment of our own country.

Russia's laws today give us the conditions we need for non-governmental and public organisations to work freely and transparently. But we will never accept for them to be used for destructive purposes. We will not accept a situation such as happened in Ukraine, when in many cases it was through non-governmental organisations that the nationalist and neo-Nazi groups and militants, who became the shock troops in the anti-constitutional coup d'état, received funding from abroad.

Meeting of the Federal Security Service board April 7, 2014 Moscow

Ella Pamfilova [newly-appointed Ombudsman for human rights]: Mr President, I must admit that since you said that I could "eat them all alive" I have become a little frightened of myself. I would like to say that if it all works out, the main thing is to be honest in our work, that is all. Honest and consistent. You can count on this.

Vladimir Putin: Being a human rights advocate is a very specific job. It envisages constant interaction with the authorities, and not just interaction, but also a critical approach to what the authorities at all levels are doing. However, without this, society cannot develop in harmony and the interests of our citizens cannot be protected in full, as much as this is at all possible. Therefore, I strongly hope to see the approach you described.

Meeting with Vladimir Lukin and Ella Pamfilova February 13, 2014 Novo-Ogaryovo, Moscow Region

M. Fedotov [Chairman of the Presidential Council on the Development of Civil Society and Human Rights]: ... We are all convinced that as the ombudsman for human rights in the Russian Federation Ella Alexandrovna [Pamfilova] will be able to bring an enormous benefit to our common cause...

L. Alekseyeva [Chairwoman, Moscow Helsinki Group]: ... The main thing is she is very pleased that human rights activists, temperamental people with difficult personalities, welcomed [her proposed candidacy] with satisfaction and hope.

V. Putin: The hope that she will devour us, a human rights activist and a woman, that she will have us for lunch, you understand? Good. (Laughter.)

Meeting with Members of Russian Human Rights Societies 23 January 2014 Novo-Ogaryovo, Moscow Region

It's clear that the opposition parties always have their opinion, even when, to put it mildly, it's not completely constructive. But they need to pronounce their own separate position. By and large, people are sensible and really don't want to do harm. But we have to convince them, not simply turn on the voting mechanism and with the help of "United Russia" force it through, but convince them. And also listen to them. I don't exclude that there may be some sort of sensible things that need to be considered in the course of working up the law.

Meeting of the Presidential Council for Culture and Art Presidium February 3, 2014 Pskov

New people appear on the political spectrum, some of them are in opposition to the government, others are not. Those who oppose us try to take a bite out of those at the top because it always raises their own rating. This is a general rule of conduct for all opposition parties in the world. It is a well-known, trivial trick, and, in principle, it is the right move for people who want to make themselves known. They jump out of their pants and get into fights, but they must be careful about it because, as they say in the country, you can lose your pants if you're not careful. It's all right if they have something to show off, but if there's nothing to brag about, they can just embarrass themselves and put an end to their political career.

News conference of Vladimir Putin December 19, 2013 Moscow

The point of conservatism is not that it obstructs movement forward and upward, but that it prevents movement backward and downward. That, in my opinion, is a very good formula, and it is the formula that I propose. There's nothing unusual for us here. Russia is a country with a very profound, ancient culture, and if we want to feel strong and grow with confidence, we must draw on this culture and these traditions, and not just focus on the future.

News conference of Vladimir Putin December 19, 2013 Moscow

For lawyers the more laws the better: you earn more fees from clients because they get completely confused by all these laws.

Meeting with students from Moscow law schools December 3, 2013 Moscow

As we know very well, when everything is open and transparent you can see immediately things such as excessively high prices and strange or sometimes completely nonsensical conditions for public procurement contracts. I cannot resist giving one example. In the Smolensk Region, they placed an order for purchasing school laboratory equipment for a value of 46 million rubles. But listen to this, the condition for the tender was that the equipment had to be capable of working in high-altitude conditions. High altitude conditions in the Smolensk Region? What mountains do they have there? Maybe there is a kind of logic to these demands, but it is certainly not clear at first glance.

State Council meeting October 4, 2013 The Kremlin, Moscow

[On the opposition] It is not enough to shout "Help, stop thief!" or "Tomorrow we will put everybody in prison for corruption," or "Tomorrow we will come and give $1,000 to each of you, and then another $5,000." It is usually all pre-election agitation. But to work systematically, quietly, without any scandal and fuss is much more difficult.

Interview to Channel One and Associated Press news agency September 4, 2013 Novo-Ogaryovo, Moscow Region

At a certain point we saw the police cracking down on the Occupy Wall Street activists. I won't call the actions of police appropriate or inappropriate. My point is that every opposition movement is good and useful if they act within the law. If they don't like the law, they should use democratic ways to change those laws. They should win voters on their side, they should get elected into legislatures so that they have a chance to influence the laws. This is the way to change things on the ground. If there are people who act outside the law, then the state must use legal means to impose law in the interests of the majority. That's the way it's done in the US, and that's the way it's done in Russia. Truth be told, we are criticized for that, but when the same thing happens in the US, it is considered to be normal. Never mind, these are double standards and we have got accustomed and pay little attention to it.

Visit to Russia Today television channel June 11, 2013 Moscow

As for comparing the events in Turkey with our NGOs, that's like comparing apples and oranges. As a Russian expression goes, a flower in the garden and an uncle in Kiev. What do the NGOs

159

have to do with anything? Is anyone closing them? Have you read the law, to start with? Look at the Russian law. It does not say anything about closing these organisations, let alone any sanctions. It talks about revealing financial data and says that if an organisation is involved in any political activity, it has to register as a foreign agent, if it receives money for those activities from abroad. But nobody is closing them.

News conference following the Russia-EU Summit   June 4, 2013 Yekaterinburg

I'm not simply ready to talk with the opposition; I talk with them already, all the time. As for what has come to be called the 'non-systemic' opposition, we offer them dialogue too. Some members of the opposition simply reject all offers of dialogue. It seems to me in any case that this concept of 'non-systemic' opposition is gradually losing its relevance. People have the right now to establish political parties with only the minimum of bureaucratic formalities involved. You need 500 people minimum, I think, to do this now, and so if you want, you can establish a fully legal political party and fight for the voters' confidence. ... Please, go ahead, take action, join the fight, enter the parliament, and prove that you're right. It's easy to sit wagging your tongue, but what do you propose actually doing?

Direct Line with Vladimir Putin April 25, 2013 Moscow

Kirill Kleymenov: Mr President, here is a question-reproach: How did you, a former KGB officer, allow the ministers in your Government to steal on a grand scale? We feel sorry for our country.

Vladimir Putin: Do you mean they should have been allowed to steal on a small scale? There must be no major or minor theft.

Direct Line with Vladimir Putin April 25, 2013 Moscow

[On Femen] Actually, I liked the protest. We knew that such a thing was being prepared. We should thank these Ukrainian girls for giving the [Hannover] fair some extra PR. Without actions such as their protest, it is quite likely that events like the fair would get less publicity. To be honest, I didn't really hear what they were shouting because the security guards stepped in very quickly. I don't really think it proper that the girls had these beefy fellows come down on them.

Press statement and answers to journalists' questions following a working visit to Germany April 8, 2013 Hannover

Meanwhile, there is one trend that I would nevertheless like to highlight. Of course everything is important but that said, we still have a transition economy and our political system is still in the making. In these conditions – and there is nothing unusual about this, the same processes occur in all countries throughout the world – a great deal of loopholes that can be exploited for corruption or used by officials for shady ventures open up. ...Our citizens' trust in public institutions in general depends on our success in addressing these issues. In turn, this impacts on the very stability and effectiveness of the state itself. ...

And there is no need to become hysterical each time violations within law enforcement agencies themselves come to light, or to think that someone has offended someone else. We need to respond to these cases professionally, in a timely fashion, and decisively rid ourselves of people who have committed misdemeanors.

Expanded meeting of the Prosecutor General Office's Board March 5, 2013 Moscow

One year, we had some severe frosts in Leningrad – this was back in Soviet times, in the 1980s; Romanov was the first secretary of the regional party committee. Incidentally, there were many tall tales about him using dishes from the Hermitage, which is all really nonsense, but there are different ways of looking at the past. And when everything froze and residential buildings began to

161

freeze, he kicked nearly the entire regional committee out onto the street, saying "If you can't govern, then go work in the streets." This may be looked at as good or as bad, but ultimately, you need governance, and working outside in the streets is not the best use of time for an administrator at that level.

News conference of Vladimir Putin December 20, 2012 Moscow

As for the fight against corruption, as I have already said, this is one of our problem areas. But it has a long history. I already mentioned the dialogue between Peter the Great and his General Prosecutor (now the Prosecutor General). When he brought up cases of theft, Peter the Great suggested that people be sent to Siberia or executed for even those minor crimes. But the General Prosecutor said to him, "Who will be left, Sire? We all steal."

News conference of Vladimir Putin December 20, 2012 Moscow

Our opposition, if you will allow me to paraphrase the hero of a famous film, has no specific work. These people are smart, but they are not liable for their decisions.

News conference of Vladimir Putin December 20, 2012 Moscow

Representatives of a very wide variety of nationalities inhabit all territories, nevertheless the regions' titular nationalities are mostly Russian. ...Other republics...are special because several ethnic groups live there that rightly consider themselves titular nations and, therefore, rightly claim that their representatives should be allowed to participate directly in governing the region. Unfortunately, in the not-so-distant past this situation led to conflicts when a minority titular nationality in a national republic said: "We will never be able to elect a president of the republic because we are in the minority, so we will think about leaving the republic." This is absolutely unacceptable. We must never allow the redistribution of territories by increasing the number of entities of our Federation. This is for both economic and social reasons.

...If we begin to further divide territories, we will increase the number of potential conflicts to infinity. This is a very dangerous thing.

Meeting of the Council of Legislators December 13, 2012 The Kremlin, Moscow

What is the difference which ethnic group an offender belongs to? It is pointless and even harmful to mention it... The important thing is the certainty of punishment. That's the first point. And the second is the fairness of the punishment, regardless of the offender's ethnic background.

Meeting of the Council of Legislators December 13, 2012 The Kremlin, Moscow

[Pussy Riot] staged an orgy in a public place. Of course, people are allowed to do whatever they want to do, as long as it's legal, but not in a public place. Again, the authorities should have looked into that. Then they uploaded the video of that orgy on the Internet. You know, some fans of group sex say it's better than one-on-one because, like in any teamwork, you don't need to hit the ball all the time. Again, it's okay if you do what you like privately, but I wouldn't be that certain about uploading your acts on the Internet. It could be the subject of legal assessment, too.

Interview to Russia Today TV Channel September 6, 2012 Novo-Ogaryovo, Moscow Region

Corruption is a problem for any country. And by the way you will find it in any country, be it in Europe or in the United States. They have legalised many things. Let's take the lobbying for private corporations – what is it, is it corruption or not? It's legalised and so formally is okay, within the law. But that depends on how you look at it.

Interview to Russia Today TV Channel September 6, 2012 Novo-Ogaryovo, Moscow Region

I remember back in the Soviet period when I worked for a well-known organization, there was a story: when a spy came to the KGB to give himself up he was asked: "Do you have a weapon?" He says: "Yes". "Then go to such and such room. And do you have means of communication? Then go to room number 5. And money?" "Yes". "Then go to room 7." And when he arrives, they ask him again: "Do you have an assignment?" "Yes". "Then go and do your work, don't bother people here who are going about their business." It was the highest manifestation of bureaucracy.

Seliger 2012 National Youth Education Forum July 31, 2012 Seliger

People are tired of everyday corruption, of bribery in the state bodies, courts, the judiciary and state-owned companies.

G20 Summit June 20, 2012 Los Cabos

Vladimir Putin: ... Although our history is, unfortunately, in large part dark, bloody and clannish, there are many instances of dedicated effort and efficiency even before Peter the Great. Isn't Alexander Nevsky an example?

Andrei Okara: Who is your favourite statesman? Or are there several?

Vladimir Putin: I like Alexander Nevsky very much. Then I like Peter the Great, and Catherine the Great in the early part of her life and statesmanship. Incidentally, Russia expanded territorially the most under Catherine. In this sense she was a more efficient monarch than Peter the Great: less blood and more acquisition.

6 February 2012 Prime Minister Vladimir Putin meets with political scientists

I haven't seen any of our opposition members doing a good job, including those who have been in power for many years. It is easy to promise everyone housing, happiness, health and wealth tomorrow but this is idle talk and it is unfair.

15 December 2011 After the Q&A session, A Conversation with Vladimir Putin: Continued, the prime minister answered journalists' questions

People in our country do not want to see the situation escalate to what happened in Kyrgyzstan, or in the recent past in Ukraine. Nobody wants chaos. In relying on the overwhelming majority of our citizens, we should conduct a dialogue with those who are in opposition and allow them to express themselves, to exercise their constitutional rights and voice their opinions. By relying on the overwhelming majority of citizens who do not want to see any chaos in the country, law enforcement agencies must organise all of this in accordance with current legislation and our nation's constitution. ...

The first thing that Secretary of State Clinton did was to provide an assessment of the elections by saying that they were unfair and unjust, even though she had not yet received the OSCE [Organization for Security and Co-operation in Europe] report. She set the tone for some of our political figures within the country, she sent a signal. They heard the signal and with the support of the State Department, they began their active work. ...

You know, when it comes to people who go to America, receive some training there, get some money and equipment and then come here and engage in provocations, dragging people into the streets and the like – first of all, you can't apply the same yardstick to these people. It's one thing when somebody comes here from abroad after being briefed and supplied with money. But it's another thing if a working man stands up, presents a problem but does not know how to solve it. He does not need to know how to solve it, it is the job of you and me to know how to solve these problems, so let's just say that everybody should do his own job.

8 December 2011 Prime Minister Vladimir Putin chairs a meeting of the Russian Popular Front's Coordinating Council

I believe that Russia enjoyed a major advantage compared with other countries during the global economic crisis, due to the coordinated work of the government and parliament. You understand that long discussions and deliberations about how things could be done better, and failure to act at a time when fast decision-making is needed, are more dangerous than taking action, even if it is imperfect.

3 November 2011 Prime Minister Vladimir Putin speaks at the closing plenary meeting of the State Duma

Let me remind you that it was the period following 1905 during which Russia suffered a humiliating defeat at the hands of Japan. That triggered very complicated processes within the country that rocked the empire. Various terrorist groups emerged. Terrorist attacks at the time claimed close to 20,000 lives, around 18,000. And at that time the Stolypin government introduced martial courts that passed death sentences on about 2,500 people. This is nothing to be proud of, to be sure. But let me remind you of something that Stolypin said at the time. I am quoting from memory so I'm not sure it'll be entirely accurate. But the gist of what he said was, "I hope that Russia will be able to distinguish blood on the hands of a doctor from blood on the hands of an executioner."

He believed that strict measures with regard to the people who were rocking the state were justified at that time. I should remind you that people who considered themselves to be progressive, above all members of the intelligentsia, unfortunately sent telegrams to the Japanese emperor congratulating him on his victory over the Russian military. I think that whatever the motives of these actions were, they were nothing less than treachery. And traitors should be treated accordingly. I do not think that all these 2,500 executions that took place in Russia were fair, not at all. It was a major tragedy. And, by the way, you know, there is no death penalty in Russia today.

15 November 2011 Prime Minister Vladimir Putin attends the plenary session of the National Forum of Rural Intelligentsia

Prime Minister Vladimir Putin toured the hospital buildings and listened carefully to the medical staff's wishes regarding the new equipment. The personnel revealed that they desperately needed a new ultrasound scanner, mammography unit, ECG machine, and dental office. At the dentist's office, Putin took a dental drill and, laughing, asked Belgorod Region Governor Yevgeny Savchenko to sit down in the dentist's chair.

"Sit down, please. If you don't buy the new equipment, I will come back and treat everyone with this," he joked.

15 November 2011 Prime Minister Vladimir Putin visits the Golovchino rural district hospital while on a working visit to the Belgorod Region

A government reshuffle only unveils the weakness of the country's leadership. This means that the leaders are either unable or unwilling to take responsibility and always shift it to someone else.

17 October 2011 Interview with Prime Minister Vladimir Putin

Roosevelt managed to get elected four times. He led the country through the harsh times of the Great Depression and World War II, and he got elected four times because he acted effectively. ...Our country, too, experienced a collapse... Only in the 2000s did we begin to rise up and establish internal peace.

17 October 2011 Interview with Prime Minister Vladimir Putin

We often face problems of abuse and corruption as soon as they learn that a new pipeline or power transmission line or road or railway is to be built. But who finds out? First and foremost, it's officials in city halls and regional governments. Immediately they start buying up all the land that would be needed for the project, and the government then is forced to buy this land from them at three times its price.

5 September 2011 Prime Minister Vladimir Putin attends a United Russia party interregional conference, Strategy of Social and Economic Development for Russia's Northwestern Regions to 2020. The Programme for 2011-2012, in Cherepovets

Vladimir Pozner: ... What's your attitude towards showing opposition activists on Channel One? ...

Vladimir Putin: ... Unfortunately, I cannot keep an eye on everything, but from time to time, I see opposition leaders on TV, including on your channel, I think. They speak openly and criticise the government quite severely.

Vladimir Pozner: So you do not take it negatively? You believe it is possible?

Vladimir Putin: Absolutely. Some radio stations do nothing but (host the opposition).

Vladimir Pozner: Radio, yes. Ekho Moskvy...

Vladimir Putin: I'll go even further... I know what goes on in reality. And when I listen to what they say and understand they're telling lies, I don't get mad about it. After all, if someone wants to hear lies, there has to be someone to tell them. Let them do it.

3 February 2011 Prime Minister Vladimir Putin visits the Channel One headquarters at Ostankino TV centre in Moscow

We often, justifiably, criticise our law-enforcement agencies. It's no accident that we have major reform plans in this sphere. But while fighting negative elements in our law-enforcement agencies, including the police, we must not tar everyone with the same brush. We need to understand that these agencies are entrusted with a vital state function and we must not treat them like dirt; otherwise our liberal intelligentsia will have to shave off their beards, don their helmets and go out onto the streets and squares to fight the radicals.

16 December 2010 Television channels Rossiya and Rossiya 24 and radio stations Mayak and Vesti FM have started broadcasting the annual Q&A session, "A Conversation with Vladimir Putin, Continued"

There was a time when I received a lot of criticism for changing the procedure for electing governors in the Russian regions. I still get criticism but one of the motives for this change was to keep criminal elements out of local governments. Unfortunately, civil society is not yet effective enough in our country, and with so-called "direct elections", nearly every candidate had a criminal looming behind his back, who tried to use his "unaccounted-for" money to influence the election campaign and its outcome and did it with a degree of success.

Now when the president proposes candidates for governors, and local deputies must vote for or against, this somehow hedges society against criminal inroads, at least at this high regional level of administration. Unfortunately, the situation in municipalities is not the same. We have direct elections of municipal administrators and criminals continue to have a say there. ... Every citizen, when going to a polling station, especially when electing local administrators, should give their vote to a candidate for his or her for personal and leadership qualities, and not on the basis of empty pledges. As a rule, people who live in small towns and villages know who backs these candidates.

16 December 2010 Television channels Rossiya and Rossiya 24 and radio stations Mayak and Vesti FM have started broadcasting the annual Q&A session, "A Conversation with Vladimir Putin, Continued"

I asked our local colleagues, the Volgograd authorities, why so few land plots had been allotted for construction, and why it took so long to allot a land plot. The answer was typical: they referred to objective difficulties, the complicated situation in the sector, lack of interest from businesses, and so on, and so forth. The general prosecutor's office conducted an audit. What were the results? The general prosecutor's office is of the opinion, and I think it is hard to disagree with them, that the main reason lies in bureaucrats' insatiable greed and the utterly corrupt and non-transparent process of allotting plots. It is striking that the Volgograd administration has allotted only 28 plots out of a total of 600 on a competitive basis over the course of two and a half years! All the other plots were allotted on non-transparent personal decisions. Bureaucrats and people close to them got land en masse.

20 August 2010 Prime Minister Vladimir Putin chairs a meeting of the Government Presidium of the Russian Federation

"What do Nemtsov, Ryzhkov, Milov and others of their ilk want, after all?"

Money and power, what else? They had a field day in their time, in the 1990s when, together with the Berezovskys and those who are now in jail and whom we recalled today, stole billions. They were dragged away from the feeding trough, they have spent much of their money and they want to come back and refill their pockets. But I think if we allow them to do so, they will not stop at billions, they will sell all Russia down the river.

16 December 2010 Television channels Rossiya and Rossiya 24 and radio stations Mayak and Vesti FM have started broadcasting the annual Q&A session, "A Conversation with Vladimir Putin, Continued"

Question: When will officials in Russia be made liable for their crimes, rather than simply resigning?"

Vladimir Putin: I must tell you that the number of persons prosecuted for malfeasance – that is, for corruption and bribes – is growing for better or worse; and in several recent years, it has been growing steadily. It is not because there are more crimes – it is because more crimes are being exposed.

16 December 2010 Television channels Rossiya and Rossiya 24 and radio stations Mayak and Vesti FM have started broadcasting the annual Q&A session, "A Conversation with Vladimir Putin, Continued"

There is nothing absolutely pure in nature. Even if there is, absolute purity can be achieved in a lab only. But we still need to strive for this. And we will do so, of course.

2 December, 2010 Prime Minister Vladimir Putin gives a news conference in Zurich after Russia wins the 2018 FIFA World Cup bid

Question: Do you think the model of democracy, the western model, is not very good, especially for Russia now?

Vladimir Putin: Can you tell me what the "western model of democracy" is? France has one, while the United States has another. A French politician told me one day: you won't get anywhere in the American elections, be they for Senate, Congress and particularly in presidential elections, without a large sack of cash. Where then is democracy? Democracy for whom? For those with lots of money? In the United States, they have a presidential republic, and in Great Britain, a monarchy. These are all elements of democracy. Which one are you referring to? There is no one concept of western democracy. It does not exist.

Let's not discuss France: I am going to visit it soon. I do not want to cite examples from French political life. Tony Blair is a good pal of mine. His party won the elections under his leadership. To a considerable extent, and I think you will agree with me here, the electorate voted for his party, its programme and also for Tony Blair himself. Then due to domestic political considerations, for party reasons, the Labour leaders decided that Blair should go, making way for another man. Tony left, with Mr Brown taking his place and automatically becoming prime minister, the top office of state. Without an election. What is that? Democracy? Yes, it is democracy, whether good or bad, such as it is.

I used to have a lot of discussions with my American colleagues. I would say: how come the majority of the population voted for one person, but got quite another as president? Through the electoral college system. The Americans responded: Don't get into it, we're used to it and it'll stay like that. We don't get involved in it. So why then do you feel you have the right to? We will sort things out and decide what to do ourselves.

10 June 2010 Prime Minister Vladimir Putin gives an interview to Agence France Presse and France 2 television channel ahead of his working visit to France

Vladimir Putin: Alisa Brunovna has given me this bell to moderate our meeting. Is everyone here? We've gathered at a very good time. This city is celebrating its birthday. The weather's good and everyone's in a good mood.

Alisa Freindlich: Well, the weather...

Vladimir Putin: ...is very good!

Alisa Freindlich: It cleared up just a minute ago, but it's been raining heavily today.

Vladimir Putin: It doesn't matter now. It's all in the past. And we should think about the future. Fine weather, good mood...

Okay, first of all, I'd like to thank Ms Chulpan Khamatova for her effort, and for gathering us together. It's a very important cause. Thank you very much. I'll also repeat it publicly, when we start the show.

The government is doing everything in its power to address at least the most acute problems more effectively than before, and we have gathered here to discuss these problems today.

As you know, a large medical centre is being constructed in Moscow for children with oncologic diseases, primarily hematologic diseases. This centre will be the largest in Europe, without exaggeration. It'll accommodate between 250 and 300 patients, servicing another 300 patients at its ambulatory clinic. Also, there will be a research lab and a hotel for the families of young patients. They will be able to come and stay there for the duration of the treatment. This option is very important for such patients. They need their family there.

The government is doing this on its own. It'll cost the budget 11 billion roubles. Construction will be finished by next June. The centre will have the latest high-tech equipment. I hope it will be able to receive its first patients at the end of next year. Construction, equipment... everything's done by our specialists and with our money, and in cooperation with doctors. Also, our European partners and friends, primarily from Germany, the leaders in this branch of medicine, have given us invaluable help. I'm mentioning them because they are very enthusiastic: They have spent so much personal time on this project, giving everything to help our specialists. And we can see the results of their efforts.

I discussed this project during my latest visit to Germany. One of the leading European and even international specialists in this area told me a very moving story. When one Swiss child fell ill, his family came to a German clinic for consultation. The German doctors said that the child should be taken to Russia because the world's number one specialist in this disease works there. I think it's great that we have such specialists in our country.

Well, we nevertheless lack the research base, equipment and other things. I hope... I'm sure that next year we'll resolve this issue almost completely.

I know that Chulpan pays special attention to these issues. She's constantly in contact with the doctors, the families of the children, and the children themselves. And she follows the progress of this centre. Do you know this story? In 2005 I received a letter from a patient at this clinic, a little boy, Dima Rogachev. He invited me for pancakes. And so I visited him.

Chulpan Khamatova: Sorry to interrupt you, he wrote that it was his sweetest dream. We ask children what their most desired dreams are, and we – and our friends and volunteers – try to make these dreams come true. Some wish for a guitar, some for a video camera. But this boy wanted to have some pancakes with the president! Vladimir Vladimirovich received this letter and came... excuse me.

Vladimir Putin: That's okay. Sadly, Dima passed away, but it was he who inspired us to build this large medical and research centre in Russia. And I've got an idea... It just occurred to me all of a sudden, and I'd like to hear your opinion... I think it would be good if we named this centre in honour of Dima Rogachev.

Chulpan Khamatova: We would need to discuss this with the doctors. His parents must have come here today. His mother comes to every concert here.

Vladimir Putin: In any case, it was he who initiated it. He was the inspiration for this idea. Not that he asked to build this centre, but...

Leonid Yarmolnik: It's a good idea. Unprecedented... No centre has been given the name of a young patient.

Vladimir Putin: Unfortunately, he died in Israel where he was being treated.

Leonid Yarmolnik: Good idea. Such centres are usually named for doctors or the person who founded them. And this centre could have the name of the boy who inspired the idea. I don't think the doctors would mind.

Chulpan Khamatova: It's their call after all.

Vladimir Putin: Okay, let's say I've finished my monologue. Now you please.

Chulpan Khamatova: Well, I was told that this should be a low key discussion, and I'll try to keep it so. First, I'd like to say while everyone's here – and we scheduled this reception before the concert, not after it – I'd like to thank everyone for coming. Some have come from other cities, not just from Moscow: Some were touring and giving other concerts. Thank you very much. When so many talented and generous people come together, they can provide a lot of positive energy... You know, when we put on these shows, I have goosebumps because I feel this energy...

I'd like to ask two questions on behalf of the fund. They're more like requests...

The problems we're facing today... I'm not sure whether I'll sound low key enough now, but still I'd like to touch on the problems that keep us from developing it as quickly as we could. I'm speaking on behalf of the Podari Zhizn [Grant a Life] fund, but I'm sure many charities are facing the same problems...

You most certainly know about the problem with orphan drugs, which are...

Vladimir Putin: ... very costly and are not mass-produced.

Chulpan Khamatova: Correct, they haven't been mass-produced because it's an unprofitable business.

Vladimir Putin: Very few patients need them, and there's no general production, therefore they're expensive.

Chulpan Khamatova: Yes. I'd like to tell you how we're dealing with this problem. Of course, it's an unprofitable business, and sometimes the situation borders on the absurd. We have to spend donated money on it. First, we need to find a doctor abroad, who agrees to give a prescription. Sometimes the same person doesn't agree to do it twice. And the drugs are needed urgently; a child's life is at stake. So we find a doctor, and even if this doctor agrees to fill the prescription, we need to find someone who'll agree to take the drug across the border, which is also difficult. Some people panic thinking that it's something illegal even if we show them all the documents. They sometimes just leave these drugs, which cost a fortune, at an airport. And they just disappear.

This is why I'm asking for your help. Ours is not the only foundation facing the problem of treating rare diseases and the procurement of rare drugs.

Vladimir Putin: Yes, this problem exists. In many countries the state makes an official list of rare diseases and rare drugs, but there's no such list in Russia, which causes problems with the import and production of drugs, if such production can be organised here. I agree that this list must be created and managed properly.

Chulpan Khamatova: And this should be done as soon as possible.

Vladimir Putin: We'll do it. The Ministry of Healthcare and Social Development has been given a directive already.

Chulpan Khamatova: I know they're doing all they can to resolve this issue but...

Remark: They need a push.

Vladimir Putin: They will finish this work on their own.

Chulpan Khamatova: They need to be prodded a little.

Vladimir Putin: I understand that a) it's a problem and b) it's an acute problem. And it will never be settled without the government's direct support because companies do not profit from it, and these drugs are produced in very small quantities.

Sergei Garmash: There is a related problem with some of the base substances that cannot be imported. If you recall, some of them are just not mentioned in our customs regulatory acts.

Vladimir Putin: Well, it's about the import of drugs from abroad. If they are not produced in Russia, and are produced in small quantities in other countries, and are not on the list of special drugs, there will be problems with customs. We'll work it out.

Chulpan Khamatova: Thank you very much, and my second question... I'd like to discuss tax benefits and tell you how it works. Unlike first aid, second aid is taxed.

Vladimir Putin: What's second aid?

Chulpan Khamatova: For example, our fund wants to help the same child twice in the same year. During the first treatment, we might purchase some inexpensive drug, then, when the child needs transplantation...

Vladimir Putin: It's taxed.

Chulpan Khamatova: Yes, and this tax is levied on the parents of this child. And they receive notification 12 months later...

Vladimir Putin: ...as the recipients of help.

Chulpan Khamatova: Yes, transplantation can cost 15,000 euros, and treatment 40,000 euros, and the parents must pay this tax even if they don't have the money.

Vladimir Putin: I see.

Chulpan Khamatova: We've prepared a draft law. It's now in the Duma. It's a big project, and we hope it will settle all the issues related to non-profit organisations. And we have a request. Could we include in this draft law a tax relief provision for the second round of treatment? Sometimes the foundation assists with organising funerals, and you can understand what bereaved parents feel when they receive a bill a year after losing their child.

Vladimir Putin: We'll need to alter the Tax Code to specify that all help received during the course of treatment be tax exempt.

Chulpan Khamatova: Yes, the whole course of treatment. It would be perfect.

Vladimir Putin: We'll do it.

Chulpan Khamatova: Thank you very much. That's all I wanted to discuss today. Thank you.

Vladimir Putin: Okay. We can actually discuss any issue, whether it's related to today's event or not. Please.

Yury Shevchuk: Vladimir Vladimirovich, may I?

Vladimir Putin: Yes.

Yury Shevchuk: You know, some aide of yours – I don't remember his name – called me yesterday and asked me not to bring up any sensitive issues, political problems and other things...

Vladimir Putin: Excuse me, could you introduce yourself?

Yury Shevchuk: Yura Shevchuk, a musician.

Vladimir Putin: Yura, it was a provocation.

Yury Shevchuk: Provocation, ah, whatever...

Vladimir Putin: My aide would never call you to say such a thing.

Yury Shevchuk: Okay, not your aide, some lunatic, yes...

Remark: It's getting funny!

Yury Shevchuk: But I've got some questions. In fact I've got a whole lot of questions. First, I'd like to thank everybody for gathering. What you see here is the emergence of a real civil society, which you speak so much about and dream about.

Here's what I'd like to discuss. I have some questions. First, freedom. Such a word, freedom... The freedom of the press, the freedom of information... What's happening in the country... We're living in a class society that has remained the same over centuries. There are rich dukes with their privileges and then the common people who toil away... And there's an immense gap between them. I'm sure you understand this.

The only way forward is making everyone equal before the law, both the dukes and the common people. Coal miners shouldn't go to work as though it's the last battle. The system must be fair. An individual should be free and have self-respect, which would result in a natural patriotism. You cannot arouse this feeling with a banner. I see what's happening now, and everyone who is intelligent and sensible can see it.

We see these banners, but it's all so superficial. It's a lame attempt to show patriotism and maybe conscience... These chants and marches... We've seen it all before. The only effective solution is civil society and equality for everyone, absolutely everyone, before the law, you, me and everyone else. Only then can we move ahead. We'll build hospitals and help children, people with disabilities and elderly people. We'll do it sincerely and willingly, it'll come from the depth of our souls.

But to this end, we need freedom of the press, which is missing. There's one paper and a half in our country. The same with television. What we see on TV cannot even be called debate; it's the same marches and chants.

The protesting electorate is growing in number, and you know it. Many are critical of the present situation. Are you honest when you say you want real liberalization and modernisation for a real country, where public organisations are not suffocated and where people don't feel scared of a policeman on the street? The police now serve their bosses and their pockets, not people.

There are a lot of persecutors in this country. I really think so. On May 31 a March of Dissent will be held in St Petersburg. My question is whether it'll be dispersed or not.

That's it.

Vladimir Putin: That's all?

Yury Shevchuk: So far yes. I can show you what we've composed. Not even composed, these are just some facts describing what's happening in our country, plus our opinion.

Vladimir Putin: Okay, thanks, I'll take a look, be sure. First of all, without democracy Russia has no future.

Yury Shevchuk: It's understood.

Vladimir Putin: It's obvious. Individuals can build on their capabilities only in a free society. And if they are able to do so, they contribute to the development of the country, its science, its industry, taking it to the highest possible level. Otherwise, society stagnates. It's an obvious fact, understood by all. It's the first point I'd like to make. Second, everyone must abide by the law. You're correct in this. But we need a professional approach to this. You mentioned coal miners...

Yury Shevchuk: Yes.

Vladimir Putin: I take to heart everything happening there [the Raspadskaya coal mine explosion].

Yury Shevchuk: Me too.

Vladimir Putin: A professional approach suggests analysing the legal and economic conditions thoroughly.

Yury Shevchuk: That's true.

Vladimir Putin: Why is it happening? What's one of the reasons? They say one reason is the base salaries at coal mines, for example, at the Raspadskaya coal mine, where the base salary accounts for about 45% of a miners' income, and the rest is bonuses. And so the workers disregard the safety rules to earn these bonuses.

Yury Shevchuk: I know.

Vladimir Putin: I made a decision and gave a directive to the government to raise the base salary to 70%. But, Yura, let me emphasise that it applies to coke mines only. You need some knowledge of this issue to understand it. In addition to coke mines, there are steam coal mines, which are less profitable. And the base salary rates depend on the price of the finished product. If we increase it thoughtlessly, steam coal mines will become unprofitable overnight and will close. If you are for a market economy, you should understand that they'll just close. And as far as I can see, you're a proponent of a market economy, not a planned economy. They'll just close. That's it. And this is only one aspect of the problem.

Now you say that policemen serve their bosses only. There are many different kinds of people working as police officers. It's a microcosm of our society in general. It's a part of our country. And these people haven't come from Mars. Many are people who risk their lives and health to faithfully serve our people. Yes, there are traffic police whose only purpose is to make money from bribes, but there also are those who would protect a child with their bodies, who use their own cars to stop criminals and who get killed. So it is unfair to tarnish the image of all these people.

Yury Shevchuk: I don't!

Vladimir Putin: No, but you said that cops serve only the officials, not the people.

Yury Shevchuk: This is true in general. For example, I will be taking part in the March of Dissent, and there will be 500 participants and maybe 2,500 special task force police. What, did we stab or kill somebody?

Vladimir Putin: I didn't interrupt you when you were talking. Don't turn the discussion into a noisy argument!

I think it is unfair to reduce everyone to the same level. We do have problems there. It's our culture: when a guy gets a license or some "stick" in his hands, he immediately begins to swing it and try to make money using it. But this applies not only to the police but in every area where people have authority and the opportunity to make illegal money.

As for these Marches of Dissent, there are rules stipulating that such events be controlled by local authorities. We should think about the rights of those who are not participating in the "dissent/approval marches." If you are going to hold a March of Dissent, pardon my sharp words, near a hospital and disturb sick children, who will allow you to do that? Of course they have the right to prohibit this!

Yury Shevchuk: May I respond?

Vladimir Putin: No! And if you want to hold a demonstration blocking a road so people cannot get to their dachas on Friday or return home on Sunday? They will curse you. And they will curse the local authorities, too.

But this does not mean that the government should make excuses and limit freedom of speech. This is an issue which should be discussed with the government.

I hope that in St. Petersburg everything will be organised in an acceptable way. People's right to express their disapproval of the government should be protected, but participants in such demonstrations should not disturb those who do not want to demonstrate, but just want to get home in time and be with their families. We have to work around that.

I really want you to understand this: That I and the other government members need people's opinions.

Yury Shevchuk: Of course.

Vladimir Putin: If I see that people go into the streets not just to talk or promote themselves but to say something important and relevant and draw the government's attention to some problem, there is nothing wrong with that. I will thank them.

Yury Shevchuk: Indeed.

Vladimir Putin: And I mean it.

Yury Shevchuk: But you also see that local authorities install amusement rides on main squares when we want to hold our protests. This is nothing but hypocrisy.

Vladimir Putin: I agree with you on that.

Yury Shevchuk: You know, last year, the whole city fought to preserve St. Petersburg's historical centre. You cannot imagine what they [the local authorities] did to block our efforts! You were born there; it's an amazing city, a wonder. But they fought us off and people got really angry. What was this all about? You carry a lot of weight, so use it...

Vladimir Putin: My weight is 76 kilograms.

Yury Shevchuk: Oh God...

Oleg Basilashvili: Vladimir Vladimirovich, let me support Yura. Just one word.

Vladimir Putin: Sure, Oleg Valerianovich.

Oleg Basilashvili: Speaking of this skyscraper. I cannot tell if it's beautiful or not, it is not my business. Maybe it is gorgeous. But most people who are concerned about St. Petersburg, who love the city and know its history say this building doesn't belong there, especially a 300–400 metre tall building.

Federal and local laws have been flagrantly violated and the authorities just laugh in our faces. We basically feel like those with power say to us, "It's you who has to abide by the law, not us, so piss off." And all the newspapers say is "it will be constructed."

I fear that this is not just about this "Gasscraper," but really about the confrontation between the government and the people whose opinion is never taken into account. Dissent has been growing and I agree with Yura on that. And this is just one small example of hundreds.

Yury Shevchuk: Millions.

Vladimir Putin: Oleg Valerianovich, this example isn't small, it's huge.

Oleg Basilashvili: Yes.

Vladimir Putin: And very tall. Of course, everyone should obey the law, it is an obvious fact. I made my position clear when answering Yury's question. If you remember, I spoke about the dictatorship of law back in the early 2000s; at the time I was criticized for that. I still believe it is an appropriate phrase. It assumes that the law must be observed by everyone: the government, ordinary people and various government officials.

I'm not going to state my final opinion on the tower. I do not want to make it in public. This is clearly an issue for the municipal government to decide. Naturally, in such cases the public needs to be consulted. This is clear.

You know, we often compare ourselves with our neighbors in the West, and we always say that we are inferior. This humiliates our national dignity. Let's look at London or Paris. How was the Pompidou Centre built? What's in the middle of the Louvre?

Oleg Basilashvili: Something really horrible!

Vladimir Putin: I am not making any assessments here. I am just saying how things are there.

Oleg Basilashvili: Let them follow our example and not the other way around. It's time to finish with these skyscrapers. Nobody builds skyscrapers any more in the world, whereas we want to put one up in the middle of the Neva.

Vladimir Putin: Oleg Valerianovich, I am not even saying whether it is good or bad. I am simply saying that this issue exists everywhere in the world. There are people who support this concept of urban development. There are people like that in our country and elsewhere in the world. Once again, I am not going to say who is right or wrong. But I certainly agree with you that when making such decisions, the authorities should consult the public and take public opinion into account.

Oleg Basilashvili: And first of all, they should be guided by the law.

Vladimir Putin: Of course, and not just guided, but must obey the law.

Oleg Basilashvili: The law that has been violated in this case. And one final point, if I may?

Vladimir Putin: Of course.

Oleg Basilashvili: If you remember, about two years ago, we discussed the law on patronage. I fully support Chulpan now. What she and her friends have been doing is truly a great thing. We should be grateful to her. And the proposals that she has made here are also very sensible, useful, and necessary.

But on the other hand, I think that the law on patronage can give an impetus to this work and make it more dynamic. We have talked about this, and you told me that the law seemed to be ready, that it was in progress and would soon be adopted. And yet there has been no movement in this respect.

It is not difficult at all. Such laws exist in almost every country in the world. It also existed in Russia before the revolution – honorable citizens, the nobility, and so on. People should not be interested in investing in yachts costing 40 billion, but in giving their money to Chulpan, to children, etc.

Vladimir Putin: Well, what can I say? I have to agree with you. Of course such activities need to be regulated. You just mentioned the fund created by Chulpan. I look at them from time to time and, frankly, I too cannot help but wonder how consistently and tenaciously they deal with these complicated and delicate matters and – what I find most appealing – without putting themselves first. And, of course, a legal framework is necessary.

You spoke about what we had in this country before the 1917 Revolution. I think it was a completely different country then and even a different civilisation, to a certain extent.

Oleg Basilashvili: Well, yes.

Vladimir Putin: Many things are different now. What is the problem? Rules are easy to write, the problem is how to enforce them. There are too many abuses.

Over the past ten or fifteen years, as soon as good ideas are put into practice, be it in the economy or in other administrative spheres, people start abusing them. They are very difficult to regulate and administer, because people start using the rules for the opposite of what they were created for.

But on the whole – Chulpan also knows this, she told me – there are things that call for special attention. We will address them, and we will make sure that no one can abuse them. This is the point.

Of course we want to do it, but we don't seem to have the brains to design them in such a way as to prevent abuses. As you know, hundreds and thousands of people work on our laws and millions are thinking of ways to evade them.

Alisa Freindlich: We are a very talented nation in that way.

Sergei Garmash: Yes. Vladimir Vladimirovich, look. We have been building a new state since the mid-1980s: many things are changing, and we are trying to change a lot of things. But for some reason no one, in my opinion, has given serious thought to comprehensive primary education reform.

New directives are issued, new textbooks are written, and we have the Single State Examination (EGE). People have been designing curricula for their universities however they like. But education is basically the same as it was in our time and in our parents' time.

But times have changed, with computers and all the new things. Granted, you and I learnt computer skills very quickly. But when it comes to the difference between computers and books... The list can go on and on, as you know.

Why hasn't anyone thought of this reform and implemented it to change the approach? I have met all sorts of people in my life, but I can't think of a single instance when I felt embarrassed because I couldn't remember one of Newton's laws or a single formula.

But if I had paid more attention to literature and history after grade six, I would be a better man now. I think the times dictate these things. But we see nothing but directives, inventions and subjects getting cut. I see the cuts they are making: just compare how much Pushkin we were taught and how much is taught now.

Orthodox education is now being introduced. There is Orthodox education even in small towns. It is being introduced into the system. The rationale is not very clear, because it costs government money.

Well, in general my question is about what I think is as important as oil and defence: comprehensive education reform.

Vladimir Putin: I think it is the most important thing, especially primary and secondary education, which is the basis of everything: higher education, science, and, consequently, the modern knowledge-based economy.

You know that Dmitry Anatolyevich [Medvedev] has come up with an initiative called Our New School. So, it would be wrong to say that no one has given it any thought and no one has been concerned about it. We simply have to do it, and we are, and here I have demographic problems in mind. Our demographics move in waves. In the coming years, the number of university students will drop sharply because of demographics. That is another challenge. Anyway, primary and secondary education is the foundation of all education, science and an innovative economy. Do you have specific proposals?

Sergei Garmash: No, I don't have specific proposals. On the one hand, I am in favour of liberalisation, but on the other hand, I have a sense that things are out of control. Let me cite a concrete example. There is a government-funded Arts Academy in the city of Samara. I was invited to give a master class there. On the way to the master class, my host tells me third-year acting students study the business of the theatre and marketing. "How many voice coaching classes are there?" "One a week." I ask, "Who designs the schedule?", and she tells me, "Our rector."

Vladimir Putin: This is a government-funded school?

Sergei Garmash: Yes.

Unidentified voice: This guy's got it coming (laughter).

Vladimir Putin: We will respond (laughs). It's in Samara?

Sergei Garmash: Yes.

Unidentified voice: Get the rector (laughter).

Ilya Lagutenko: I have a not very serious question from the Far East. My name is Ilya. In addition to singing songs about Vladivostok, I help an organisation that is trying to save the Siberian tiger. I know that you have given an order to organise a "tiger summit" in Vladivostok.

Vladimir Putin: Yes, we have agreed that there will be a summit... Honestly, I am not sure that all those present know that the tiger summit will be a very high-level event. Heads of state and government are taking part.

Ilya Lagutenko: Yes, I have met many of them, and I've travelled to Washington. But a couple of days ago rumours began to circulate that the governor of Primorye said that he has no money and Vladivostok does not have the necessary infrastructure to host the event.

Vladimir Putin: We will hold the tiger summit, but unfortunately, we cannot hold it in Vladivostok.

Ilya Lagutenko: So, it's true....

Vladimir Putin: No, it's not that he has no money. The problem is that we are organising a major international APEC event, and all the construction capacity, both local and from other Russian regions, has been committed to preparing for that event. Vladivostok is, in fact, one big construction site today. You come from Vladivostok yourself and you see what is going on. We are building a brand new airport there. We are making the best use of it. It was originally my idea to hold this major international event, the Pacific summit. We are building a new airport there with a new runway, which I believe will be 3,400 (metres).

Ilya Lagutenko: We will eclipse Hong Kong.

Vladimir Putin: It will be a good, modern airport. We never had such an airport in the east of the country. We are building several roads and two bridges. One of them is truly unique – a bridge to Russky Island. Almost every pylon has hundreds of meters, making it possible to monitor them from space. It will be a good and major event. The summit will be held on Russky Island, where a whole new city is being built. Later it will be used for a new research and education centre, a new university.

Andrei Makarevich: While we're on the subject of laws, we have been struggling for over six years to improve the law on the protection of animals. The current law is full of flaws. It doesn't make owners responsible for their pets, like elsewhere in the world. That is why we have a staggering number of homeless animals, who are killed in very cruel ways in secret. Our efforts have hit a wall.

Voice: Makarevich doesn't have enough clout.

Andrei Makarevich: I met with Luzhkov [mayor of Moscow] four times in Moscow to discuss the matter.

Vladimir Putin: Where is this draft now?

Andrei Makarevich: I have it here. Actually, we have reworked it since the State Duma sent it back seven years ago. I am prepared to submit it.

Vladimir Putin: OK. We will revisit the issue. I'll ask our party at the Duma to take it up again and go over it together with you.

Andrei Makarevich: Thank you.

Vladimir Putin: I watch your programmes in which you crawl under water. Aren't you afraid?

Sergei Garmash: It's not as frightening as the streets of Moscow.

Vladimir Putin: No, no, no. He has very interesting programmes, very beautiful. I don't have the time to watch all of them, but what I've seen is great.

Leonid Yarmolnik: Vladimir Vladimirovich, there is something I want to tell you. First, I would like to thank you for being with us today. Over the last ten years, I've witnessed how whatever you pay attention to somehow works out. That is very important. My heart aches for children, above all. As most of those present are actors, who age and get sick... In our country you basically have to live from hand to mouth. As long as you work, you can get by. But if you drop out for three months, the money runs out. There is a fund I would like to tell you about. It is the Artist Fund created by Masha Mironova and Zhenya Mironov. I am a member of its board of trustees. We have ways to raise money, to ask for money. It is funded, and much has been done. What worries me is that many charitable funds are used as fronts for money laundering. Of course, not all funds are like that. We had a lot of problems, and I told my colleagues, "I'll talk to such and such people and they'll shell out the money." But you are up against such odds.

Here is a fund; lots of resources can be raised to be invested for a profit, which the fund would use. But we just don't have that kind of mechanism.

Vladimir Putin: Sure we do.

Leonid Yarmolnik: No, Zhenya and I have been racking our brains...

Vladimir Putin: There is a mechanism. It can be done.

Leonid Yarmolnik: Because this is the most painful thing...We have already lost so many actors. They died in poverty and misery.

Vladimir Putin: If the fund has raised a great deal of money it can live off the interest on its capital.

Leonid Yarmolnik: Yes, of course, but it is all very complicated. I was involved in it myself. Sberbank was advising us. There is always something in the law that needs to be changed. Because, again, there are so many actors... And they are all proud and decent people... They don't talk about their hardships. We only hear about it when it is too late to treat them and help them.

Generations have been raised on the work of these actors, including you and me. It is horrible, a disgrace. There is so much neglect. So, we would like to be able to reach you more quickly in case something crops up that can't be resolved without you.

Vladimir Putin: Leonid, you simply have to formulate it... Chulpan has been specific: a decision is needed on rare drugs and we will do this, we will respond. No tax on second-time assistance. I assure you we will follow through on it. These are specific things. When you say that you have problems, I need to know exactly what problems. Be specific.

Leonid Yarmolnik: OK. I understand.

Sergey Garmash: I propose that before the Health Ministry implements this law we ask Vladimir Vladimirovich to bring us medicine. Surely he won't get checked at customs.

Vladimir Putin: You want me to import drugs? Work as a shuttle merchant? (laughter)

Vladimir Kekhman: I have a follow-up on the theatre. Since we are in a theatre... We think of you as a theatre person. I am new to this field. I've been a theatre director for three years...

Vladimir Putin: Yes, we've heard. As we were coming here, I said, "Were you the guy who imported bananas?" "Yes," he says. I say, "We have opened a new line linking St.Petersburg to Latin America, so you should help us even more."

Vladimir Kekhman: Moreover, we are beginning production in Ecuador together with you.

Vladimir Putin: What?

Vladimir Kekhman: We are starting production in Venezuela... and now also in Ecuador. Ecuador accounts for 95%.

Vladimir Putin: That much?

Vladimir Kekhman: A million metric tonnes. We are the biggest firm. We control 30% of production in Ecuador and 5% of world production.

Vladimir Putin: What is your turnover?

Vladimir Kekhman: Our company? Our company's turnover is 680 million.

Leonid Yarmolnik: Are we talking about fish? (laughter)

Vladimir Putin: You'll get it in a moment. We are going to discuss charity for your fund.

Leonid Yarmolnik: Thank you.

Vladimir Kekhman: I wanted to say one more important thing. Two issues. One very critical issue is succession. After a difficult twenty years at the Musical Theatre we no longer have choreographers or teachers – some have left, some have died.

Presidential grants ensure that we are doing well financially. Therefore, the most important thing is this: there is a law on persons working in the area of culture (an umbrella law), but there is no law on theatre workers, which is very important because these are different things. Librarians are not the same as theatre actors. When it comes to money, all is well, but as far as the law on theatre workers is concerned... there should be a separate law because a theatre, be it musical, drama or any other theatre, needs continuity in order to exist.

Vladimir Putin: I see.

Vladimir Kekhman: That is the first issue. And the second issue is a very important one about the budget, the cultural budget really. There are rumours that it will be cut. Is this true?

Vladimir Putin: First of all, I would like to say that although Vladimir and I began our discussion with bananas, he has done a great deal for the theatre. It's true. His contribution can be seen with the naked eye. So I should be the one thanking you.

Now, about the law on theatre workers. Let me be frank. I am not prepared to answer it now. Why? You see, we have been having a lot of discussions about the law on youth, for example. Those who oppose it argue, "why a law on youth, why not a law on middle-aged and older people?" You're talking about theatre workers. And next we will need a law on librarians, and then a law on other cultural workers. Maybe we need that kind of specificity, or perhaps it is enough to have one good, big law. I don't know.

Vladimir Kekhman: Can I propose an initiative?

Vladimir Putin: You are welcome to. I think we have the Culture Minister here. You can speak to him directly.

Vladimir Kekhman: Thank you.

Vladimir Putin: There was a second part to your question.

Vladimir Kekhman: It's about the overall budget for Russian culture. For example, Tatarstan is the leader today. They spend 1% of their budget on culture.

Vladimir Putin: Not only that. They spend it wisely.

Vladimir Kekhman: That is true. Maybe we spend 2%, and we should at least leave it at that level.

Vladimir Putin: You know that our economy has contracted because of the crisis. Even though oil prices are pretty high, $70 on average, and could still go higher, all the same, the overall budget revenue has dropped significantly. Regardless of the price of oil, the economy has contracted a bit. That means we will have to cut certain items, because now we are financing our budget deficit using the savings we accumulated over the past few years. But this deficit cannot last forever. Why? Because if we go down that road, we will quickly find ourselves in the same situation as Greece. And we will not have Germany by our side to open its purse and pay for us.

Our situation is different. We have to be sure that we can, relying on our own resources and through playing a worthy role in the world economy, resolve the numerous challenges that confront us: defence, medicine, education, security, counter-terrorism and so on – and culture.

Unfortunately, there will be a slight cut compared to last year. If my memory serves me right, it will not be less than in 2008, which was a good year, before the crisis. Last year we added a bit extra to respond to the crisis. But we'll see what can be done.

Vladimir Kekhman: Please, if there is any chance at all, we are not talking about an awful lot of money, 75 billion.

Vladimir Putin: I know. When I addressed the Duma...

Liya Akhedzhakova: Seventy-five billion. We can't raise 40,000 for a child, and he says 75 billion is not a lot of money.

Vladimir Kekhman: It's for all culture.

Liya Akhedzhakova: Well, I never.

Oleg Basilashvili: Liya, it's money for the entire national culture. It's the country's entire culture budget.

Vladimir Putin: Leave Liya alone. She's right. It is a lot of money.

Liya Akhedzhakova: This is outrageous.

Diana Arbenina: Excuse me, can I go back to the issue of childhood?

Vladimir Putin: Yes, of course.

Diana Arbenina: I gave birth to twins four months ago and I want to breast-feed them.

Vladimir Putin: Congratulations.

Diana Arbenina: Thank you very much. I am doing just that. But recently I was involved in an incident at Koltsovo airport because they didn't want to let me board the plane with a bottle of breast milk. Like many mothers in our country (and actresses among them), I can't always feed my children in person. And I do what I've got to do every day to make sure that my twins get nothing but their mother's milk.

I would like our laws to have a clear provision concerning this vital liquid. I do not want mothers like me, who are prevented by circumstance from being with their children 24/7, to have to present a paper certifying that milk is vital for babies. This would be like something out of a Bulgakov novel. I would like this to be established by law.

Because each time I go on tour I have to go through this ordeal at the airport. I never know whether they will let me in or not.

Marina Neyelova: You have to do it in front of them.

Diana Arbenina: That won't help. I have two of them.

Marina Neyelova: It's a great idea.

Leonid Yarmolnik: It's wonderful.

Emmanuil Vitorgan: It's like in that joke.

Vladimir Putin: The first thing I can say, Diana Sergeevna, is that we all understand the reason for this.

Diana Arbenina: Yes, terrorism, I know.

Vladimir Putin: The need to fight terrorism. But I admit that there is a lot of formalism.

Diana Arbenina: That's what Yura Shevchuk spoke about. Everything depends on the person. The official. Either he is a good person with a kind heart, not callous, or...

Leonid Yarmolnik: The human factor.

Vladimir Putin: You know that last year – I am not sure of the exact figures, but passengers tried to smuggle tonnes of flammable substances onto planes. Tonnes. Can you imagine?

Diana Arbenina: Can't they check if it is milk or something else?

Vladimir Putin: Well, they can, but you wouldn't let them taste it, would you? I just said there's a lot of formalism. It's true. But how can we keep passengers safe and avoid formalism? It's not an easy question. I'll ask that it be reviewed again.

Diana Arbenina: Good, I hope they'll do something about it before my children grow up.

Leonid Yarmolnik: Marina (Neyelova) and I were wondering – if this were to be allowed, there could be a new type of substance that terrorists can take advantage of. It cuts both ways, you know.

Ilya Lagutenko: But breast feeding is allowed on board. Technically it is allowed.

Diana Arbenina: Not in the past.

Chulpan Khamatova: And what if the child is not with you, if the child is at home?

Leonid Yarmolnik: Vladimir Vladimirovich, you have asked so many questions that I don't feel like speaking any more.

Vladimir Putin: You see, another problem is that they keep inventing new methods.

Liya Akhedzhakova: What is frightening is that a terrorist can bribe his way anywhere.

Oleg Basilashvili: You mean if you are not a terrorist you can't?

Vladimir Putin: For a bribe?

Liya Akhedzhakova: Arbenina cannot get in, but a suicide bomber can.

Vladimir Putin: She can get through. In the end they let you pass, don't they? Liya Medzhidovna, even so, she can get through and she does eventually. She is annoyed because it takes so much time. But she can handle it.

Yuri Shevchuk: I suggest having a drink before we get down to work. Can I propose a toast? To our children... whether they live in a country that is bleak, corrupt, totalitarian, authoritarian, with one party, one anthem, one thought...

Vladimir Putin: A country should have one anthem.

Yuri Shevchuk: ... or a bright, democratic country where all are equal before the law. That is all that is needed. Unfortunately, this is not yet the case. I would like our children to live in this country and to get well. This is my toast.

Leonid Yarmolnik: Wonderful.

Vladimir Putin: The drink suits the toast. (Laughter)

Yuri Shevchuk: By the way, children should stay away from alcohol.

Vladimir Putin: That is true. But with regard to the anthem, Yura, you went a bit too far. The bit about "one anthem" was a Freudian slip, as they say. In the early 2000s, when we looked at the constitutions and the charters of the Russian regions and republics, we found a lot of democracy. They had everything: sovereignty, their own borders and property. The only thing that was lacking was some indication that they were part of the Russian Federation.

So, I completely agree with what has been said. Democracy and law and order always go hand in hand. Rule of law is impossible without democracy, but democracy is impossible without adherence to the law. I think this is obvious.

Yuri Shevchuk: Ours is an ignorant nation. Nobody knows this.

Vladimir Putin: Many know it...

Yuri Shevchuk: We should educate people. That is what we do.

Vladimir Putin: And if we speak about it more often in the presence of such highly respected people as are present here today, there will be more such people and things will be better still.

29 May 2010 Prime Minister Vladimir Putin meets with participants and organisers of the charity show The Little Prince

The report by the Prosecutor General's Office shows ... there are still a lot of instances when officials impose irrelevant requirements on companies seeking to receive a license, such as collecting expert certificates, supporting documentation, and references. Moreover, regulatory and supervisory measures have turned into a profitable business that involves hiring crony firms and organisations. ... And of course, these "compulsory" services are overpriced. ... Blatant misdeeds were revealed, including secret bribery of officials and employees at government agencies. It is not considered disgraceful to receive contributions from the companies that officials are supposed to be overseeing.

15 October 2009 Prime Minister Vladimir Putin chaired a Government meeting

Everywhere in the world there is a triangle: at the bottom are soldiers and junior officers, and higher up the pyramid there are fewer positions, generals, admirals, etc. In this country it is an inverted pyramid. At the lower level, those who fight and make critical decisions on the battlefield, there are not enough people, and the top is overcrowded.

6 April 2009 Prime Minister Vladimir Putin reported to the State Duma on the Russian Government's performance in 2008

On August 31, 2008, Vladimir Putin and Emergencies Minister Sergey Shoigu visited the Ussuri Reserve, which has been carrying out a programme to protect the Amur tiger. ... The group received a message from researchers from a special team working in the forest saying that a five-year-old tigress had been trapped. ... Putin took a shot at the animal with the air gun loaded with syringes containing a tranquilliser. The tigress fell asleep a moment later.

Putin pointed to the tigress' open eyes.

"That's the way it should be," one of the researchers said.

"Does she see anything?" Shoigu asked.

"Yes, she does and she'll remember you," Putin joked.

While the tigress was asleep, the researchers measured her body length, weight, blood pressure and pulse rate, and also took a blood test.

"There isn't any alcohol in her blood?" Vladimir Putin joked again and then asked: "How long will the animal go on like this?"

"It can be prolonged, but normally it lasts 30 or 40 minutes," the researcher said.

"Then she'll start eating us, a snack of sorts," Putin remarked. "As for you, it's okay, you have been in for it. And why us? There are others who can eat us, apart from her!"

Vladimir Putin's Visit to the Ussuri Nature Reserve

Any country, as soon as it makes concessions to terrorists, ultimately suffers greater losses than those that are incurred in the course of special operations. In the long run it destroys the state and increases the number of victims.

31 May 2008 Prime Minister Vladimir Putin gave an interview to the French newspaper Le Monde

And finally, one last comment. Vladimir Volfovich [Zhirinovsky] said that we need to pay attention to the elite and work with them, because from workers and peasants – you said, I wrote it down word for word – you only get insignificant little people. I myself am from a workers family, Vladimir Volfovich. I absolutely do not agree with you. No, no, I wrote it down word for word. We have a talented people. We need to fight poverty and resolve the problem of education. And it is not the people who are to blame that part of the population in our country is being degraded in connection with poverty, in which we have pushed them into over the past 15 years. It is our fault, mine and yours. Fifteen years ago I personally was not at and did not work in such high and mighty government posts. Today we are here, and it is our fault and our responsibility to fight poverty and resolve the problems of health care and education.

Transcript of the Meeting with State Duma Leadership and Faction Leaders March 11, 2008 The Kremlin, Moscow

I do not think that we should heap ashes on our heads and turn to self-flagellation in an attempt to prove to all how good we are.

Transcript of Annual Big Press Conference February 14, 2008 The Kremlin, Moscow

Organising government is one of the most complex issues. Government should be sufficiently strong to be able to guarantee sovereignty, security and defence capability. It should be sufficiently strong to protect the country's territorial integrity, but it should also be sensitive to regional and municipal issues and sensitive to the needs of individuals. Such government cannot be achieved if citizens do not feel any connection with the state and do not think they have any influence on the authorities, and so government must therefore be democratic. The balance between strong and sensitive government is of crucial importance. This is very fine and delicate work and we need to be very much aware of what stage of development society has reached, what is acceptable and what is not possible.

Interview with Time Magazine December 19, 2007 Given December 12, 2007

The government really has made mistakes. You can and should criticize it for that. We see the problems ourselves and we are working to resolve them. But the political speculation on these difficulties has caused at the very least some perplexity. And who is responsible for it? Those who for decades had guided Russia, and at the end of the 1980s left people without the most basic services and goods: no sugar, no meat, no salt, no matches. And of course their policies were responsible for the collapse of the Soviet Union.

There has also been speculation on the part of those who only a decade ago controlled key positions in the Federal Assembly and the government cabinet. These are the people who occupied high positions in the 90s and acted to the detriment of society and the state, served the interests of oligarchic structures and bargained away our national assets. These are the ones who are telling us how to live today, the ones who, by the way, made corruption the principal means of economic and political competition. These are the ones who year after year accepted unbalanced, totally irresponsible budgets, finally resulting in default, collapse and a precipitous fall in living standards for the citizens of our country. ...In short, it is all those who at the end of the last century brought mass poverty and an epidemic of corruption to Russia, something we have been fighting ever since.

And do not labour under any illusions, dear friends! All these people have not left the political scene. ...They want to take revenge, to return to power, to regain their spheres of influence, and to gradually restore an oligarchical regime based on corruption and lies. ...Now they have even taken to the streets. They have learned a little from Western specialists and have trained in neighbouring republics. Now they will organize provocations here. Overall, I think that there can be no doubt: these gentlemen can only do one thing if returned to power, rob millions of people again, fill their pockets, and do so with their characteristic brilliance and cynicism. Of that there can be no doubt.

Today, everyone can see that Russia has accumulated vast resources. Some want to take it all away again, divide it up, and then reduce it to rock bottom. They have done this more than once in the past. Still others want to ransack and steal everything again.

Dear friends! I appeal to you, to all like-minded people, to everyone who wants to make Russia a strong and prosperous country, a country of free and happy people, a country open to an honest dialogue with all peoples of the world. ...Be sure to participate in the elections and vote for United Russia.

Speech to a Gathering of the Supporters of the President of Russia November 21, 2007 Luzhniki Stadium, Moscow

In the medium term future, Russia will need strong presidential power. I cannot imagine another system. I already mentioned that we need to strengthen and develop the multiparty system. What kind of parliamentary republic could we have unless we first have normal political parties? It would be chaos. Even countries with a well developed multiparty system sometimes run into problems. ... Look at what is happening in Belgium where they have not been able to form a government for months now. …

At the beginning of the 1990s, ...We decided to introduce the principles of parliamentary democracy at the city level [in St Petersburg]. After all, we were talking about a city of five million people – the population of a European country like Finland. As I said, almost all power was in the hands of the Legislative Assembly and it was decided that the Legislative Assembly would appoint ministers to the city government. The whole thing turned into an endless nightmare. It would take half a year or more to get ministers appointed and the city's economy was beginning to suffer. Then the deputies themselves began to fear that everything would soon fall apart and people would start taking to the streets, and they decided at that point to elect a mayor – and in terms of his functions, the mayor is, at city level, like the president at national level – and give him the main powers. Without a real multiparty system, each deputy is in reality backed by this or that business organisation or this or that political lobby group. Without internal discipline and an ideology binding people together, this all leads to chaos.

Meeting with Members of the Valdai International Discussion Club September 14, 2007 Sochi

After working in the intelligence services for a few years some people start looking for spies everywhere, even under the bed.

Meeting with Members of the Valdai International Discussion Club September 14, 2007 Sochi

If you think that we should let anyone and everyone break windows in the streets and hold demonstrations in violation of the law, you should allow the same in your own countries. But you do not allow this in your own countries. Look at how firmly the police acts in Paris, Berlin and other European capitals!

Meeting with Members of the Valdai International Discussion Club September 14, 2007 Sochi

When people deliberately provoke the law enforcement agencies and deliberately go to places where they are obviously going to cause disruption to normal city life, the authorities have to respond and enforce order. Thankfully, we have never had to use the extreme methods that are used in some Western European countries.

Interview with Newspaper Journalists from G8 Member Countries June 4, 2007

Recently there have been a lot of cases where corruption has come to light. But I consider that this is good. You know how bad it would be if people in Russia felt that they were surrounded by corruption and not by the prosecution of corruption.

Transcript of Press Conference with the Russian and Foreign Media February 1, 2007 Round Hall, the Kremlin, Moscow

We shall not allow organisations that deal with problems of internal policy to be financed from abroad. That is the issue. And that is the most important problem. We want and will support the development of civil society in every possible way, including non-governmental organisations that work towards helping the environment, the population, the struggle against corruption. We are going to support all this and many other things. But we will not support and we shall not encourage foreign states to send money into Russia in hidden ways, through the special services, and for these organisations to carry out political activity inside the Russian Federation. And I think that such an attitude is absolutely correct, if we want to provide for Russia's sovereignty and that of the Federal Republic of Germany. And I wish you the same.

Interview with ZDF Television Channel (Germany) July 13, 2006

The ability to manipulate public opinion is no less in western countries, the so-called developed democracies, than it is here. And civil society should do everything to resist these tendencies.

Interview with ZDF Television Channel (Germany) July 13, 2006

Without a free press and without civil society we will not be able to fight such problems as corruption, for example. We understand this very well. But if a free press is interpreted as being the chance for the oligarchs you mentioned to buy up all the media outlets and then use them to advance their own corporate and group interests, above all their own financial interests, I do not think that is a free press.

Interview with TF-1 Television Channel (France) July 12, 2006

Some of our partners still have the desire to influence our foreign and domestic policy. They need to put aside these desires so that we can start building a normal and equal partnership. Using the democratisation of Russia as an instrument to pursue one's own foreign policy aims with respect to our country is unacceptable.

Interview with TF-1 Television Channel (France) July 12, 2006

Corruption flourishes in growing economies and countries going through a transition period. It has become a regrettably serious problem in Russia, I think, not only because our economy has undergone such immense change during this transition from a planned system to a market economy, but also because the old system of moral values that prevailed in the Soviet era has collapsed but the state apparatus has not changed much.

Transcript of the Interactive Webcast with the President of Russia July 6, 2006
The Kremlin, Moscow

Russia has no future unless we develop democracy, media freedom and civil society. If we do not do this, Russia will not succeed in resolving problems such as corruption that we have mentioned and will not be able to maintain high economic growth rates because there will not be a sufficient level of economic freedom. We chose this road ourselves, not because we were forced to do so, but because we decided that this is the best way forward for our country's development, and we will remain on this road.

Transcript of the Interactive Webcast with the President of Russia July 6, 2006
The Kremlin, Moscow

Everyone is ready to talk about human rights, but of some other country – about their own country nobody wants to discuss this subject.

Excerpts from Transcript of Meeting with Participants in the International Forum of Non-governmental Organisations Civil G8-2006   July 4, 2006 International Trade Centre, Moscow

Where you have the state you also have corruption, this is always and everywhere the case.

Excerpts from Transcript of Meeting with Participants in the International Forum of Non-governmental Organisations Civil G8-2006   July 4, 2006 International Trade Centre, Moscow

The civil service in any country is, unfortunately, a fairly closed caste that tries to defend its uniform and its caste interests, so to speak, though it should above all be thinking about the interests of the citizens.

Transcript of the Press Conference for the Russian and Foreign Media January 31, 2006 Circular Hall, The Kremlin, Moscow

I worked in intelligence and know how information and information bulletins are made. After all, this is determined to a considerable extent by the political attitudes and bias of those who do it. Screening of information may be done in such a way that your opinion is formed in advance, on the strength of the screening itself.

Interview to CBS anchor Mike Wallace May 9, 2005

Conditions for corruption in the country as a whole arise when business representatives penetrate government bodies to solve their clan or private interests.

Interview to CBS anchor Mike Wallace May 9, 2005

Our bureaucratic apparatus is still largely an exclusive and often arrogant caste that regards state service as an alternative form of business.

Annual Address to the Federal Assembly of the Russian Federation April 25, 2005 The Kremlin, Moscow

Americans are not especially interested in what people abroad think of their domestic affairs. That is quite right and is the way it should be in any country, including in Russia, in my view.

Interview with Egyptian Newspaper Al Ahram April 25, 2005 The Kremlin, Moscow

All countries have problems with democracy, including those who like to talk about it more than anyone else.

Interview with Egyptian Newspaper Al Ahram April 25, 2005 The Kremlin, Moscow

The main characters in a famous Italian film say, "A real man must always try, and a genuine girl must always resist." The same goes for the media and the authorities. The authorities have always tried to ensure their interests, reduce criticism, and so on, while the press and other media have always found out everything they could to draw the attention of the authorities and society to the current authorities' mistakes.

Press Conference with Russian and Foreign Media December 23, 2004 The Kremlin, Moscow

I am simply convinced that from time to time, the personnel of such key structures in the state need to be changed. ...People get used to their high positions, and they become surrounded by hangers-on, minions, cling to old ideas, and begin to value their place too highly, instead of working hard and thinking about the development of the area they work in and the country as a whole.

Meeting with journalists March 27, 2004 Bocharov Ruchei residence, Sochi

If we have to deal with such instances as the recent criminal treatment of conscripts, then we cannot talk about attracting new people into law-enforcement and security structures. I feel that not everyone knows what happened. Conscripts were left on an airfield in the wind and sub-zero temperatures while their plane was being re-fuelled. They are all now in hospital. Incidentally, their recruitment offices had sent them to serve in border-guard units. This case, of course, must be thoroughly investigated and the guilty parties punished.

Speech at an Enlarged Session of the Russian Federal Security Service Board January 15, 2004 Moscow

Of course, a court and a prosecutor's office are not places which give awards, certificates, orders, medals and cash prizes. The prosecutor's position is that cash prizes have already been received, and it is necessary to find out whether they were received legally.

Press Statement and Answers to Questions at a Joint News Conference with Italian Prime Minister Silvio Berlusconi November 5, 2003 Rome

In general, we have introduced many elements of democracy on the basis of what we have witnessed happening in the countries of established democracy, including the so-called dirty pre-election technologies. I do not want this to be taken as any kind of justification on our part. There is nothing good here for us either. In this context I want to cite an old proverb we have in Russia: Do not blame the mirror when your mug is crooked.

Interview to The New York Times October 4, 2003 Novo-Ogaryovo

Chechnya did not become independent. We never recognised the independence de jure, but we practically recognised it de facto: all our armed forces, the prosecutor's office and the police left. The vacuum was instantly filled by destructive elements from radical Islamic organisations, from international Islamic organisations. By the way, this should be borne in mind in the course of settlement in Iraq. Of course we are dealing with an internal political problem and Iraq is an international problem, but we have to be mindful of this and we should on no account create a power vacuum.

Speech and Answers to Questions at Columbia University September 26, 2003 New York

In democratic countries a great deal is subordinated not to solving existing problems in the country and international problems, but instead to tactical problems linked to elections. As one famous figure said, a good politician thinks about elections, but a statesman thinks about future generations.

Interview with American Television Channels   September 20, 2003   Novo-Ogaryovo

The institution of democracy is not developed enough in our country. That is the key element. When our political parties and non-governmental organisations come into their own, the state will naturally withdraw from the sphere of economic regulation wherever its presence is more of a hindrance than help. Unfortunately, you cannot achieve this overnight. But I think we are on the right track.

Extracts from a Transcript of the Meeting with the Finalists of the Student Essay Competition "My Home, My City, My Country"   June 5, 2003   The Kremlin, Moscow

Question: Is there anything the President would very much like to do but can't?

Vladimir Putin: What can't the President do? The President cannot go beyond the Constitution of the Russian Federation. But sometimes the temptation to do so is great.

Extracts from a Transcript of the Meeting with the Finalists of the Student Essay Competition "My Home, My City, My Country"   June 5, 2003   The Kremlin, Moscow

Question: What do you think about allowing the country's President to serve three and more terms in a row?

Vladimir Putin: When a person stays in power too long, even if he is a very good person, his incentives are blunted, he doesn't have "fire in his belly", like at the start of the journey. Secondly, he comes to be surrounded by all sorts of groups, which are known as the camarilla. It is a great hindrance to the leader himself and to the goals for the sake of which he came to power. So I think two terms in office is enough. It is hard to say whether two four-year terms are enough. It is a matter of taste. One can have two five-year terms, but not more. I don't think it is a relevant matter for Russia today because we must respect the country's Constitution. We should not allow it to be changed to suit the tastes of the people who happen to be in power at the moment. One must handle the Constitution carefully. I am categorically against amending it.

Extracts from a Transcript of the Meeting with the Finalists of the Student Essay Competition "My Home, My City, My Country" June 5, 2003 The Kremlin, Moscow

If we have made a promise to the people, then we must deliver on that promise. Otherwise it is better not to make such promises in the first place.

Annual Address to the Federal Assembly of the Russian Federation May 16, 2003 Marble Hall, the Kremlin, Moscow

A truly developed civil society only emerges when the functions of the state machine are radically reduced, and distrust between various social groups is overcome.

Annual Address to the Federal Assembly of the Russian Federation May 16, 2003 Marble Hall, the Kremlin, Moscow

During my work as President I have become convinced that any state is by nature a huge and lazy animal.

Transcript of a Meeting with the French Regional Press and TV Channels February 12, 2003 Bordeaux

Very often people's perception of the whole state greatly depends on how policemen treat citizens.

Excerpts from a Transcript of a TV and Radio Broadcast (Hotline with the President of Russia) December 19, 2002 The Kremlin, Moscow

Question: The Russian Government says that it is fighting terrorism in Chechnya. How are antipersonnel mines and high explosives used? They claim thousands of lives. Don't you think that by trying to eliminate terrorism in Chechnya in this way you are exterminating its population?

Vladimir Putin: ...If you want to become an Islamic radical and are ready to be circumcised, I invite you to Moscow. We are a multi-faith country and we have experts who can do it. And I would advise them to carry out that operation in such a way that nothing would grow in that place again.

Excerpts from the Transcript of a News Conference following Russia-European Union Summit November 11, 2002 Brussels

Want to make a mess of something? Entrust a commission with the matter, set up a working group – and the thing will die there.

Answers to the Questions at a Joint News Conference with Finnish President Tarja Halonen October 5, 2002 St Petersburg

Question: Before flying to Kananaskis you talked to the governors of the southern regions of Russia. How do you evaluate the performance of the federal and local governments in bringing relief to the victims of the natural disaster?

Vladimir Putin: Unfortunately, there are many victims and it was a very large-scale disaster. As always the least well-off people suffer most. ... And I think the local authorities could have acted more efficiently in a preventive way.

Talk with Journalists June 27, 2002 Kananaskis, Canada

Allow me once again to cordially welcome you to Moscow. It is a great honour to host such a large number of major European specialists on financial auditing. I noticed that the name of the

212

German representative is Mr Engels. Thank God, he is not accompanied by Marx.

Speech at the 5th Congress of the European Organisation of Supreme Audit Institutions (EUROSAI) May 27, 2002 Moscow

No problem has ever been solved by imposing bans. ...Any ban in the political sphere leads to radicalisation.

Excerpts from a Talk with German and Russian Media April 7, 2002

Tougher punishment unfortunately, as much as we would like it to be the case, does not in itself decrease crime rates. For internal political consumption, it may be useful to project an image of a strong leader who is prepared to shoot or electrocute people. But even the knowledge I acquired at St Petersburg University entitles me to maintain that in order to effectively fight crime – not by slogans or populist actions but to do it in a serious and responsible way – one has to act on a broad front. It calls for hard work, effort and financial resources. It calls for the strengthening of the law-enforcement bodies, improvement of the country's economy, above all the eradication of poverty, as well as for legal education and the spread of legal culture and simply for a higher overall cultural level and much else.

Although I could probably score some points in purely political terms by announcing a return to the death penalty and close that problem for myself, leaving it to those who succeed me to sort things out. I think it would amount to cheating the population and the nation. I have no right to do that.

Excerpts from a Talk with German and Russian Media April 7, 2002

Question: There is said to be great mistrust in Russia of the law enforcement agencies... Of late several prominent businessmen have been arrested, including Goldovsky, Titov and so on. And there are other people, bureaucrats like Borodin, whom nobody touches. Don't you see some double standards in this approach?

Vladimir Putin: You mentioned mistrust of the law enforcement agencies. I think we should speak not about mistrust of the law enforcement agencies but more broadly a certain mistrust of the state. For decades the state was separated from the population, it existed by itself in the context of a totalitarian system and the population existed by itself. There was no way the people could influence the actions of the state, and a measure of alienation developed.

As for the gentlemen you have mentioned, I very much doubt that it has caused a negative reaction among the people and contributed to their mistrust of the actions of the state or the law enforcement agencies. I think, on the contrary, it tends to improve people's impression of the activities of the state and the law enforcement bodies because people see that at least something is being done. As for Borodin, for example, if the law enforcement agencies have ruled that he has committed no crime, one has to defer to that opinion. As regards Goldovsky, nobody has yet convicted him. A preliminary investigation is underway. As in any other country, a person can be declared guilty only after a court indictment has come into force.

You know, there is a joke, which goes like this: "Doctor, you have pulled out my healthy tooth. "Never mind, we'll get to the sick one in due course." I don't think it would be right if we proceed in this way. So, of course we must improve our law enforcement system. But the worst we could do is to prevent them from doing anything at all.

Interview with the Wall Street Journal February 11, 2002

Question: Were you worried that these politicians could turn against you, considering that they had concentrated great resources in their hands?

Vladimir Putin: Of course, I can't afford not to think about it. But I was not elected by the people who own fortunes, but by the citizens of Russia so that I could restore order in the country. I don't think that oligarchy is the best way for Russia. On the contrary, I think it would be a disaster for our country. And in this connection I would like to repeat: in my opinion, we must improve the court system, we must see to it that there are no miscarriages of justice, that labels are not stuck on people, but we should not create conditions in which a person or group of persons feel absolutely secure no matter what they are doing, even if they are breaking the law.

Interview with the Wall Street Journal February 11, 2002

If civilized countries have de facto, and I stress, de facto, two, three or four functioning parties, why should Russia have 350 or 5000? That is bacchanal and not democracy. The only result is that people are unable to determine their political sympathies. So, people choose not between ideologies, between programmes, but between persons, between personalities.

Excerpts from the Transcript of a Press Conference for Russian and Foreign Journalists July 18, 2001 The Kremlin, Moscow

The extent to which people trust the state depends directly on how well the state protects them from the arbitrary actions of racketeers, bandits and bribe takers.

Annual Address to the Federal Assembly of the Russian Federation April 3, 2001 Moscow, the Kremlin

We will develop political processes in a way that is traditional for Western democracies, and I would like to stress that. But it does not mean that anarchy and permissiveness should hold sway in Russia. Some people inside the country and abroad don't like our attempts to put our house in order in that sense. ... I suspect that there are people who would like to live according to former rules and fish in troubled waters. But that will not happen.

Excerpts of a Transcript from President Putin's Internet Conference March 6, 2001 Moscow

Total calm can be achieved only in a cemetery. And where there are living people, there are clashes of opinions and views, and there is nothing strange about it.

From an Interview with the Canadian CBC and CTV Channels, the Globe and Mail Newspaper and the Russian RTR Television December 14, 2000

On Constitution Day, we are particularly aware of the magnitude of our common responsibility to Russia, especially the responsibility of those who work for the state. Those who must keep the state machinery in working order and prevent it from running down, stalling or idling. And, last but not least, those who guarantee that this sophisticated and costly vehicle does not cut political corners, that political shadow players and gamblers do not take over its controls.

Address at a Gala Reception on Constitution Day December 12, 2000 The Kremlin, Moscow

Russia must not and will not be a police state.

Interview with the Izvestia Newspaper July 14, 2000

Is there a danger that the measures to strengthen the Russian state will bring totalitarian rule back? It is my deep belief that a liberal economy is impossible without democratic government, democratic freedoms or civilian institutions. But do not confuse democracy with anarchy.

An Interview to Public Russian Television, Reuters International News Agency and Japanese NHK Television Company July 11, 2000

The communist idea is no more than a beautiful and to some extent harmful fairy-tale – for society and the state.

From the Transcript of an Interview with the American NBC News Channel
June 2, 2000

In performing my duties as the President of the Russian Federation, I pledge to respect and protect the rights and liberties of every citizen; to observe and protect the Constitution of the Russian Federation; to protect the sovereignty and independence, security and integrity of the state and to serve the people faithfully.

Inauguration Ceremony May 7, 2000 The Great Kremlin Palace, Moscow

Nikolai Svanidze: How would you assess the actions of law-enforcement agencies at present? Do you have any serious complaints about them?

Vladimir Putin: There are always problems. There is a pike in the lake to keep the fish awake.

Interview with the RTR TV Channel January 23, 2000

In fact, the people that scare the public with the allegedly approaching dictatorship are the very same people who tell me, "Order the Duma to vote the way they should. We know how they should vote. Just give the order." Some of them go even further in private conversations. They say, "You were the FSB director only recently. Just show them who is boss, and they will do what they have to." Do you remember the old joke where one person asks, "How is your health?" and the other answers, "Don't waste your time waiting."

Interview with the RTR TV Channel January 23, 2000

We'll chase the terrorists everywhere. In the airport – in the airport. That means, you'll excuse me, we'll catch them in the toilet and waste them in the outhouse in the end. That's it, the issue is resolved once and for all.

Statement to the media September 24, 1999

We must do away with revolutions and act in such a way that there are no paupers in the country. Flourishing states do not have paupers.

Speech to the State Duma August 16, 1999

The moral right to govern will be kept by the one who will change the life of the ordinary person for the better.

Meeting with Journalists August 9, 1999

Chapter 3

SOCIETY

Dmitry Medvedev: For all residents in our country the housing sector is a space for socializing and recreation and, of course, this space must be a cozy, intelligible, comfortable space where people can enjoy talking to each other and relax. Two thirds of our cities' residents and altogether two thirds of our country's residents live in apartment buildings so, in one way or another, they interact every day in these surroundings. I propose discussing this too.

Vladimir Putin: To play dominoes.

Dmitry Medvedev: Including that [laughter]. But even dominoes need to be played in comfortable surroundings.

Meeting with United Russia parliamentary party and experts   September 6, 2016 The Kremlin

[Journalist]: When I flew here on Korean airlines I had a choice of two films to watch: one was Doctor Zhivago, and the other was the Godfather. Which would you recommend to somebody trying to understand Russia?

Vladimir Putin [laughter]: I do not know. You see, we have a famous poem, which goes: "You will not grasp her with your mind or cover with a common label, for Russia is one of a kind – believe in her, if you are able."

But the Russian culture is multifaceted and diverse. That is why if you want to understand, to feel Russia, you should certainly read books – Tolstoy, Chekhov, Gogol, Turgenev – listen to Tchaikovsky's music and watch our classical ballet. But the most important thing that one should do is talk to people. I assure you: as soon as you start to meet average ordinary people you will understand that Russians, whether they are Tatars, Mordovians, Chechens, Daghestanis, are very open-hearted people. They are open and a bit naïve.

But there is one characteristic feature, which many nations must have but it is particularly evident in Russians. It is a pursuit of justice. It seems to me that it is one of the dominant features in the Russian mentality. And another component of the Russian mentality is a pursuit of some [ideals]... Of course, this is a common feature, there are millions of people and all people are different from each other, but on the average we certainly want to be well off and I will strive to do my best for people to live better and to improve their living standards. Notwithstanding all this, there is a pursuit of some high moral ideal, some moral values in Russian people's mentality and heart. This is the thing that for sure – and I am convinced of it – is our positive distinctive feature.

Interview to Bloomberg September 5, 2016 Vladivostok

Attempts are made to weaken us from within, make us more acquiescent and make us toe their line. What is the easiest way of doing this? It is to spread distrust for the ruling authorities and the bodies of power within society and to set people against each other. This was brilliantly used during the tragic years of World War I, when the country was simply brought to the point of disintegration. Today, this is an exercise in futility.

Truth and Justice regional and local media forum April 7, 2016 St Petersburg

You must personally monitor the conditions in prisons and detention centres and make sure that they have modern standards of detention and healthcare. I remember well my visit to Kresty [a pre-trial detention centre in St Petersburg]. True, this was many years ago, but people were getting teeth removed there without receiving any anaesthetic. What kind of situation is this? What century are we living in? I hope that nothing of this sort is going on today.

Expanded Meeting of Prosecutor General Office's Board March 23, 2016 Moscow

Here is what I would like you to focus on: First, ensuring safety in public places. In 2015, the number of crimes committed in the streets grew by 9 percent. You need to regroup, improve the work of the duty details and make broader use of technical equipment. You have to make full use of public assistance as well. We have already created a legislative basis for this and some 200,000 people's guards and Cossacks are helping the police to patrol the streets.

Expanded Meeting of the Interior Ministry Board March 15, 2016 Moscow

(Responding to a question about his personal attitude to the founder of the Soviet state Vladimir Lenin and his removal from the Mausoleum and burial) As for the burial and other such matters, you know, I believe we should be very careful here, so as not to take any steps that would divide our society. We need to unite it. This is what matters.

Meeting of the Russian Popular Front's (ONF) interregional forum January 25, 2016 Stavropol

[Question]: The country is going through very hard times, and you know this better than we do. What is your forecast for the future?

Vladimir Putin: ... Two friends meet and one asks the other: "How are you?" The other says: "My life is all stripes – black stripes followed by white ones." – "So which one is it now?" – "Now I'm in the black one." Another six months pass, they meet again: "How's life? I know it's all stripes, but which one is it now?" – "It's black now." – "But it was black last time!" – "Looks like it was white last time."

Vladimir Putin's annual news conference December 17, 2015 Moscow

Today, nearly half of the criminal cases brought to court concern petty crimes or misdemeanours, but those who committed them, including very young people, go to prison for them. A prison term, even the conviction itself, usually has a highly negative impact on these people's lives, often creating a situation in which they commit new crimes. I ask the State Duma to approve the Supreme Court's proposal that a number of offences in the Criminal Code be decriminalized and that crimes not presenting a big danger to society be reclassified as administrative offences, but with an important reservation: a repeated offence must be classified as a criminal act.

Presidential Address to the Federal Assembly December 3, 2015, The Kremlin, Moscow

We have more than fulfilled our obligations under the Kyoto Protocol: from 1991 to 2012, not only did Russia have no increase in greenhouse gas emissions; it substantially reduced its emissions over this time. This has saved the equivalent of around 40 billion tonnes of carbon dioxide gas from entering the atmosphere. For comparison, let me tell you, colleagues, that total emissions by all countries in 2012 came to 46 billion tonnes. In other words, Russia's efforts have made it possible to slow down global warming by nearly a year. ... Over this same time, Russia's GDP nearly doubled. This shows that it is entirely possible to put the focus on economic growth while at the same time looking after the environment.

Conference of the Parties to the UN Framework Convention on Climate Change November 30, 2015 Paris

We are learning to objectively and carefully treat and respect our history and the centuries-long uninterrupted road our country has travelled. This road was full of great achievements, sharp turns, mistakes, and outstanding victories. We need to know and study this difficult experience with its many aspects and dimensions, take pride in it, learn lessons from it, of course, and feel and understand its spiritual and moral significance. ...

I recall Boris Yeltsin's words, which the whole country knows now: Look after Russia! Those words were addressed to all of us, to present and future generations. Boris Yeltsin wanted our country to become strong, prosperous and happy. We have already done a lot to achieve these aims. We have overcome many difficulties, and we will without question resolve the tasks ahead.

Opening of the Boris Yeltsin Presidential Centre   November 25, 2015 Yekaterinburg

Responsibility must always be personal. And it's absolutely certain that athletes who are far from doping, who have never touched drugs and do not do this, should not have to answer for those who break the rules.

Meeting on preparing Russian athletes for 2016 Olympics in Brazil November 11, 2015 Sochi

The Soviet collapse left 25 million Russians abroad. This just happened overnight and no one ever asked them. I repeat my argument that the Russian people became the world's biggest divided nation, and this was unquestionably a tragedy. That is not to mention the socioeconomic dimension. The Soviet collapse brought down the social system and economy with it. Yes, the old economy was not very effective, but its collapse threw millions of people into poverty, and this was also a tragedy for individual people and families.

Meeting of the Valdai International Discussion Club October 22, 2015 Sochi

It is impossible to solve the health problems of millions of people with the help of pills. People need to put into practice and have a passion for a healthy lifestyle, fitness and sports.

Interview to American TV channel CBS and PBS September 29, 2015 Novo-Ogaryovo, Moscow Region

I have heard people tell sad jokes about how the latest village facility has just closed down and the only medicine available to them now is garlic. In some cases, it's hard to know what even to say in reply. Therefore, we must, of course, pay more attention to healthcare in the countryside.

Russian Popular Front forum For Quality and Affordable Medicine! September 7, 2015 Moscow

As you know, a census was conducted in Crimea last October, and more than 96 percent of the people indicated their ethnic identity. This is objective data, reliable and obtained through professional work. There are people from 175 different ethnic groups living in Crimea today. Russians make up the biggest ethnic group (68 percent), followed by Ukrainians (16 percent), and Crimean Tatars (more than 10 percent). The census also gave us information on people's native languages. Eighty-four percent of Crimean residents said they consider Russian their native language, nearly 8 percent said Crimean Tatar is their native language, 3.7 percent Tatar, and 3.3 percent Ukrainian.

Meeting with representatives of Crimean ethnic groups' public associations August 17, 2015 Yalta

Are we ready and willing to sharply raise the retirement age? I believe not. I'll tell you why. Yes, life expectancy is increasing, but for men it is 65 and a half years, and setting the retirement age for men at 65 means that, pardon me for this straightforward expression: you've done your fair share, here's your wooden overcoat, have a nice ride? That's impossible.

Direct Line with Vladimir Putin April 16, 2015

Colleagues, today I would like to touch on the sensitive topic of freedom of creativity. This is a right guaranteed by our nation's Constitution. And we all know that culture can live and achieve its heights under two key conditions: staying true to historical traditions and, of course, giving broad freedom to creativity, thought, and spiritual development.

Nobody, no government, can dictate to an artist, a writer, a film director, or actually to any person what kind of creative work gifted people should do and in what way. Often, they see something that was once considered unacceptable and today is a standard in their own new way. Anyway, you understand what I'm talking about. And we must treat this particular quality of being ahead of the times carefully and with respect.

Of course, we need to take into account the fact that today, society has set a moral requirement of a sort to all those engaged in cultural activity. It can be explained because often, creative freedom is turned around with pseudo-cultural substitutes, simply in an attempt to earn more. But indeed, there is nothing unusual or new about this.

Joint session of State Council and Council for Culture and Art December 24, 2014 The Kremlin, Moscow

I want to stress that Russia was and will certainly be an integral part of global civilisation. Our multi-ethnic culture has always been characterised by openness and friendliness. It has always responded to global trends in art and enriched itself and largely formed these global trends. We not only value these traditions, but will also do everything possible to develop and enhance them. We need to remember to expand our cultural influence on the world and we should not isolate ourselves.

Joint session of State Council and Council for Culture and Art December 24, 2014 The Kremlin, Moscow

One major issue is to make sure we stop – as soon as possible – resorting to any form of ideologisation regarding our history and culture. Undoubtedly, every stage of our state's development had its positive and dark sides. We have to analyse them impartially, as seen by modern man and use this to make sure nothing holds us back. Naturally, here we have to properly assess and draw the required attention to the activity of our outstanding compatriots of the past.

Joint session of State Council and Council for Culture and Art December 24, 2014 The Kremlin, Moscow

Alexander Solzhenitsyn drew attention to the problems of our society not because he was hostile. On the contrary, he was a patriot, he wanted to keep his country from falling apart, but it did fall apart because back then we did not pay attention to the things he focused on.

Joint session of State Council and Council for Culture and Art December 24, 2014 The Kremlin, Moscow

Something I would like to single out and support here is that we have to pay attention to the Soviet period as well. Everything you said here about the achievements of the Soviet era was absolutely true and we should not use ideological reasons to defile any of the achievements of our country and our people during that very important period of our history.

Joint session of State Council and Council for Culture and Art December 24, 2014 The Kremlin, Moscow

Especially if we understand the times we are living in and what has brought us here, if we talk about increasing patriotism in the country, then as one close acquaintance of mine said yesterday (he is a finance expert and entrepreneur), "The best expression of patriotism is not to steal."

Meeting with Federal Assembly members December 22, 2014 The Kremlin, Moscow

If we want to live longer, if we want our people to be healthy and go to skating rinks instead of liquor shops, then skating rinks must be available. We need to create new football fields, hockey rinks and fitness centres. Importantly, people should spend their money on gym memberships rather than on partying with friends. We need to create a culture where people practise physical fitness and sports. Then the life expectancy in Russia will be more than the current 70–71 years.

News conference of Vladimir Putin December 18, 2014 Moscow

There is elite wine, there are elite resorts. There are no elite people. You know what the Russian elite is? It's a worker. A farmer. Someone who carries our entire country on his shoulders. Has been carrying it for centuries, and will carry it for centuries to come. All other levels, including elites and others, are absolutely groundless. There are rich people and poor people, sick people and healthy people. But they are all equal before the country and before the law.

News conference of Vladimir Putin December 18, 2014 Moscow

I spoke about a healthy traditional family and a healthy nation. This is without question our priority. But there is an implicit hint here, which you noted and highlighted just now, namely, we make families of the traditional kind our priority. But this does not mean that we are going to persecute people of non-traditional orientation. You understand? People have tried to stick this label on us, even people who use criminal law to persecute people of non-traditional orientation. Some US states make it a crime, and though as far as I know these laws are not actually applied and the Supreme Court has suspended them, but they are nevertheless still on the books. We have no criminal penalties.

Meeting with members of the Council for Civil Society and Human Rights and federal and regional human rights commissioners December 5, 2014 The Kremlin, Moscow

On the idea of a broad amnesty to coincide with the 70th anniversary of Victory, I am in favour of an amnesty, but the thing is, for a start, we cannot make these amnesties too frequent otherwise there won't be anyone left in the prisons.

Meeting with members of the Council for Civil Society and Human Rights and federal and regional human rights commissioners   December 5, 2014   The Kremlin, Moscow

Now with regard to restrictive trends in the media. Naturally, I also hear about this, but I do not see us having any real trends. Just look, for example: the western experts themselves are saying that western media create a parallel reality with regard to events in Ukraine. What is that? It is an order from the authorities, and the media are carrying out that political order. I suppose we have something similar in certain areas. Is that good or bad? It's bad. If the press wants people to believe it, it should remain objective, providing information about events and developments comprehensively. They can, of course, comment on them as well, but then it should be made clear that it is an author's personal opinion.

Meeting with members of the Council for Civil Society and Human Rights and federal and regional human rights commissioners   December 5, 2014   The Kremlin, Moscow

Andrei Vandenko [TASS]: One more quote. Nikolai Berdyaev: "A Russian loves Russia, but is not used to feeling himself responsible for Russia."

Vladimir Putin: ... As a rule, an ordinary Russian person had nothing of his own and permanently worked for his master. So, what was left over for him was a blessing, and he knew that they could snatch away everything. It all stems from the times of serfdom.

We cannot say that there was no responsibility for the country. There could have been no proper attitude to current affairs, business and property. It had not been formed like it had in the countries with a developed market system, where a person is aware that he must struggle for his own wealth and for his family's. Our mindset and mentality hinge on community life. This is good and not so good at the same time. It is good because there is a sense of community. It is not so good because there is no individual responsibility. ...

I would say that I personally feel responsible. All depends on the person on the whole... The simpler the person is, the closer he is to his roots, the more responsible he feels for his Motherland. I will also explain why. He has no other Motherland, he is not going to either board a plane, train or mount a horse to leave or buzz off from here. He knows that he will be living here on this land, his children, grandchildren and great-grandchildren will be living here as well. He must take care of them. ... An ordinary person has it more, but in general this is the common mentality of all Russian people. ... Yes, those who have billions feel like global citizens. They feel more free, particularly if their money is in offshore banking accounts. They have gone abroad and stay there, feeling good...

Andrei Vandenko: Is this bad?

Vladimir Putin: I think this is bad. This is certainly bad. A man cutting off his roots eventually regrets it. There is nothing more near-and-dear than your native land, friends, relatives and the culture, in which one was raised.

Andrei Vandenko: The world has no borders now.

Vladimir Putin: It has always been without borders. Was it different in the times of Lermontov or, for example, Pushkin? Just pack your bags and go. People went to spa resorts in Europe or travelled by sea to America. This is what we see again today. On the whole, nothing has changed much. There was a relatively short period of time in history, when the world isolated with borders.

Andrei Vandenko: Are we trying now to set up new 'curtains'?

Vladimir Putin: No, not us – and we will not. We realize the fatality of the 'iron curtain' for us. There were periods in the history of other countries, which tried to isolate themselves from the rest of the world and paid very dearly for that, practically by degradation and collapse. Undoubtedly, we are not taking this path. And nobody is going to build a wall around us. It is impossible!

Interview to TASS News Agency November 24, 2014

We should pay special attention to interethnic and inter-religious relations and fully support the culture, traditions and identity of the peoples living in a given area, town or city. This is a very delicate job, but you know what can happen if it is left undone.

The second area is work with the younger generation. It is among them that the leaders of extremist organisations are trying to find followers and conduct their propaganda, primarily using the internet. Extremist ideology is gaining momentum in the virtual world, spilling out into the real one.

Society is justly concerned about such negative tendencies. Clearly, here prevention also comes to the fore. The strategy for countering extremism contains a whole range of issues directed at organising young people's leisure, at teaching patriotic values and the ability to resist socially dangerous behaviour.

The third important area is the improvement of the migration policy. We still have quite a few problems here that have to do with illegal, uncontrolled migration. We know that this breeds crime, interethnic tensions and extremism. We need greater control over compliance with regulations covering migrants' stay in Russia and we have to take practical measures to promote their social and cultural adaptation and protect their labour and other rights.

Security Council meeting November 20, 2014 The Kremlin, Moscow

We should not ban anything in general except what is purely criminal in nature, and the legislators view these things in just this way – as something criminal. As for things that have a negative impact but are not actually criminal as such, the only way to combat them is to offer a more solidly justified and better explained view in their place.

We noticed that during the civil war period, which was a very difficult time for our entire nation, for better or for worse, the Bolsheviks' slogans and posters were more vivid and concise and no doubt more effective in their impact. Aside from anything else, they also rode the fashion of the moment because no one wanted to keep fighting and so they called for an end to the war. They duped society, of course. You all know the slogan of "Land to the peasants, factories to the workers and peace to the people!" They did not give the people peace because the civil war broke out, and they took the factories and land and nationalised them. So this was complete and total deception.

Meeting with young academics and history teachers   November 5, 2014 Moscow

All these wars, invasions, the wars against the Mongol-Tatars and so on, why did it all happen? Yaroslav the Wise was very wise of course and did a lot to develop the country, but he did not institute a system of succession like the system used in some Western countries. The procedure for succession to the throne in Russia was very complicated and tangled and created fragmentation. …

Yesterday, I was talking to someone, a very well-known individual, highly respected and very educated. But she did not know that National Unity Day honours the liberation of Moscow by militia members who were headed by an ethnic Tatar. This was surprising – how could this be? But it's amazing. He collected money and gave away all his belongings in order to gather a militia, appealed to the prince and essentially put him at the head of the militia. He collected the money, you see, to save Russia.

This says a great deal. It speaks to the internal unity of the multi-ethnic Russian people, which keenly feels the danger of a rift, from the division of the nation, from fragmentation.

Meeting with young academics and history teachers   November 5, 2014 Moscow

This year, we spoke a great deal about World War I and, I feel, we presented information about that war very well and quite objectively. In practice, we revived the names of many of our forgotten heroes and gave new, unbiased assessments to the events that happened then and the result that was so tragic for Russia. Why was it so? Where did this result come from? After all, we were not beaten in battles on the front. We were torn apart from within, that's what happened. Russia declared itself a loser. To whom did it lose? To the nation that ultimately lost the war itself. Overall, it's crazy. I think this is an entirely unique situation in history. Russia lost enormous territories, did not achieve anything aside from colossal losses. We must know this as well, that we suffered enormous losses out of some sort of political considerations. I am not even certain whether we were able to recoup those losses fully.

Yes, we won the Great Patriotic War; we were winners in World War II. This was also likely no accident, because those who took part in World War I – they were essentially the people leading the main operations, supervising the fronts and the general staff. Who were those leaders? Military experts who fought in the First World War. There were some new commanders as well, an entirely new generation so to speak, especially after the 1937 repression. But the military experts who had made it through the furnace of World War I were at the forefront. And this also played a certain role. The cruelty of the leadership likely played a certain role as well.

We could, of course, argue about this and give political assessments. It's just hard to say whether we could have won the war if the leaders had not been so cruel, if they were more like those in Nicholas II's time. It's very hard to say. And what would the consequences have been if we'd lost? The consequences would have been simply catastrophic. They were going to physically exterminate the Slavic people, and not just ethnic Russians, but many other peoples, including the Jews, the Gypsies and the Poles. In other words, if you weigh it, it is hard to say what is worse. We must study it and assess it, but those assessments must be as objective as possible. ...

As for the role of the Soviet Union and our allies in World War II, all this is also highly important. We cannot deny the enormous input of our allies into the victory over Nazi Germany. But we must compare the victims sacrificed at the altar of this common victory, the efforts and significance. And to do this, we simply need to restore some information: how many German divisions were on the Eastern Front, and how many fought on the Western Front? Simply the number of tanks, artillery, planes on the Eastern Front and the Western Front. ... How many victims were there? How many people died in World War II in Great Britain? How many, 350,000? The US lost about half a million, somewhere between 350,000 and half a million, that's it. Yes, that is an enormous number, it is terrible, but you see, it is not the 25 million victims lost by the Soviet Union.

Meeting with young academics and history teachers   November 5, 2014
Moscow

Healthy conservatism is about using the best of all that is new and promising for progressive development.

However, before we tear down the old, the foundations that brought us to where we are today in terms of development, we first need to understand how the new mechanisms will work. This is extremely important. This means that if we want to survive, we need to support the basic pillars upon which we have built our society over the centuries. These basic pillars include looking after mothers and children, preserving and cherishing our own history and achievements, and looking after our traditions and our traditional faiths. Russia has four traditional religions recognised by law and is a very diverse country.

We therefore need to create a solid base out of everything that helps us to shape our identity as the multi-ethnic Russian nation, the multi-ethnic Russian community, while at the same time remaining open to everything new and effective in the world, everything that can contribute to growth.

Meeting of the Valdai International Discussion Club October 24, 2014 Sochi

Mass protests and rallies are an entirely legitimate method for expressing one's opinion and fighting for one's interests, but all of this needs to happen within the framework of the law. Revolutions are bad. We have had more than enough of these revolutions in the 20th century. What we need is evolution. ... Incidentally, with regard to mass demonstrations, let's look at Occupy Wall Street. Where is that movement? It was nipped in the bud. And nobody says that they were treated badly. They were treated well, but they were suppressed. They were embraced so tightly that nobody had time to say a word, and it is unclear where it all dissipated. In this regard, we need to give them credit: they work well.

Meeting of the Valdai International Discussion Club October 24, 2014 Sochi

Countering tobacco use is a very relevant task for our nation. We have done public surveys: around 2010, I believe 40% of our population smoked. We have passed a plan to counter tobacco use and are implementing it. In the past year, the number of people who regularly consume tobacco decreased in our country by 16 or 17%. Overall, we will continue following this path: carefully, so as not to infringe on the rights of individuals to their freedom of choice on what to do and how to live.

Meeting with Director General of the WHO Margaret Chan October 13, 2014 Novo-Ogaryovo, Moscow Region

People are dissatisfied with the condition and functioning of social services. The range of economic and social problems also affects our demographic situation. Incidentally, it results in a curious situation, an unusual one compared to other regions in Russia: we are seeing natural population growth in the Far East, and this is a very good sign. However, because of the migration flow, the number of residents in the region is still declining, which, of course, is alarming. In other words, the demographic indicators for birth rates and mortality are generally improving and birth rates are good; however, there is a continued outflow from the region.

People are going to places where it's easier to find interesting work and decent salaries, get modern education and quality medical care.

Meeting on state support for investment projects and priority development areas in the Far East September 1, 2014

The time is long since ripe in our society for a new and modern policy towards senior citizens. It has to be based on a differentiated approach and on creating conditions for ensuring both active old age and effective support for those who really do need help. ... However, the medical service they receive often leaves something to be desired; much needs to be changed here. It is not okay when elderly people encounter indifference, spend long hours in queues, often simply to get a prescription, and thus lose a whole day. ...

First of all, in any civilised society and state, it is always a direct duty of government institutions and public organisations to take care of the elderly. And second, I want to stress that this concerns not only senior citizens, but the entire nation, people of all ages. Because when people see and know that the government cares about its senior citizens, they treat their country and their government differently; they even plan their lives differently, in the sense that there is a reliable system of state support and care for people. And this always creates internal stability in any nation, in any society. This is no less important for us than any other nation.

State Council Presidium meeting on developing social protection system for senior citizens August 5, 2014 Voronezh

I would like to note that despite certain stereotypes that exist regarding Russia, including on the so-called issues of sexual minorities, to a large extent this is a fictional idea. I would like to remind you that, unlike some other states, Russia does not have criminal prosecution for homosexuality and other types of unconventional sexual behaviour. We do not have criminal sanctions against this, while in other countries, including some very big ones that consider themselves democratic states, such a criminal offence is envisaged by law. Just as the death penalty, which, as opposed to many other countries, Russia does not have and does not apply.

Press statements and answers to journalists' questions following Russian-Austrian talks June 24, 2014 Vienna

Question (via interpreter): There have always been periods of strict order and authoritarian power in Russia. But in the age of the Internet, can a country develop by restricting freedoms?

Vladimir Putin: It is impossible and we are not restricting the Internet. ... You know, whatever we do, someone tries to find something that goes against democratic principles, including the Internet. Are there any restrictions in Russia? I don't believe so. Some of our opponents say there are unacceptable restrictions. What kind of restrictions do we have? For example, we have banned the promotion of suicide, drugs and pedophilia. These are our restrictions. What's wrong with that?

Question (via interpreter): And homosexuality. It is not pedophilia, it's a different story.

Vladimir Putin: That's not true, we did not ban homosexuality. We banned the promotion of homosexuality among minors. You see, these are two different things. In the United States, since we have talked about it, homosexuality is illegal in some states. We impose no criminal liability whatsoever. We banned only promoting homosexuality among minors. It is our right to protect our children and we will do it.

Vladimir Putin's interview with Radio Europe 1 and TF1 TV channel June 4, 2014

Russia is part of the modern world, not the world of the past but the modern world. And I believe it has an even greater future than some other countries that can't take care of their young people, of the new generations, of their children, and believe that they can just let things slide.

Vladimir Putin's interview with Radio Europe 1 and TF1 TV channel June 4, 2014

Everything goes through servers located in the United States, everything is monitored there. You should simply always bear in mind that such is the reality created by the Americans. They are the ones who did it. You know that it all began initially, when the Internet first appeared, as a special CIA project.

Media Forum of Independent Local and Regional Media April 24, 2014 St Petersburg

Our human rights movement has deep roots. It was born during a totalitarian regime, when there was no free press, no option for citizens to express themselves, and no real public life. Having gotten used to opposing the authorities, they do not seem to have another area of activity today. The truth is, the authorities need to be improved too. Indeed, all the discussions we are holding now also speak to this.

In this regard, all of you are human rights activists, too; you are standing up for our citizens' interests. This type of work has great significance in any nation, including ours, if it is aimed at promoting the interests of one's own nation and not promoting the interests of other nations with regard to the Russian Federation.

Again, the shift in political human rights activism has historical roots, and many of these human rights organisations, particularly if they were created during previous decades and have permanent relations, including financial, with sponsors abroad, find it difficult to turn away from the hand that feeds them.

That is why we have passed a law on so-called foreign agents – not spies, of course. ... There is nothing offensive or reprehensible about this. We simply need to know who they are and what the money they get from abroad is being spent on. But we should not paint everyone with the same brush. I repeat, in and of itself, the human rights movement is very much needed. I say this completely sincerely. ...Only one thing is unacceptable: to serve the interests of a foreign state with regard to Russia.

Media Forum of Independent Local and Regional Media April 24, 2014 St Petersburg

The rural areas are home to around 37 million people today. In 2000, if you recall, the figure was 40 million. People continue to leave the countryside. Villages with ten or fewer residents now make up 24 percent of the total. The cities have always been a magnet of course, and we see pretty much the same process happening everywhere else around the world too. But the countryside today is often pushing people into leaving because of no employment prospects, no housing, poor everyday living conditions, and a general sense of having no purpose and place to put oneself to use.

Joint meeting of State Council and Council for Implementation of Priority National Projects and Demographic Policy April 21, 2014 The Kremlin, Moscow

It is not the severity of the punishment but its unavoidability.

Direct Line with Vladimir Putin April 17, 2014 Moscow

We all know in Russia, in St Petersburg and around the entire world how great a tragedy the people of Leningrad lived through over 900 days under siege. We all know about the 125 grams of bread that civilians received as their daily ration, though not everyone got it. We know all this, and we know how many people died. Among Leningrad's civilian population, 360,000 people died over four months alone, at the end of 1941 and the start of 1942, from December through to March. This is almost as many people as Britain lost in the whole of World War II. You see the difference between the number of victims that the Soviet people and other countries sacrificed upon the altar of common victory?

We know all of this, but at the same time, it is our duty to make new facts better known, and to make sure that nothing is ever forgotten. This is most important of all – to let nothing go forgotten, to ensure that people here and abroad remember this tragedy, remember the courage and heroism of the Soviet people and the people of Leningrad, and do everything they can to make sure that nothing like this ever happens again anywhere around the world.

Beginning of meeting with Great Patriotic War veterans who fought in the battle for Leningrad, and people who lived through the Leningrad siege January 27, 2014 Kirovsk, Leningrad Region

History, just like other humanities, should teach students to think independently, to analyse and compare different points of view. However, I would like to repeat that the backbone of the entire history course should be fairness and a lack of bias, respect for our past and love for our homeland.

Meeting with designers of a new concept for a school textbook on Russian history January 16, 2014 The Kremlin, Moscow

Can you tell me what the big difference is between Cromwell and Stalin? There is none. From the point of view of the liberal part of our political establishment, they are both bloody dictators. The former was actually a very cunning man who played a somewhat controversial part in the history of Britain; however, his monument is there, nobody is tearing it down. …Though I have to admit that Cromwell lived quite some time ago, while for us this is still a very sensitive issue. We have to treat every period of our history with care. It is best, of course, not to create any commotion, not to blow people's minds with some untimely actions that could divide society.

News conference of Vladimir Putin December 19, 2013 Moscow

I once said, as you may know, that the collapse of the Soviet Union was a tragedy of the 20th century. Some of my colleagues raised an uproar, accusing me of some sort of hegemonism, of a desire to restore the empire. This is all rubbish! I was referring to the humanitarian side of the issue first and foremost. You are right: people used to live in a single united country, there was no difference between Ukraine, Russia, Belarus or Kazakhstan – all were equal. There was no difference between them. This, in fact, was the huge advantage of living together in such a big single state. It had its benefits; it gave us an edge in competition. However, it so happened that people woke up one day, and the country was gone – and nobody asked them. They suddenly realised they were living abroad. All sorts of things started happening, including ethnic conflicts. People found themselves in a crisis, often without work, without any prospects for the future.

News conference of Vladimir Putin December 19, 2013 Moscow

The most important topic requiring frank discussion in our society today is interethnic relations. This one topic concentrates many of our problems: challenges relating to socio-economic and regional development, corruption, shortcomings in the work of public institutions, and of course failures in educational and cultural policies, which often produce a distorted understanding of the true causes of interethnic tensions.

Such tensions are not provoked by representatives of particular nationalities, but by people devoid of culture and respect for traditions, both their own and those of others. They represent a kind of Amoral International, which comprises rowdy, insolent people from certain southern Russian regions, corrupt law enforcement officials who cover for ethnic mafias, so-called Russian nationalists, and various kinds of separatists who are ready to turn any common tragedy into an excuse for vandalism and bloody rampage.

Together we must rise to the challenge; we must safeguard interethnic peace and thus the unity of our society, the unity and integrity of the Russian state.

Presidential Address to the Federal Assembly   December 12, 2013   The Kremlin, Moscow

Interethnic relations are an extremely sensitive, crucial area of our lives. Over 80% of our population consists of ethnic Russians, and they are certainly the group that drives our nation's development, both culturally and demographically. But Russia's strength lies in the fact that it is a multi-ethnic and multi-faith nation. If we want to preserve this, we must give this matter our utmost attention. And there is just one correct approach: all citizens of the Russian Federation are equal regardless of their faith or ethnicity. This means everyone must respect our laws equally, and everyone must be held equally responsible if they violate those laws, also regardless of national, ethnic or religious affiliation. And nobody should hide behind their exceptionality and demand any sort of special rights for themselves. That is what's most important.

Russian Popular Front conference December 5, 2013 Moscow

An extremely important area, I don't need to talk about it, everyone understands anyway – is how we live and where we live, each of us, imagine – even me. Even where I live the water from the pipes is sometimes rusty – it's funny but true. It's shameful to even talk about it, you understand, although it is a government property. Maybe that's why? I don't know. It's an absolutely exceptional question, because it affects almost every resident in the country.

Russian Popular Front conference December 5, 2013 Moscow

Without the participation of citizens, their direct support, including financial, it is impossible to solve several problems and tasks. For example sports facilities... In several European countries ... citizens make their contribution ... and with their membership booklet...have access to the sports facilities in their city, region, or the building where they live. ... But they know that they have paid, they have the right, and they came with their booklet – the children are allowed onto the playground and they take care that everything is kept neat and tidy.

Russian Popular Front conference December 5, 2013 Moscow

The subject we are dealing with is a very big issue not just for Russia but for practically all developed countries. You know how serious these problems are in Europe, North America and other parts of the world. Some of our colleagues in Europe have spoken of their ethnic policy's failure over the last decade. We cannot allow ourselves to even contemplate such an outcome because Russia is a multi-ethnic country.

Meeting of Council for Interethnic Relations October 22, 2013

I cannot but agree with the colleagues who say that we must improve our labour laws. This is indeed the case. What we are seeing, after all, is more like wild capitalism letting out another belch – forgive the crude metaphor – something not much different from the auctions for shares that were carried out with assets at one time. Using cheap migrant labour is above all an economic problem. But there is certainly a need for firm, consistent and civilised measures to put the situation in order.

Meeting of Council for Interethnic Relations October 22, 2013

Our labour market needs additional workers for jobs that are not being filled by Russians. So we must examine this labour market more carefully and deal more professionally with the question of which jobs are open to migrants and which ones are not.

Moreover, and I have already said this many times, all migrants must clearly understand that if they come to the Russian Federation, they must speak the language and be familiar with the history and culture of the peoples in the region they are coming to, and they must respect our traditions, our laws and our culture. Law enforcement agencies must react accordingly. Here, public monitoring of law enforcement agencies is very important to put an end to any form of corruption.

As for Siberia and the Far East, it is impossible to force either Russian citizens or migrants wishing to live in Russia to go there; or at least, it is impossible to force them to move there. We must create favourable social and economic conditions, and that will be the main factor contributing to the success of those regions' development.

Press statement and answers to journalists' questions following the APEC summit October 8, 2013 Bali, Indonesia

We must create an environment in which it will be the norm, a way of life and a vital demand for the young generation to have an all-round education and be at home with classical and modern art, music and literature. ... As for pre-school establishments, children need to start learning about good taste there too, while they are still at this young and most receptive age. This is the way to educate people who are literate and want quality arts products, and this in turn will lower the number of people who look only to mass culture, often of low quality.

Meeting of the Council for Culture and Art October 2, 2013 The Kremlin, Moscow

[Every country] has to have military, technological and economic strength, but nevertheless the main thing that will determine success is the quality of citizens, the quality of society: their intellectual, spiritual and moral strength. After all, in the end economic growth, prosperity and geopolitical influence are all derived from societal conditions.

Meanwhile, today Russia's national identity is experiencing not only objective pressures stemming from globalisation, but also the consequences of the national catastrophes of the twentieth century, when we experienced the collapse of our state two different times. The result was a devastating blow to our nation's cultural and spiritual codes; we were faced with the disruption of traditions and the consonance of history, with the demoralisation of society, with a deficit of trust and responsibility. These are the root causes of many pressing problems we face.

Meeting of the Valdai International Discussion Club   September 19, 2013
Novgorod Region

Berlusconi is currently on trial for living with women, but nobody would lay a finger on him if he were gay.

Meeting of the Valdai International Discussion Club   September 19, 2013
Novgorod Region

It's not just the question of elites; in society, there are always some kinds of bacillus that destroy this social or public organism. But they become active when the immunity decreases, when problems arise, when the mass of people, millions of people, begin to suffer. These millions already believe that things cannot get any worse, let's change something at any price, we shall destroy everything there, "we shall build our new world, and he who was nothing will become everything." In fact, it did not happen as one wished it to be.

As for the loyalty or disloyalty of the elites, perhaps, it is possible that such a specific problem exists. I think, it was Pushkin – by the way, no one would suspect him to be a state or a tsar's satrap, on the contrary, he was a freedom lover, a friend of the Decembrists, and there is certainly no one who doubts it – but even he once said, "We have a lot of people who oppose not the government, but Russia." Unfortunately, our intelligentsia has such a tradition. But this is due to the fact that people always want to emphasise their civility, their level of education; people always want to be guided by the best examples. Well, maybe it's inevitable at some stage of development, but, beyond any doubt, this loss of the state self-identity both during the Russian Empire's collapse and during the Soviet Union's breakup was disastrous and destructive. We need to understand it in advance and prevent the state from being in the condition it was at the final stage of the First World War or, for example, in the last years of Soviet Union, when even soap was sold by coupons.

Do you remember an anecdote when one family comes to visit another family and they ask their guests:

- Do you take your tea with sugar?

- Yes, with sugar.

- Well, then, you will have to wash your hands without soap.

You may laugh at it but it seems that people were thinking that things could not get any worse. But we all have to understand that once revolutionary changes, not evolutionary, but revolutionary changes begin, things can become worse, much worse. And I believe that the intelligentsia should be the first to understand this. And the intelligentsia, realising it, should prevent any abrupt steps and revolutions of different types and nature. We have just had enough; we have already experienced so much, both in terms of revolutions and wars, that we need decades of calm and smooth development.

Interview to Channel One and Associated Press news agency September 4, 2013 Novo-Ogaryovo, Moscow Region

Yekaterina Rovinskaya: We have a very serious problem. I live two kilometres away from the Moscow Ring Road in barracks built by German prisoners in 1950. Eighty-five percent of the house is decrepit. It is dangerous to even enter it, but we live there because we have nowhere else. ...In 2000 we were promised relocation. ...Please help us. I have documents, and if possible I'll give them to you.

Vladimir Putin: Yes, of course.

I'm afraid to misquote figures but it's true that, unfortunately, we have a great deal of dilapidated housing. Not merely uninhabitable but downright dangerous, and not only in the Moscow Region, but throughout the entire country. Seven years ago we first began allocating federal resources for relocation... But of course there are cases that are completely out of the ordinary. If this is your case, then of course we will do our best to help you...

Seliger 2013 Youth Forum August 2, 2013 Seliger

Mikhail Tantsura: Mr President, ...Let me tell you what foreigners are writing about Russia, since most of the guidebooks about Russia are foreign.

Take TripAdvisor, for example, which comes up first in Google: "If you're hungry and in a hurry, go to McDonalds, you can be sure you won't get food poisoning there." Or take my favourite, Lonely Planet, they come up fourth in Google: "Don't drink in Russia if you're not prepared. After a night in a bar in winter you might stumble into a snowdrift, fall fast asleep and never wake up again."

Vladimir Putin: Well, there's truth in that really. It all depends how much you drink, but such cases do happen. ... Of course it's a good thing to have visitors from abroad, but those who say that we don't have the necessary infrastructure aren't really just making it up, you know.

Seliger 2013 Youth Forum August 2, 2013 Seliger

It is not social policy that leads to the consequences Europe is facing today, but rather living beyond its means, losing control of the general economic situation and structural distortions. Moreover, many European countries are witnessing a rise of a dependency mentality when not working is often much more beneficial than working. This type of mentality endangers not only the economy but also the moral basis of society. It is no secret that many citizens of less developed countries come to Europe intentionally to live off welfare, like they call it in Germany.

Interview to RIA Novosti News Agency June 14, 2013

You're starting to get on my nerves with these same-sex marriages. No matter where you go, I go to Europe and they're out waving banners there, I come here, and you're after me again on the issue. I already stated my opinion on this matter overall. I think that our legislation is very liberal in this respect and there is no discrimination of any sort. People in our country work and pursue their careers regardless of their sexual orientation. We give them state recognition for their achievements in the specific areas in which they work. I think that there are no problems here.

I think indeed that we should all be more tolerant of each other and less aggressive towards each other, no matter whether we're talking about heterosexuals or homosexuals. Less aggression and less song and dance about these issues would be the best thing for everybody. As for a law banning gay couples abroad from adopting children from Russia, I have not seen such a draft law yet. If our country's parliament passes such a law, I will sign it.

News conference following the Russia-EU Summit   June 4, 2013
Yekaterinburg

Good afternoon, friends,

Today, on the eve of International Children's Day, we are presenting the Order of Parental Glory here at the Kremlin in Moscow. ... I congratulate you all and wish you all success with all my heart. ...

We all know how hard it is to be a parent, but the children's smiles and family gatherings around the table more than make up for all the difficulties involved. There is always room for everyone and enough love, warmth and attention to go round. The heroes receiving their decorations today are happy people. Your lives are filled with true purpose, wisdom and generosity.

Many of you have ten or more children, and in the upbringing you provide you show that in today's often contradictory world nothing can replace goodness and warmth, parental love and care, the traditional values that have for centuries created the bonds between state, peoples and values that have always given Russia such a solid foundation.

A ceremony awarding the Order of Parental Glory took place at the Kremlin May 31, 2013 The Kremlin, Moscow

I have always felt outraged when our Western partners, as well as your colleagues from the Western media, referred to our terrorists who committed brutal, bloody, appalling crimes on the territory of our country, as "insurgents". They were hardly ever referred to as terrorists. They provided assistance to them, information support, financial and political support – sometimes directly and sometimes indirectly, but it always accompanied their activities on the territory of the Russian Federation.

One can endlessly speculate on the tragedy of the Chechen people during their deportation from Chechnya by Stalin's regime. But were Chechens the only victims of repression? The first and the biggest victim was the Russian nation, which suffered the most as a result of repression. This is our common history.

Direct Line with Vladimir Putin April 25, 2013 Moscow

Someone is writing poetry, and someone is in Siberia. ... "Someone is in prison, and Vasilyeva is walking around her posh apartment" and so on. You know, just because some are in prison, especially if they were imprisoned wrongfully, does not mean that Ms Vasilyeva and others like her should be imprisoned too. We mustn't look at whether or not she is in prison, but whether other people have been rightly convicted. ...

We do not need to go back to the dark period of 1937. If they are guilty they will be punished. And if some parties are innocent then this will need to be communicated clearly and understandably. We will have to explain this to people and show it. The fact that there are currently many such cases that resonate within society, as they say, is, I think, no bad thing. People must know what's going on. Then perhaps officials at different levels of government will also realise that in the end no one can breach the law with impunity.

Direct Line with Vladimir Putin April 25, 2013 Moscow

I understand people's outrage and their desire to see criminals punished. The question is: what is the most effective measure. Why do you say that such criminals as this will go free eventually? One type of punishment available to us is life imprisonment. I assure you, prisons are no holiday resorts.

Direct Line with Vladimir Putin April 25, 2013 Moscow

Kirill Kleymenov: Mr President, we are literally swamped with questions about rising housing and utilities sector bills. I asked viewers to send in copies of their housing and utilities bills before this broadcast. ... We have this completely absurd case, ...this woman...paid 1,258 rubles before for her one room, but now she got sent a bill for 6,657 rubles. Her neighbour, Vladimir, who lives two rooms down from her, got a bill for 13,551 rubles. There is supposed to be a rule keeping cost increases within a six-percent limit. The system is totally non-transparent.

Vladimir Putin: This is appalling! ...Of course there are a lot of problems in the housing and utilities sector. We know that more than 60 percent of the infrastructure is in unsatisfactory condition and the sector as a whole needs modernisation and investment. But this is no excuse to resort to such barbaric means and place the whole burden on ordinary people. Local authorities did not take timely steps earlier to gradually raise costs and ended up creating a huge gap between needed revenue and the costs people were actually paying, and now they heap all the consequences of this situation overnight on people's shoulders. This is not right and we cannot let this happen.

Direct Line with Vladimir Putin April 25, 2013 Moscow

Question from Izhevsk: Hello, my name is Yevgeny. When the snow melts, our roads melt too. I get the impression the authorities find it more to their advantage to write off funds for road repairs rather than build actual normal roads.

Tatyana Remezova: Mr President, before you answer the question, let me read a few text messages sent in on the same subject:

"The roads in Volgograd [formerly Stalingrad] remind one of footage from wartime newsreels." We've had a huge number of calls from Volgograd about the road problem, actually.

Here's another short message: "I pay my taxes. Where are my roads?"

Vladimir Putin: Yes, roads have long been known as one of Russia's traditional problems. ...We have a vast territory but only a small road network. You know that it was only not so long ago that we built the road connecting Chita and Khabarovsk. We didn't even have a road connecting the eastern and European parts of the country. ...Of course, I cannot go and inspect all the roads in the country. This is something that the Government and the regional authorities need to organise at their level.

Maria Sittel: Unfortunately, it looks like without your personal involvement, Mr President, nothing gets sorted out.

Vladimir Putin: This is an age-old problem in Russia. We just need to organise regular on-going work.

Maria Sittel: Other countries seem quite good at resolving this problem.

Vladimir Putin: Other countries have tackled it in various different ways, including during crisis periods. In Germany in the 1930s, for example, they built roads there as a way of fighting unemployment. They took extraordinary road construction measures. We have also examined various possibilities for using road construction as an anti-crisis measure and a measure to get people in employment and pump up the economy.

Direct Line with Vladimir Putin April 25, 2013 Moscow

History teacher Anton Molev: Mr President, as you probably know, your proposal to introduce a standard history textbook on which you have even issued specific instructions has provoked a heated debate.

Vladimir Putin: ...I think that there should be a unified concept of this textbook, a set of textbooks that would show us the chronology of events and their formal assessment. Without a formal assessment, students will lack a fundamental understanding of the events that took place in our country over the past centuries and decades.

Last year, if I'm not mistaken, we had 41 history textbook versions for Grade 10, and this year, there are 65 recommended history textbook options for Grade 10. Is this normal? I remember, even people of very liberal views, who now seem happy to criticise and even disparage, some of them came to me a few years ago and showed me, look what they're writing, they're completely off their rocker. Sometimes it's not even clear who won World War II...

This does not mean that we should return to totalitarian thinking. If there is a general line, an official point of view, the textbook can present more than one position, and it is the teacher's job (and our teachers are talented people) to draw the students' attention to the fact that there are different assessments of the same events and to teach young people to think and reason for themselves.

Direct Line with Vladimir Putin April 25, 2013 Moscow

Maria Sittel: To what extent would you characterise yourself as the president of this or that generation? Are you the pensioners' and workers president?

Vladimir Putin: When it comes to being the pensioners' and workers president, well, I'm from a working class family myself and I have immense respect for workers. They are the main ones holding up the whole country on their shoulders. As for pensioners, you saw the veterans taking part in the discussion just before, and my parents too, they lived through the siege of Leningrad, my father fought in the Great Patriotic War, was a war invalid, and so I feel in my marrow just what sort of people these are. What's wrong with being their president? I would just like to thank them for all the support they give me.

If we're looking at today's workers though, being a worker today is certainly not just about using your muscles. Workers' jobs today are becoming more and more skilled and demand ever more intellectual input. Some of the public discussions today show that members of the modern working class, the working class' elite, are in every measure equal to other social groups. When you look at it, after all, who are scientists, doctors, teachers – they're all workers, all people just hard at work in their jobs, and I rely on their support too.

Direct Line with Vladimir Putin April 25, 2013 Moscow

Maria Sittel: "Will cannabis be legalised in Russia?"

Vladimir Putin: No, it won't. Industrial hemp, which is a derivative of cannabis, can be used in agriculture and to make fabrics, but I am strictly opposed to legalising the drug. In some countries – my trip to the Netherlands was mentioned earlier – soft drugs have been legalised for a long time, and the point of this was to create a legal alternative to hard drugs. Practice shows that this is not effective: it becomes the first step to hard drugs and severe addiction, and we do not need that.

Direct Line with Vladimir Putin April 25, 2013 Moscow

I believe it is my duty to protect the rights of sexual minorities, but let's face it: gay marriages do not produce children. Both Europe and Russia are facing a demographic crisis. Of course, we can address this problem by increasing the number of immigrants, and that is one way to resolve this problem. But I would like to see an increase in births primarily among the so-called titular nations: Russians, Tatars, Chechens, Bashkirs, Daghestanis, Jews, and so on – that is, among the peoples who consider Russia their homeland.

Press statement and answers to journalists' questions following Russian-Dutch talks April 8, 2013 Amsterdam

Alexei Semenov: We see maths, like the humanities, as a science about people, about the way we think, reason, prove and argue. In this respect, we see a need for a common policy for developing maths education in Russia...

Vladimir Putin: When you started talking about maths, I remembered a well-known joke from back in the Soviet era: the teacher in maths class asks Givi what two plus two makes, and he replies, "Are we buying or selling?"

Conference of the Russian Popular Front March 29, 2013 Rostov-on-Don

Yana Lantratova: Just recently when I was passing by a playground, I overheard a conversation between two schoolchildren. The older child was instructing the younger one, saying: "You know, be patient, I have heard that they will adopt a law so that you can complain about your parents and they will be punished."...

Vladimir Putin: ...Eavesdropping is not good, I learned this during my time working for the KGB, so I don't do that. ...But I ask you to think about how to help us reduce violence against children in the family. Unfortunately, we still have this problem, and these facts are often ignored.

Conference of the Russian Popular Front March 29, 2013 Rostov-on-Don

Often, and sometimes rightly, we criticise everything that happened in Soviet times, but I must say that quality education in the Soviet Union really did contribute to upward social mobility. I know this from my friends, my acquaintances, and my personal experience. It is well-known that I come from a working class family: my father was a blue-collar worker and my mother was simply a general labourer. Family income was extremely modest.

I just recalled my time in the KGB. I was already working in the KGB, but we were still living in a shared apartment without any modern amenities. And if it were not for the opportunities the Soviet regime provided to young people like me – to get a decent education, then go abroad to work, be invited to work at a university as the rector's assistant, and then the Leningrad City Council and so on – I would have never had a chance to do all this. And perhaps today it is quite difficult to do this, and this is our common misfortune. We need to return this quality to our education – make it work as a means of social mobility.

Conference of the Russian Popular Front March 29, 2013 Rostov-on-Don

Vladimir Putin: It is the case that problems related to medical care are among the priorities for Russian citizens. People are watching very closely what is happening in this field. And of course the desire of citizens to improve the quality of services, while preserving what is currently free of charge, is very big and well founded. For that reason we must and will do everything possible to save the free, compulsory aspects of care for citizens of the Russian Federation. According to our Constitution our citizens have this right and it must be ensured. That is the first thing I would like to say.

What percentage of our GDP is currently devoted to medicine? 3.6 percent?

Veronika Skvortsova: 3.7 percent.

Vladimir Putin: 3.7 percent. I would draw your attention to the fact that this is probably not enough, and some countries allocate more funds.

I would also draw your attention to the fact that we spend 2.5 percent on defence. …

I also want to draw your attention to the fact that in 2000 30 percent of our citizens were living below the poverty line, that is one in three Russians lived in poverty. Now the figures are changing: it was 15 percent and then 17 percent. The numbers vary in the light of certain calculations. How many are there now?

Reply: 11.2 percent.

Vladimir Putin: 11.2 percent living below the poverty line and before that it was 30 percent; this still represents significant progress. But 11.2 percent is undoubtedly a lot and for that reason one of our principal objectives and most important tasks remains combating poverty.

Conference of the Russian Popular Front March 29, 2013 Rostov-on-Don

We talk a lot about patriotism today, even argue about it. Argue about its meaning and the aspirations and values it should contain. But there are people whose very lives give us clear answers to these questions. Without question Alexander Pokryshkin, who showed us just how much a person can do for his homeland, was one of these people.

He had just one goal – to liberate his native land. His talent, brilliance and fame inspired fighters the whole length of the front, spurring them on to new deeds. Thirty of the pilots who went through Pokryshkin's school became Heroes of the Soviet Union, and three of them were decorated with the title twice.

His military history counts only victories and not a single defeat. He made more than 600 combat flights. It was there, in the danger-filled wartime skies that he honed his unique science of victory, and back on the ground he analysed these air combats in every detail and came up with new tactics. Great attention went into every last detail of each of his bold manoeuvres.

For young pilots and for his fellow soldiers he was more than a commander – he was a true comrade in arms. Everyone knew that Pokryshkin would never abandon a comrade to his fate. Everyone remembered his words: "My boys mean more to me than shooting down another plane. Together, we'll down even more of them."

The fighter plane division under his command shot down 1,147 enemy planes and wrote itself into the glorious pages of the Great Patriotic War's history.

100th anniversary of the birth of Alexander Pokryshkin   March 6, 2013
Novosibirsk

Any wage is better than welfare benefits. This is extremely important. Our people are really interested not in receiving handouts from the government but in seeing the government help create new jobs and help women to actively participate in the workforce, well, in dignified work activities of course. We talk about this all the time – about creating 25 million new jobs, well paid, high technology jobs, etc. It seems to me that is the main direction. In several other countries, welfare benefits are going up, meanwhile these people don't reenter the workforce. On the contrary, there is a redirection, the creation of a general government welfare, and these people lose any motivation to work.

Meeting of the Council for the Implementation of Priority National Projects and Demographic Policy February 26, 2013 Novo-Ogaryovo, Moscow Region

The situation in the sector is not improving. ... Surveys show that more than a third of our people have problems with cold water supply, 40 percent of apartment blocks have problems with hot water supply, and more than a quarter of households say they have problems with electricity supply. At the same time though, they are seeing their housing and utilities bills going up all the time. ...

We keep talking about improving quality but little actually changes.

Another issue concerns management of apartment buildings. ... There are still problems and loopholes in the law, and they create fertile soil for all kinds of abuses. ... There has been a growing number of so-called 'raider takeovers' of residential buildings, when managing companies battle between themselves for the right to collect people's money. They don't compete to provide quality services, but just to collect people's money.

Meeting on improving the quality of housing and utilities services February 4, 2013 Sochi

[On the migration issue] This is a very important, very sensitive and delicate topic for any nation, because it is a relevant problem for all developed nations that appeal to migrants. Europe has the same problems, as does the US. Incidentally, here in Russia, we have approximately the same number of emigrants from CIS nations, about ten to twelve million, as in Europe and the US – they have about the same number of undocumented emigrants. A nation as ethnically diverse as ours also faces domestic problems, there are specific issues, but they are still less pronounced than abroad. For example, some European nations that are famous for their liberalism have already declared the collapse of their multicultural policy.

It is a highly controversial idea, but it has become quite pointed there. Incidentally, I have long-standing personal relations with many European leaders. Even ten years ago, I was saying, "Listen, if the government does not react to what is happening with immigration, it will lead to an increase in right-wing, far right and quasi-fascist sentiments, because the local citizens will not feel protected against an influx of immigrants, from seeing them take local jobs and push local citizens out of the labour market." ... They don't respect the customs and so forth. There are some very crazy things for Europeans. In Holland a few days ago representatives of one of the parties addressed the local parliament with a call to ban owning dogs in the city centre. ... It seems ridiculous at first glance but it raised a storm of protest among the local citizens because that is part of their culture. ...

Of course nobody is saying we must only toughen the registration [of migrants]. ... After all, why do people come here, for example, from the North Caucasus? Because the unemployment rate there is very high. ... Naturally, we need to primarily focus our attention there on developing the economy, creating new jobs so that the people who are born and grow up in those regions do not feel like they want to move somewhere else; this is an obvious fact. Clearly, we cannot do this in one day. We have a development programme for the south of Russia... This means not only creating production facilities and jobs, but also the social sector, services, medicine and education. ... But that does not mean we shouldn't work with the people who come here, to the European or central part of our nation, to our large cities with over one million residents. They must certainly follow the local rules; that is clear. Just as those who come to other territories must be respectful of the cultures and customs of the local people.

Meeting with regional human rights ombudspersons August 16, 2012 The Kremlin, Moscow

Women will always be mothers, sisters and loved ones. They should always remain women, even if they achieve outstanding results in their respective fields of activity. One such example is the lady sitting across from me. As for men, they are designed by the Lord to be defenders, providers and protectors. We should not cross the line. Let women remain women, and men remain men.

23 September 2011 Prime Minister Vladimir Putin takes part in the United Russia conference session "Civil Society: Partnership and Justice"

Elvira Protsenko: Mr Putin, our problem is as follows: there are five nurseries owned by the Defence Ministry in Vladivostok. ... They are about to literally throw us out of already existing nurseries. ... The only problem is that these nurseries are located on the ground floors of blocks of flats. ...

Vladimir Putin: I think there are two problems. The first has to do with the existing rules – after all, children need to have some space to walk around, and so forth. If a kindergarten is located on the ground floor of a residential building, they wouldn't have this opportunity. This allows the Defence Ministry to say that kindergartens do not meet the standards, even though they have existed there up until now... Secondly, as far as I can tell, these kindergartens are very well equipped. Considering the shortage of preschool institutions, shutting them down seems completely impractical. ... We will guarantee the interests of the defence ministry as well. Nobody there was planning to snatch up these premises. They were most likely thinking about using these premises as housing for officers. ... I think we'll set things right with these small sites.

Elvira Protsenko: Thank you very much. ...

Vladimir Putin: Mr Shuvalov, please look into this issue.

8 September 2011 Prime Minister Vladimir Putin receives people at the public reception room of the United Russia chairman in Vladivostok. The reception was attended by First Deputy Prime Minister Igor Shuvalov

When the USSR broke up, its former external perimeter began to be guarded by the newly independent states. Because of their financial problems, this border is guarded in a satisfactory manner, but not an excellent one. And Russia has never maintained any borders with these republics. As a result, the gate was flung wide open. As you know, Afghanistan accounts for 90% of global heroin production. And so, this heroin has flooded into the Russian territory.

5 September 2011 Prime Minister Vladimir Putin attends a United Russia party interregional conference, Strategy of Social and Economic Development for Russia's Northwestern Regions to 2020. The Programme for 2011-2012, in Cherepovets

Alexei Kharin: Do you think it is possible to consider the possibility of spending maternity capital on buying a car? A car is a real help for running all sorts of errands, especially in rural areas...

Vladimir Putin: The issue concerns securing the interests of children and women. You know, you can spend this money to buy a car or go on a vacation, or do something else. My concern is that this money will be simply squandered. Buying a car is tricky. One day you buy it, the next day you sell or total it, and so much for owning a car.

5 September 2011 Prime Minister Vladimir Putin attends a United Russia party interregional conference, Strategy of Social and Economic Development for Russia's Northwestern Regions to 2020. The Programme for 2011-2012, in Cherepovets

The modernisation of healthcare cannot be postponed. We have discussed certain accomplishments today. But look how short the average life expectancy is, unfortunately. We were saying an upward trend is a good result – indeed we raised it from 65 to 69 in four years. I know that's good; but it's not much. It is still 8–10 years below developed countries. The death toll for vascular diseases is four to five times greater than in Western Europe, and the infant mortality rate is 50–100% higher. Over 30% of Russian hospitals do not have hot water. Thirty percent! Over 8% have no running water at all, and 9% have no sewage system. A quarter of all medical centres require an overhaul, not to mention their obsolete equipment.

20 April 2011 Prime Minister Vladimir Putin delivers a report on the government's performance in 2010 in the State Duma

Question: In general, how do you feel about the fact that people have the right to keep firearms at home?

Vladimir Putin: Negatively, I am categorically against it. Moreover, I think we should tighten the rules for the sale of non-lethal weapons. ... It is allowed in some countries, for example in the United States. We know the tragic incident: a congresswoman was advocating the free possession of guns and herself became a victim. One has to understand that this has a lot to do with tradition, and we do not have such a tradition. I am sure that the free circulation of firearms would cause great harm and pose a great threat for us. ... People have too many weapons as it is.

3 February 2011 Prime Minister Vladimir Putin visits the Channel One headquarters at Ostankino TV centre in Moscow

It is not only fear that drives people, sometimes it is conscience.

29 December 2010 Vladimir Putin wishes government pool journalists a happy new year and answers their questions at the government press centre

You know that this is a European trend: radical elements try to blend in with sports fans and use them as a ram, like the Teutonic knights used the "pig" formation to break enemy ranks. Of course, they are young people, but they are not brainless. I hope they understand that somebody is trying to use them.

29 December 2010 Vladimir Putin wishes government pool journalists a happy new year and answers their questions at the government press centre

Question: Hello, Mr Prime Minister, in November you were on a working visit to our town to estimate the progress made on the modernisation of our healthcare system. Honestly, I think our authorities outdid themselves in putting on a show for your visit. They rushed to prepare the hospitals for your visit. They provided temporary equipment to the hospitals, for example the region's main hospital, only to remove it shortly after your visit. They made nurses tell you that their monthly salaries were 12,000 roubles and that doctors received cheques for 30,000 roubles. But it's all false. Our salaries aren't that high. My salary is 3,650 roubles, lower than the subsistence level. I have to work two and a half shifts, for which I get 14,000 roubles. Senior nurses get a maximum of 5,000 roubles.

What you saw in the wards also has little to do with the real situation. Most of the patients were asked to leave the hospital on the day of your visit, and in some wards the patients were disguised as members of the hospital's staff. As I understand it, you were shown that everything is going as planned and that the money is being used properly. Can you comment on this please? (Applause.)

Vladimir Putin: I can't understand why you are applauding. Because of the cunning of the local authorities or because of the doctor's audacity? Excuse me, you didn't introduce yourself... Well, yes, I was in Ivanovo. Governor Mikhail Men is a very experienced leader, a very good one. I'm surprised to hear what you're saying. I can't see the need for these hasty preparations. We announced our visit beforehand. We didn't really have to go to that particular hospital... Well, as I know, one part of the hospital's building has been renovated, and there is the other part they haven't gotten to yet, but it is on the renovation plan. The governor told me which part was renovated and which would be renovated later.

But if you are saying that some equipment was installed in this renovated part of the building and then it was dismantled and removed, this issue needs to be investigated by the supervising authorities. We will certainly look into this. This also applies to salaries, in particular the salaries of mid-level medical personnel. ... Next week a commission of the Ministry of Healthcare will be sent to the Ivanovo Region.

16 December 2010 Television channels Rossiya and Rossiya 24 and radio stations Mayak and Vesti FM have started broadcasting the annual Q&A session, "A Conversation with Vladimir Putin, Continued"

To make sure people feel at home everywhere in Russia, we must all behave appropriately, so that a person from the Caucasus feels safe walking around Moscow, and Russians of Slavic ethnicity feel safe living in the North Caucasus. People of all ages must have a shared awareness that they have one homeland. One of our main objectives here is to ensure that all people can live and feel safe and comfortable everywhere in the country.

16 December 2010 Television channels Rossiya and Rossiya 24 and radio stations Mayak and Vesti FM have started broadcasting the annual Q&A session, "A Conversation with Vladimir Putin, Continued"

Do you know what the problem is with our educational system? The problem, unfortunately, is that there is a disconnect between how professionals are educated and what the labour market actually needs. Our goal, the government's goal is to first of all combine these two components. And here there are several ways to address this problem. One of them is early internships at companies that are interested in recruiting particular specialists. Such a practice is now becoming more widespread. This is the first line of endeavour.

Second, major companies are themselves organising specific courses and teaching departments, providing them with financial support and recruiting professionals in advance. But it would be inappropriate for the government to force companies to do this. They would still not use this method. We can't force anything. We can't force graduates or companies to do anything.

14 July 2010 Prime Minister Vladimir Putin meets with representatives of student construction brigades in Sochi

I do not want to say that everything is perfect. You know that all over the world, wherever you point a finger, authorities always try to put a better face on things and to curb the media to some extent. But in any country with a well-developed civil society these attempts, as a rule, do not succeed. Where society is immature or weak, authorities find it easier to manipulate it. In this sense, our goal is for our civil society to mature, grow, gain in strength and understand its own strength.

10 June 2010 Prime Minister Vladimir Putin gives an interview to Agence France Presse and France 2 television channel ahead of his working visit to France

This is a special day for our countries and our people. It is dedicated to our shared memory of the past and to Russia's and Poland's common future. For the first time ever, the prime ministers of Russia and Poland have paid their respects to the victims buried at Katyn together. This step was necessary to advance Russian-Polish relations. It was motivated by our shared desire to have a relationship as true partners and neighbours. The truth about the past is important to Poles and Russians alike, however harsh and uncomfortable this truth might be. We will do everything possible to let the public know the truth. ...

I invited Mr Tusk to come here today. I did this deliberately, out of deep respect for the Polish people. I did this to stress once again that we do not have any banned subjects in Russia and that we denounce all the crimes committed by the totalitarian regime. I did this to emphasize that 4,000 Polish officers and 8,000 Soviet citizens killed in the 1930s, as well as many more Soviet soldiers massacred by the Nazis lie in the soil of Katyn. This is a painful part of our common history. But we believe that the truth cleanses. ...

I would like to stress once again that the Russian nation was the first to fall victim to the totalitarian regime. ...

Naturally, one is prompted to ask why some people were exiled to Siberia, and others executed. There is no rational explanation for this. The documents say nothing about this. The motives and goal of this crime remain unclear. We have talked today, and I can say as frankly as I have told the Prime Minister of my own understanding after a meeting with scholars. I'm ashamed to say that I didn't know this before. It turns out that Josef Stalin had personally supervised a military operation in the 1920 Soviet-Polish War. I didn't know anything about this. The Red Army was defeated at the time, and many Soviet soldiers were taken prisoner. The latest records show that 32,000 Red Army soldiers died from famine and diseases in Polish captivity. In my opinion, and I repeat, this is just my opinion, Stalin felt personally responsible for that tragedy. Perhaps, he organised this execution as an act of vengeance. Although this does not justify the crime, it may explain something about its motive.

7 April 2010 Prime Minister Vladimir Putin and Polish Prime Minister Donald Tusk hold a joint news conference

[Question]: "Do you consider Stalin's role on the whole to be positive or negative?"

Vladimir Putin: I don't think it would be right to give a blanket assessment. Obviously, between 1924 and 1953, when Stalin led the country, it changed dramatically: It turned from an agrarian country into an industrialized one. True, there were no peasants left and we all remember well the problems, especially in the final period, with agriculture, the food queues, etc. All that happened in the rural areas had no positive impact. But industrialisation was accomplished.

We won the Great Patriotic War. Whoever and whatever one might say, victory had been won. Even if we go back to the question of casualties, you know, nobody can today throw stones at those who organised and led us to victory because if we had lost that war, the consequences to our country would have been far more catastrophic. They are hard to imagine.

All the undeniable positive things, however, had been accomplished at an unacceptable price. Repressions did take place. It is a fact. Millions of our fellow citizens suffered from them. Such a method of running the state, of achieving results is unacceptable. It is impossible. Undoubtedly, during that period we were confronted not only with a personality cult, but with massive crimes against our own people. That is a fact too. We must not forget about it either. Any historical event should be analysed in its entirety. That is what I would like to say.

3 December 2009 Special TV programme "Conversation with Vladimir Putin: To Be Continued"

Question: What in your opinion impedes Russia's development most of all?

Vladimir Putin: One can philosophise on that score endlessly. ...In the sphere of mentality, of course, it is the socialised consciousness, the expectation that the state should solve all the problems. That of course restricts individual initiative.

3 December 2009 Special TV programme "Conversation with Vladimir Putin: To Be Continued"

I must honestly say that those young people in our country that are involved in these art forms, and I'm not afraid to say this, bring their Russian charm (to them). Because although it may be crude, rap, even urban and street rap, already has social content and addresses the problems of youth. Graffiti is becoming refined and polished, like a real art form. Breakdancing is something completely unique. Breakdancing truly promotes a healthy lifestyle, because it is difficult to imagine how it could be related to drug use. It would be impossible to perform so-called low-risk breakdancing, and still less high-risk breakdancing, especially when you see the acrobatics some of these guys do. This really does command respect.

13 November 2009 Prime Minister Vladimir Putin presented awards to the winners of the "Battle for Respect: Start Today" competition on Muz-TV

Our eco-system is very vulnerable. It is amazing that the Earth still survives today. Our planet evolved through a combination of billions of circumstances and continues to exist thanks to the fact these billions of circumstances somehow interact and work together. Our planet, which is in constant movement through what is essentially the hostile environment of outer space, is faced with the constant threat of destruction. It could be hit by large cosmic bodies. We have a very thin ozone layer and our atmosphere in general is really quite thin. There is a very fine line beyond which damage becomes irreversible, and we might not even notice that we have crossed this line.

Interview with Time Magazine December 19, 2007 Given December 12, 2007

They took the step towards destroying a system that the Russian people could endure no longer. I am not sure I would have been able to take such a step. Gorbachev took the first step and Yeltsin completed what I think was a historic and very important transition for Russia and its people. Both of them, Yeltsin above all, of course, gave Russia freedom, and this is indisputably the historic achievement of the Yeltsin era. ...The tragedy is that people's hopes were disappointed because freedom to do as one pleased was called democracy, and the theft of millions to enrich a few, the plunder of immense resources that belonged to the whole people, was called the market and market relations.

What did the collapse of the Soviet Union mean? Twenty-five million Soviet citizens who were ethnic Russians found themselves outside Russia's border and no one gave them any thought. This is equivalent to the population of a large European country. They found themselves suddenly in the position of being foreigners without ever having been asked about what they themselves wanted.

Interview with Time Magazine December 19, 2007 Given December 12, 2007

First, I think that the death penalty is senseless and counterproductive. History over the centuries, right down to modern civilisation, has proven the senselessness of the death penalty. I will quote an example I have already given in the past. Pickpockets in ancient Rome were sentenced to public execution, and it was precisely during these public executions that the greatest number of pockets were picked because huge crowds gathered to watch the spectacle and the pickpockets had a field day. Tougher penalties, right up to the death penalty, are not in themselves a remedy and are not the most effective instrument in the fight against crime. Lawyers will understand me for they know that the most effective weapon in the fight against crime is the certainty of being punished (this is common knowledge), and not the severity of the punishment.

Second, it is my conviction that by passing the death sentence on its citizens, even if they are criminals, the state instills cruelty in its citizens and breeds ever new examples of citizens showing cruelty towards each other and towards the state itself. This is also harmful and counterproductive. In order to fight crime effectively we need an effective economic policy, an effective social policy, and competent, modern and civilised prisons and law enforcement agencies. It is harder to achieve all of this than to bring back the death penalty, but we should not take the populist road, and to be honest, there is no need today. Russia feels confident today and has entered a period of economic growth and political stability.

Meeting with Members of the Valdai International Discussion Club September 14, 2007 Sochi

In the old days we told this joke: When you ask a General: "Can a General's son become a General?" he says: "Yes, he can." "And can a General's son become a Marshal?" "No, he cannot." "Why not?" "Because Marshals have their own children."

Meeting with Members of the Valdai International Discussion Club September 14, 2007 Sochi

It used to be said that Russia had two big problems – roads and fools. I think that we have two other big problems today – incompetence and corruption. These are two of the biggest problems facing Russia today. Young people can do a great deal in this respect. I say this in all seriousness because young people are not burdened with the negative experience of the past and have more energy and more modern knowledge.

Excerpts from Transcript of Meeting with Members of Russian Youth Organisations July 24, 2007 Zavidovo, Tver Region

We do have bleak chapters in our history; just look at events starting from 1937. And we should not forget these moments of our past. But other countries have also known their bleak and terrible moments. In any event, we have never used nuclear weapons against civilians, and we have never dumped chemicals on thousands of kilometres of land or dropped more bombs on a tiny country than were dropped during the entire Second World War, as was the case in Vietnam. We have not had such bleak pages as was the case of Nazism, for example. All states and peoples have had their ups and downs through history.

Excerpts from Transcript of Meeting with Participants in the National Russian Conference of Humanities and Social Sciences Teachers June 21, 2007 Novo-Ogaryovo

Looking at the problems we have yet to resolve, one of the biggest is the huge income gap between the people at the top and the bottom of the scale. Combating poverty is obviously one of our top priorities in the immediate term and we still have to do a lot to improve our pension system too because the correlation between pensions and the average wage is still lower here than in Europe. The gap between incomes at the top and bottom end of the scale is still high here – a 15.6 to 15.7-fold difference. This is less than in the United States today (they have a figure of 15.9) but more than in the UK or Italy (where they have 13.6–13.8). But this remains a big gap for us and fighting poverty is one of our biggest priorities.

Interview with Newspaper Journalists from G8 Member Countries June 4, 2007

"In the working out of a great national program which seeks the primary good of the greater number, it is true that the toes of some people are being stepped on and are going to be stepped on. But these toes belong to the comparative few who seek to retain or to gain position or riches or both by some short cut which is harmful to the greater good."

These are fine words and it is a pity that it was not I who thought them up. It was Franklin Delano Roosevelt, the President of the United States of America, in 1934. These words were spoken as the country was emerging from the great depression. Many countries have faced similar problems, just as we are today, and many have found worthy ways to overcome them.

Annual Address to the Federal Assembly   May 10, 2006   Marble Hall, the Kremlin, Moscow

And now for the most important matter. What is most important for our country? The Defence Ministry knows what is most important. Indeed, what I want to talk about is love, women, children. I want to talk about the family, about the most acute problem facing our country today – the demographic problem. ... I propose measures to support young families and support women who decide to give birth and raise children. Our aim should be at the least to encourage families to have a second child. ... The state should provide such women with an initial maternity capital that will raise their social status and help to resolve future problems.

Annual Address to the Federal Assembly   May 10, 2006   Marble Hall, the Kremlin, Moscow

As you know, we lived for many decades in the Soviet Union under the slogan that rather than thinking about the present generation, we must think of the future one. In the end, by not thinking of the people living today, we destroyed the country.

Joint Press-Conference with the President of the United States, George W. Bush September 16, 2005   Washington

The law has to be obeyed at all times, and not just when they've grabbed you by your private parts.

Interview with the ANSA Italian News Agency, Corriere della Sera Newspaper and the RAI Television Company November 3, 2003   The Kremlin, Moscow

[On the official visit to the United Kingdom] I won't be divulging any secrets if I tell you that it was the first time in my life that I wore tails, and I can't say that I liked it. ...But there are certain traditions in the United Kingdom and although they are somewhat archaic, there is a certain standard set by the state protocol and many follow it. In general, I think it is good that the traditions have survived. I think many will agree with me that when we lost our own traditions we felt the poorer for that. We are trying hard to restore our Russian traditions.

Statement to the Press and Answers to Journalists' Questions at a Joint Press Conference with Polish President Alexander Kwasniewski   June 28, 2003   Baltiisk

V. K. Dolzhenkova: Mr. President, first of all, I have been asked to pass on the best wishes of the Vedyashkin family. If you recall, you were at their wedding, and you urged them then not to "put things off." They have asked me to tell you that Russia will soon have a new little citizen. But now, getting on to serious matters...

Vladimir Putin: No, what you just said is very serious. What could be more serious, especially given the demographic situation today in Russia? This is a very serious issue throughout the whole of Europe. Please wish them happiness on my behalf.

Press Conference with Russian and Foreign Media   June 20, 2003   The Kremlin, Moscow

Question: When will the Russian provinces cease to be "the backwater"?

Vladimir Putin: You know, Russia has its backwater, America has its backwater and France has its backwater. A province is a province. But in economically developed countries with a developed infrastructure the living standards by and large are comparable to the standards in big cities. This is not the case in our country because under the former administrative command system, with a shortage of resources, priority was given to big cities or communities where state interests were concentrated, mainly defence-related. But in a society with a strong market economy those differences should gradually disappear. Of course it takes time. And nobody can tell you how much time. It will depend on the rate of economic development in Russia. The infrastructure will develop. As for the spiritual legacy, I am sure

271

that the backwater is in many ways superior to the metropolises. There everything is more honest, more open and more transparent, and the relations among people there are often genuine and not ephemeral and prompted by concerns about career and money. If our provinces manage to preserve all that as the infrastructure and living standards improve, I think life there will change for the better. I hope it will happen in the lifetime of your generation.

Extracts from a Transcript of the Meeting with the Finalists of the Student Essay Competition "My Home, My City, My Country" June 5, 2003 The Kremlin, Moscow

People and the human race are developing and are becoming better and better from decade to decade, from century to century and from millennium to millennium. There is more and more information available, the horizons are broader, there are more opportunities and life is becoming more interesting.

Extracts from a Transcript of the Meeting with the Finalists of the Student Essay Competition "My Home, My City, My Country" June 5, 2003 The Kremlin, Moscow

If there is something you don't like you have to correct it. It does not depend on the country, but on us.

Extracts from a Transcript of the Meeting with the Finalists of the Student Essay Competition "My Home, My City, My Country" June 5, 2003 The Kremlin, Moscow

You shouldn't wait for some good guys to do something for you. You have to fight for your rights.

Answers to Questions at a Meeting with the Students at Ufa State Oil Technical University January 4, 2003 Ufa

They say that Moses led his people in the desert for forty years in order to be free from the past and form a new man. For us that is too much and we have to remove all that is negative that was laid in previous years connected with the monopoly of power by one party, with totalitarianism and the lack of freedoms. And in this sense, the education of the independent man is an extremely important task. All this must be coupled with fostering patriotism. The one does not hinder the other, but on the contrary, they must complement each other.

Extracts from the Transcript of a Meeting with the Professors and Teachers at the Ufa State Oil Technical University January 4, 2003 Ufa

I think every person must have a moral and spiritual core. It does not matter what denomination he belongs to. All denominations have been invented by people. And if God exists, he must be in a person's heart. For such a country as Russia, religious philosophy is very, very important because the dominant communist ideology, which effectively replaced Christianity as the state religion, has ceased to exist, and nothing in a person's soul can replace universal human values as effectively as religion. And besides, religion makes a person spiritually richer. I would say no more. I don't want to enlarge upon it because I think it is a very personal matter. I don't think it is a sphere that one should parade, let alone use for political purposes or comment on for the media.

Interview with the Wall Street Journal February 11, 2002

Question: How do you think the fall of the Taliban government will affect women's rights?

President Bush: ...I want Vladimir to discuss that. He knows about women's rights and the importance of them because he's raising two teenage daughters...

Vladimir Putin: I agree with the President that such a problem exists. What we see in Afghanistan is an extreme manifestation of this. Unfortunately, women there overall are not treated as people in the full sense of the word. ...A whole program must be developed to change this, starting with the education of young girls. There are many programs and many people who are devoted to implementing these programs and achieving certain goals. And what we must fear and must not allow as a result of implementing these programs and achieving goals is for a woman to be turned into a man. (Laughter and applause.)

Transcript of the Meeting with Students of Crawford High School November 15, 2001 Crawford, Texas

It never pays to argue with a woman.

Interview with the American Broadcasting Company ABC November 7, 2001

We in Russia have a joke: when men meet at work they discuss women, and when they meet women outside working hours they discuss work.

News Conference Following Russian-British Talks November 21, 2000 The Kremlin, Moscow

All of us – young people and older people – must be efficient. The state as a whole must be more efficient. It depends on how well we adapt to the new living conditions. We should remember what happened to the dinosaurs.

Excerpts from a Transcript of the Meeting with the Professors and Students at Novosibirsk State University November 17, 2000 Novosibirsk

Question: What do you think about the security of graduates in the new millennium, about their employment opportunities? Twenty years ago our parents, for example, had job placement for graduates.

Vladimir Putin: You are asking me whether we will return to a situation when certain things are guaranteed. You have mentioned your parents. They were guaranteed a salary of 120–130 roubles, and sausage cost 2.2 roubles a kilo. There was nothing else in the shops. But there was sausage at 2.2 roubles a kilo. Everybody was promised a state-owned flat, but nobody actually got one. But everybody had that promise. Everybody knew they were entitled to it. It reminds me of an old joke. An old woman comes to a lawyer and asks him: "Sonny, do I have the right?" And he replies: "You do, granny." She says: "I would like to know whether I have the right?" He replies: "You do." She says: "Wait a bit, I want to know whether I can or can't?" He replies: "No, granny, you can't."

Excerpts from a Transcript of the Meeting with the Professors and Students at Novosibirsk State University November 17, 2000 Novosibirsk

A decent person remains decent under the communist system and in a democratic society. And, vice versa, a dishonest person will remain dishonest in any social system.

Interview with the French Newspaper Le Figaro October 26, 2000

There is only one way [to fight religious extremism]: to enhance the prosperity of the Muslim population or Muslim countries generally and to introduce universal human values.

Interview with the French Weekly Paris-Match July 6, 2000

Taking wealth from the rich and giving it to the poor is the most dreadful thing that can be done. We must do the opposite – to strengthen the institution of property and give every owner – small or large – a sense of absolute confidence that he will be able not only to keep his property, but increase it and use it and dispose of it in the Russian Federation.

Interview with the French Weekly Paris-Match July 6, 2000

Society must be mature enough to understand that investing in human resources, in young specialists, is far more effective than dividing and spreading everything evenly.

Excerpts from Transcript of a Meeting with Students at the Irkutsk State University February 18, 2000 Irkutsk

Chapter 4

BUSINESS AND THE ECONOMY

Elvira Nabiullina: Banks collapse for non-economic reasons, but actually because of –

Vladimir Putin: Rogue operations.

Elvira Nabiullina: Yes. Embezzlement. We came across unique cases, for example, when some banks took money from clients and never documented the operation, which means they stole the money the moment they took it from the people. We could not find it, because the transaction was not reflected in the documents. In those cases, only law enforcement agencies can put an end to this and guarantee the inevitability of punishment. The inevitability of punishment is certainly key to preventing similar acts by other bankers. Unfortunately, in many cases bankers flee the country after having transferred the money, which also needs to be brought back to Russia – not just to punish the culprits, but also to return the money. This is hard work.

Vladimir Putin: But to punish them, you also need to repatriate them.

Elvira Nabiullina: Yes.

Vladimir Putin: Or better yet not let them flee in the first place.

Elvira Nabiullina: Maybe we need to adjust the legislation, to consider this: there are laws that prevent debtors who do not pay for utilities or traffic fines from going abroad, so when bankers with such amounts of debts just leave… It is clear that you cannot obtain a court order in two days, but it is necessary to think about a system.

Vladimir Putin: We have to be very careful, of course, so as not to restrict the freedom of travel, but we still need to protect the government and society, and bank depositors, from all criminal acts, that much is clear.

Meeting with head of Central Bank Elvira Nabiullina September 13, 2016
The Kremlin, Moscow

The defence industry requires our particular attention. Your task here is to bring to light 'grey schemes' for siphoning off budget money and cases of buying equipment for modernising defence enterprises at inflated prices, and generally help to ensure stricter budget discipline.

Expanded Meeting of Prosecutor General Office's Board   March 23, 2016
Moscow

Robotics is certainly one of the most promising areas both for our economy and the defence sector. You know that right now, many leading armies of the world are switching to ground and air vehicles that have no live operator, no pilot or tank crewperson. This is a very promising direction. There is even an opinion that (although it would be better if we did not have conflicts at all) future conflicts will end when one team of robots beats the other. So that people do not have to suffer.

Visit to the North Caucasus Federal University January 25, 2016 Stavropol

[Question]: Sanctions are in force, oil prices are falling and there are not only sanctions but also a crisis. Will Russia have enough resources for all this?

Vladimir Putin: … Some of the resources that we earmarked for military training and exercises – we simply retargeted them to the operations of our Aerospace Defence Forces in Syria. Something needs to be thrown in, but this does not have any significant impact on the budget. … It is difficult to think of a better training exercise.

Vladimir Putin's annual news conference December 17, 2015 Moscow

A whole army of inspectors continues to hinder the operation of good businesses. ... During 2014, the investigative authorities opened nearly 200,000 cases on so-called economic crimes. But only 46,000 of 200,000 cases were actually taken to court, and 15,000 cases were thrown out during the hearings. Simple math suggests that only 15 percent of all cases ended with a conviction. At the same time, the vast majority, over 80 percent, or specifically, 83 percent of entrepreneurs who faced criminal charges fully or partially lost their business – they got harassed, intimidated, robbed and then released. This certainly isn't what we need in terms of a business climate. This is actually the opposite, the direct destruction of the business climate. I ask the investigative authorities and the prosecutor's office to pay special attention to this.

Presidential Address to the Federal Assembly December 3, 2015 The Kremlin, Moscow

A unilateral imposition of sanctions is a violation of international law. Well, whatever, let's put aside the legal aspect of the matter. Of course, they do damage, but they are not the main reason for the slowdown in the growth rates of the Russian economy or other problems related to inflation. For us, the main reason is, of course, the decrease in prices in the world markets of our traditional export goods, first, of oil and consequently of gas and some other products. This is the core factor. Sanctions, of course, have a certain impact, but they are not of crucial and fundamental importance to our economy.

Interview to American TV channel CBS and PBS September 29, 2015 Novo-Ogaryovo, Moscow Region

I often hear comments about Russia's turn towards the East. ... Everything is developing faster there than in other places. So should we turn down our chance? The projects we are working on were planned long ago, even before the most recent problems occurred in the global or Russian economy. We are simply implementing our long-time plans. ... We will be able to link together the western and eastern gas pipeline systems and promptly rechannel resources back and forth when needed, depending on the international market. This is very important.

News conference of Vladimir Putin December 18, 2014 Moscow

As for the so-called profiteers, it is not a crime to play on the currency market. These market players can be foreigners or various funds, which are present on the Russian market and have been operating quite actively there. Or they can be Russian companies. Overall, as I said at the beginning of this meeting, this is an accepted practice in a market economy. Profiteers always appear when there is a chance to make some money.

News conference of Vladimir Putin December 18, 2014 Moscow

First of all, I am talking about specific steps to increase the efficiency of state corporations and companies with state participation, where the state owns 50 percent or more of the shares. We have 52 such companies. They hold leading positions in key sectors of the economy: in infrastructure, energy and the military industrial complex; they have close economic and cooperative ties with many companies across the country.

In this regard, I will stress again: state companies should prioritise placing orders with Russian organisations, first and foremost, with small and midsize businesses. It is of course necessary to buy abroad, but we must import only unique equipment and technologies without which we cannot develop, or will develop less effectively, worse than we would like. We are talking first and foremost about technologies and equipment that do not have equivalents in Russia. ...

It is clear that the state's participation in state companies' capital provides significant advantages, such as strong support in carrying out complex projects and the opportunity to strengthen positions in foreign markets. At the same time, the government as the major shareholder certainly has the right to expect corresponding returns.

I want to remind you that we agreed on the general principle as regards payment of dividends to the state: no less than 25% of net profits. However, based on the results of the past two years, this requirement is met by just over half of state-owned companies, and some even managed to get individual government resolutions allowing them not to pay dividends or significantly reduce their size.

It is clear that all of us here are grown-up, experienced people, and it is clear that the arguments are always solid and based on the need for capital investments. Let's agree that if decisions are made, they need to be fulfilled. And if they are not fulfilled, then new decisions are needed, reasonable and systemic, not piecemeal ones, or ones in favour of individual enterprises that ran to some high official.

Meeting on improving the efficiency of state companies December 9, 2014
The Kremlin, Moscow

But some of what we see is cause for question. Prices for petroleum products rose by 10 percent as of December 1, even though global oil prices have dropped by 35 percent. The questions do not end here. The whole situation would not be such cause for question if it were not for the fact that most of the price growth is in the retail segment, while wholesale prices are dropping. What are we to make of this? Where is the Federal Anti-Monopoly Service? I'd like to hear a few words on these issues.

Meeting with Government members December 9, 2014 The Kremlin, Moscow

We face some challenges today. I will not dwell on this now. This affects our cooperation in various areas and directly concerns you too in terms of restrictions now in place on some types of advanced technology transfers to our country. This is not a good thing, but at the same time, we could turn it into an opportunity. It was easier to simply buy something abroad, but now we will have to invest funds and create what we need ourselves. I realise that this is not easy, it's a difficult task, but in the current situation it does offer a clear advantage in that it gives us a powerful impetus for our own scientific and technological development. ...

I want to make clear that when I often talk about import substitution, I always specify that it concerns cases where this substitution is appropriate. Regardless of who might want to create difficulties around us, and how, it is impossible to close off everything in the modern world, especially if the nation in question is open to the world; it is totally impossible. This means we do not need to substitute all imports. Can we grow bananas? Yes. But should we? No, because they would be expensive and we can certainly buy bananas somewhere else.

Meeting of the Presidential Council for Science and Education December 8, 2014 St Petersburg

It is essential to lift restrictions on business as much as possible and free it from intrusive supervision and control... Every inspection should become public. Next year, a special register will be launched, with information on what agency has initiated an inspection, for what purpose, and what results it has produced. This will make it possible to stop unwarranted and, worse still, 'paid to order' visits from oversight agencies. Finally, it's crucial to abandon the basic principle of total, endless control... There are so many inspection agencies that if every one of them comes at least once, then that's it, the company would just fold.

Presidential Address to the Federal Assembly December 4, 2014 The Kremlin, Moscow

I propose a full amnesty for capital returning to Russia. I stress, full amnesty. Of course, it is essential to explain to the people who will make these decisions what full amnesty means. It means that if a person legalises his holdings and property in Russia, he will receive firm legal guarantees that he will not be summoned to various agencies, including law enforcement agencies, that they will not "put the squeeze" on him...

We all understand that the sources of assets are different, that they were earned or acquired in various ways. However, I am confident that we should finally close, turn the "offshore page" in the history of our economy and our country. It is very important and necessary to do this. I expect that after the well-known events in Cyprus and with the on-going sanctions campaign, our business has finally realised that its interests abroad are not reckoned with and that it can even be fleeced like a sheep.

Presidential Address to the Federal Assembly December 4, 2014 The Kremlin, Moscow

Diversion or embezzlement of budget funds allocated for federal defence contracts should be treated as a direct threat to national security and dealt with seriously and severely, as in the suppression of the financing of terrorism. I mention this for a reason... On certain positions, prices double, triple or quadruple, and in one case they grew 11 times.

Presidential Address to the Federal Assembly December 4, 2014 The Kremlin, Moscow

The authorities are putting considerable investment into road construction and repair, but this investment has not always been very efficient in producing returns. Even recently built roads often do not measure up to the required standards, wear out fast, cannot withstand today's traffic burden and so on. We need to take measures to make the estimates and project documentation for road works more accurate and exact. Many of the methods used are clearly outdated and the result is that we still have these 'black holes' into which the allocated funds disappear. We repair the same roads over and over, year after year, instead of gradually expanding the amount of high-quality road construction. ...

Another big problem is the unjustified rise of costs for the so-called inert road construction materials, that is, gravel, sand and so on. It happens that the construction or repair of a piece of road infrastructure has not even been officially announced yet and all the neighbouring land that could be used for quarrying is already bought up and the entrepreneurs then dictate monopolist high prices during the actual construction work. We need to check in each particular case with whom the entrepreneurs behaving in this way are linked with. The Government should pay attention to this problem and develop the needed mechanisms. For your reference, I can tell you that the price of gravel has gone up by 46 percent over the last five years, and the price of sand by 79.7 percent. Do we really have this kind of inflation? ... We cannot help but ask about the role corruption is playing here.

Meeting of the State Council Presidium on improving Russia's road network October 8, 2014 Novosibirsk

I believe we have to thank those of our colleagues who are pursuing certain political goals by introducing the economic limitations we all are aware of, because this makes us work. This is very good. Whatever programmes we put on paper regarding the need to diversify the economy, we do not have enough stimulus to implement them if we are doing fine selling the oil and gas that we have and buying everything we need abroad, and it is rather difficult to create such a stimulus artificially. However, when life sets us certain challenges, we are forced to tackle them one way or another and we do.

Meeting with young nuclear scientists September 19, 2014 Sarov

Russia is a very unique country in some ways. We made our nobles grow long beards, then made them shave them off, then made them grow them long again, then cut them off again. Why do we do this? It's the same with the economy.

If you look around, when individual countries' economies or the global economy goes into crisis, the level of state regulation increases and people say that this is necessary, and that the state needs to take this or take that. As soon as the economy recovers from the crisis, people say that state regulation is just a set of shackles, puts chains on the economy and stops it from moving ahead. They say the market is self-regulating. And so then you got this liberal movement that did indeed help to speed up development, but crisis phenomena build up even faster and are inevitable, and so some amount of state regulation is then needed again.

It is the same too in the way society and the state are organised. We cannot rely only on our past experience of course. We do need to keep hold of our traditional values, but they must not prevent us from moving forward. We need to look at the situation in society, the circumstances of the moment.

During the Soviet years for example, for all the criticism of that period there was a time when the economy did grow very fast and the country strengthened rapidly. Whatever people might say about the number of victims in World War II and the Great Patriotic War, we did win in the end. We can criticise the commanders and Stalin all we like, but can anyone say with certainty that a different approach would have enabled us to win? No one denies that Stalin was a tyrant and that we had the labour camps and the personality cult, but we need to be able to look at issues from every angle.

Seliger 2014 National Youth Forum August 29, 2014 Seliger, Tver Region

We are about to take another major step in the development of promising oil and gas fields in the Arctic. ... All this great work was made possible by uniting the efforts of Rosneft and our US partner, ExxonMobil. ... In spite of the difficult current political situation, pragmatism and common sense still have the upper hand, and that is very gratifying.

Video linkup with West Alpha drilling rig in Kara Sea August 9, 2014 Sochi

D. Grishin [CEO Mail.ru]: ...There is, you can say, a preconception, that any contact with the authorities, in general, will not lead to anything good.

V. Putin: That's right. (Laughter)

D. Grishin: In principle, if you can hide and suppose they won't notice, it's better to hide.

V. Putin: That's not right. ... First of all, it makes no difference, there is nowhere you can hide from us. (Laughter.) Secondly, it's simply unworthy for representatives of such a promising business as yours to hide from somebody. Why do so? You have to crawl out from under the driftwood and associate with people. However unpleasant it is, you have to get together with society and the government and search for common solutions.

Internet Entrepreneurship in Russia Forum June 10, 2014 Moscow

The problem of offshoring does not just apply to Russia; it is an epidemic in the global economy today. ... A product is created in one country while the profits are generated in a totally different place, and that country never sees them. This, of course, should be changed. ... And naturally, we must do more than scare our companies, dragging them away from the offshores through some sort of administrative measures; we must first and foremost develop – and this is most important – economic and legal measures to protect the interests of the owner, the investor, and all participants in this process.

Internet Entrepreneurship in Russia Forum June 10, 2014 Moscow

We have a very important and sensitive topic to discuss today, which is well known and, I would even say, painful: single-industry towns. ...Overall, we have more than 300 such towns in Russia, which are home to over 15 million people. We fully understand that it would be very dangerous to maintain this situation, where the wellbeing of many individuals essentially depends on one or two local companies.

As you know, the government has supported single-industry towns that found themselves in difficult circumstances, and provided funding for the development of infrastructure and the creation of new factories for supporting employment, including at small and midsize businesses, within the framework of anti-crisis measures. At the same time, it would be wrong to rely only on federal support to resolve the problems of single-industry towns. We need to get regional leaders personally involved in this process, as well as the heads of municipal organisations and, of course, the owners of the local companies and potential investors. ...I want to once again remind employers about their social responsibility. When restructuring production in single-industry towns, they must always think about the people, taking into account whether the city or district has alternative jobs.

Meeting on stable development of single-industry towns   April 28, 2014 Petrozavodsk

We will review the results of our military technology cooperation in 2013 today. As the results confirm once again, Russia is a global leader in this market and is solidly in second place in arms supply volumes. I remind you that the USA holds 29 percent of the market, Russia 27 percent, Germany 7 percent, China 6 percent, and France 5 percent. ... Russia supplies goods to 65 countries and has signed and is implementing military technology cooperation agreements with 89 countries.

Meeting of the Commission for Military Technology Cooperation with Foreign States April 25, 2014 The Kremlin, Moscow

Back in the day, in Soviet times, when people wanted to buy the works of Valentin Pikul they were obliged to buy the complete works of Leonid Brezhnev too. The desire of insurance companies to try to sell a little more is natural ... but as far as forcing services onto people, we must of course fight this.

Media Forum of Independent Local and Regional Media April 24, 2014 St Petersburg

The Government has issued a resolution whereby salaries of executives in publicly funded institutions should be no more than eight times higher than the average salary in that particular institution. This difference is high enough to provide a decent salary to senior executives and recognise their managerial abilities and qualifications. Anything above that is unacceptable. I do not rule out the possibility of violations in this area. We will get back to this and take a look at this issue at the local level.

Direct Line with Vladimir Putin April 17, 2014 Moscow

Our goal is not merely to limit the possibilities of using offshore schemes. We know that we will not get anywhere by simply banning things. Our efforts are mainly directed at making the Russian jurisdiction more attractive, at improving the business climate, strengthening legal guarantees of property protection, and improving the judiciary, including courts of arbitration. We will work on all these issues consistently and I expect to be working in close contact with you as well.

Naturally, once national companies start paying taxes in Russia, once they stop evading any responsibility for this country, this will lead to the growth of overall trust in business in general (I am sure you understand this too), trust in private property and to the values of economic and business freedom. This is key to the progressive development of our nation.

Congress of the Russian Union of Industrialists and Entrepreneurs March 20, 2014 Moscow

The modernisation of the housing and utilities sector requires huge resources, as we all know. We have to apply break-through technologies and new materials to make the infrastructure reliable, safe and lasting. We need to have more sources of funding, primarily by stimulating private investment and making greater use of public-private partnerships.

Something I would like to focus on in this connection is that honest companies should benefit from participation in the housing and utilities sector. Therefore the implementation of such projects requires long-term guarantees, taking into account their long payback period. This has to do primarily with tariffs. This is the basis, as we see it, of economics in this type of business.

At the same time, the work must be done on schedule and with high quality, and any attempts to channel the money in some other direction should be nipped in the bud. I would like to hear your specific proposals, including those on ways of controlling this sphere of activity.

I also believe that only companies with a transparent ownership structure and with relevant market experience should be able to take part in such modernisation projects. We have already mentioned that even in this sector some management and other companies are registered in offshore zones, which is absurd.

Economic Council Presidium meeting   January 30, 2014   Novo-Ogaryovo, Moscow Region

We are more than double behind the developed economies in labour productivity. This gap between consumption levels and productivity is unquestionably dangerous. Living off natural resources at our future generations' expense, spending a fortune we did not earn and dividing up this unearned fortune cannot be sustainable long term.

Russia Calling! Investment Forum October 2, 2013 Moscow

It is no secret that considerable amounts of speculative and sometimes blatantly criminal capital are accumulated in offshore zones. And the countries and territories where it is registered often have very little understanding of the money's owners or its origin.

The sudden emergence and uncontrolled movement of these funds has an extremely negative effect on the global financial system.

The outflow of capital to offshore zones reduces the tax base, decreases tax revenues and threatens national fiscal sovereignty. Against such a background, it is difficult to talk about building a fair taxation system. We have all seen not so long ago the head of Apple answer awkward questions from senators about the fact that his company keeps tens of billions of dollars earned in the United States outside the American tax boundaries.

Interview to RIA Novosti News Agency June 14, 2013

We cannot solve the pension system's problems by increasing the tax burden on business, and by suppressing entrepreneurial activity and economic growth. We must create tax conditions so as to ensure that investing money in Russia is more advantageous than hiding it on some island or spending it on luxury items. Letting the growth of social spending outstrip the growth of the economy will lead us to a dead end.

2014–2016 Budget Policy Address June 13, 2013 The Kremlin, Moscow

You know, concerning that difficult question, which you mentioned second: either agree with our partners so that they open up their markets to us and not use various procedures within the framework of the WTO to close their markets to us, or introduce such rules as theirs. I think that the second path is more realistic because we know them very well, they are very intelligent people, attractive, well-educated and know how to speak well and correctly lay out their position, and that always sounds very convincing, liberal, and market-oriented. But to agree with them so that they concede even one millimeter is impossible unless in response we have to concede at minimum half a meter of our interests.

But agree we nevertheless have to and we will try to do it, and will strive for this, drawing on our patience and conducting negotiations on each issue. At the same time, in the framework of the current rules, without violating the WTO rules, we need to use everything that our friends, partners, and competitors use, in the framework of the World Trade Organization.

Meeting with Russian entrepreneurs May 23, 2013 Voronezh

Alexander Prokhanov: An unfair system and inequality – financial, social, status inequality – are dividing society and driving people apart. Is it not time to introduce a luxury tax? This could be the first step in eliminating the terrible and divisive unfairness in society. We must tax these palaces of gold and the diamonds in which oligarchs' wives and lovers drape themselves from head to foot...

Vladimir Putin: How do you tell the oligarchs' wives from their lovers, by their fragrance?

Reply: By their age.

Vladimir Putin: Oh, by their age. ...I am in favour of a luxury tax. The issue of social justice and the huge income gap is a very serious one, not just for Russia. In some countries with developed economies, the USA too, this is becoming an ever more serious issue. Europe in this respect deserves credit for having made more effort to give a social dimension to its economy, and so the divides are not as great there. I think therefore that we would do well to study Europe's best practice and traditions in this area and see what we can try out here at home.

Direct Line with Vladimir Putin April 25, 2013 Moscow

Maria Sittel: When will everything be all right?

Vladimir Putin: People who are fond of drink say that you can't drink all the vodka but that is the goal you must aspire to. Everything will probably never be all right. But we will aspire to it.

Direct Line with Vladimir Putin April 25, 2013 Moscow

As for Mr Khodorkovsky, there is no personal prosecution in this case. I remember very well how it developed. There still are attempts to present it as a political case. Was Mr Khodorkovsky engaged in politics? Was he a State Duma deputy? Was he a leader of a political party? No, he wasn't any of those things. It's a purely economic offence and the court made a ruling.

News conference of Vladimir Putin December 20, 2012 Moscow

It is difficult to demand public respect for property acquired in corrupt deals.

G20 Summit June 20, 2012 Los Cabos

The fact of the matter is that we did not produce anything that people actually demanded... No one bought the galoshes we produced except in Africa, to wear them in the hot sand.

State Duma plenary session May 8, 2012 Moscow

However, as we all know we still have a big material gap. The incomes of the wealthiest people – and I'd like to speak about this issue because this is really a problem for us – are about 16 times higher than those of the poorest. Regrettably, this gap has remained practically unchanged in the last few years. We must pay very close attention to this problem. It is fraught with enormous social, political and economic risks. I'll quote some figures to show how we compare with other countries in this respect. In Germany, Austria and France the gap between the richest and the poorest is 5–7 times and the majority of experts consider it the best ratio. In the United States the gap is 15 times, almost the same as we have, while Brazil, a BRICS country, has a much bigger gap – 39 times.

11 April 2012   Prime Minister Vladimir Putin delivers his report on the government's performance in 2011 to the State Duma

Embarking down the path of providing loans at rates that are economically ungrounded is very dangerous. ... This is akin to printing money, quite simply. After this, it is only a matter of time until a crisis. It would be unavoidable. The same thing happened with mortgage loans in the United States, when banks did not even check the solvency of borrowers and simply handed out huge amounts of money for mortgages.

5 September 2011 Prime Minister Vladimir Putin attends a United Russia party interregional conference, Strategy of Social and Economic Development for Russia's Northwestern Regions to 2020. The Programme for 2011-2012, in Cherepovets

Sergey Ponkratov: We make quality food. Take poultry. Isn't our chicken meat incomparably better than American deep-frozen "Bush legs"?

Vladimir Putin: The West overuses antibiotics. That's a constant problem. Now, contaminated vegetables have appeared out of the blue. Where did it come from? Nobody knows. I think it's due to overuse of herbicides, which leads to mutant viruses and bacteria.

Sergey Ponkratov: They are using genetic engineering. They manufacture genetically modified products with crazy changes. God knows what these foods can lead to. We should treat nature with more respect.

Vladimir Putin: That's right. It takes nature millennia to make a change man accomplishes within a season.

23 June 2011   While on a working trip to the Rostov Region, Prime Minister Vladimir Putin visits an agricultural cooperative and talks to its workers

Oleg Shein (A Just Russia): Mr Putin, the Audit Chamber has uncovered the unlawful diversion of billions of roubles allocated to the Federal Agency for Fishery for the construction of special vessels. It concluded contracts with companies that lacked any production capacity, labour resources, or work experience. As a result, no vessels have been built, and the money has been rotating through banks. ...

Vladimir Putin: As for responsibility, don't worry. After completing any undertaking, those who have stood aside and done nothing are usually rewarded here, while those who are innocent are punished. As for the Federal Agency for Fishery and the contracts for the construction of vessels, we must look into this matter attentively. It goes without saying that if there are elements of manipulation, those responsible will be identified and taken to task.

20 April 2011   Prime Minister Vladimir Putin delivers a report on the government's performance in 2010 in the State Duma

If they are proven guilty, then they must be punished. Such people should be given guilty verdicts when there is embezzlement and other crimes. But no one should be the victim of unfounded accusations. We should not forget about the presumption of innocence. Or are we to treat all people in this country as thieves?

29 December 2010 Vladimir Putin wishes government pool journalists a happy new year and answers their questions at the government press centre

Question: Mr Putin, you have always supported business, and during the recent economic crisis you helped businesses get loans. However, you emphasised that this money is not a gift. Do they repay the money?

Vladimir Putin: This is a really important issue. We spent a lot of money to support the real economy in various ways. As for Norilsk Nickel and some other similar enterprises, we passed a special law and spent over 11 billion dollars from our foreign exchange reserves via our state bank, Vnesheconombank, to restructure the debt our large companies owed to foreign lenders.

We tried and did avoid a situation in which, as a result of a margin call (I won't go into details now and explain what it is), they found themselves in a difficult situation in their relations with foreign banks, further aggravated by a decline in capitalisation. As these are strategic assets, we did not want this to happen, and so we gave them money to pay their loans to foreign banks and allowed them to refinance their loans in state domestic banks. We spent 11.5 billion dollars on it, through Vnesheconombank. I would like to stress this. All this money was paid back to Vnesheconombank and returned to the Central Bank of Russia and the country's foreign exchange reserves – all the money. This is the first way we supported businesses.

By the way, Vnesheconombank not only returned the money to the Central Bank of Russia, but also earned 400 million dollars from these transactions, from payments from these companies.

The second way we supported the real economy was by spending 175 billion roubles from the National Wealth Fund through Vnesheconombank to support the stock market for Russian companies, whose shares started losing value during the crisis. This could have negatively affected the economy of the entire country.

Vnesheconombank got this money and propped up the value of the shares of Russian companies listed on the stock exchange. It started buying shares and stabilised the situation. This was followed by a short period of stabilisation, after which the value of shares started rising. In order to avoid the destabilisation and collapse of the market, Vnesheconombank started selling these shares on the market (which is not a secret by now). Vnesheconombank earned 100 billion roubles from these operations. This money was distributed in the following way: 50 billion roubles were spent on large state projects, including Olympic construction in Sochi, and another 50 billion roubles were spent to lower mortgage rates.

16 December 2010 Television channels Rossiya and Rossiya 24 and radio stations Mayak and Vesti FM have started broadcasting the annual Q&A session, "A Conversation with Vladimir Putin, Continued"

I am quite critical of the leaders of big business. I am not even talking about what was happening in the 1990s. Even so, the way many big business people behaved at the height of the crisis in 2009 pleased me and even came as a bit of a surprise. It was strange and unexpected for me, but they displayed a sense of responsibility and showed no signs of being greedy or stingy during the crisis period. They were prepared to sacrifice their capital and give freely of their time and actually put their own destinies on the line. Because when someone was on the brink of ruin, and was not afraid of it, but did as we had agreed – developing production, supporting the workforce – and mortgaged almost all their property and put themselves entirely at the mercy of the state in that sense, I was very surprised that many were ready to give everything they had to the state.

On the one hand, and I can understand it, they did not know what the outcome of all this would be and felt it would be better to cash in, as they say in some business circles, getting money from the state and absolving themselves of responsibility. But many behaved as I have just told you, and I found it very heartening. When the crisis began to recede, the fight for control of the companies began among them. In my opinion, it has more to do with ambitions. Not money, but a clash of ambitions. I don't think that is good. It certainly damages the economy and production.

27 August 2010 Vladimir Putin answers questions from Russian journalists while driving a Lada Kalina car down the new Amur motorway

Ernest Mackevicius: When will Khodorkovsky be released?

Vladimir Putin: This notorious personage is in prison because of a court decision. It is not important when he will be released, it is important to avoid repeating such crimes in this country. This is a matter of economic crimes. By the way, the Yukos bankruptcy proceedings were initiated by Western creditors and banks. And all these proceedings were carried out in accordance with Russian law. ...

The money that was once stolen from the people must be returned to them. And not to a vague group, but to the actual people who have found themselves in trouble as a result of the difficult, I'd even say tragic, economic developments of the early and mid-1990s. These funds should help the least well-off citizens of the Russian Federation. And so the 240 billion roubles earned from auctioning Yukos assets were used to create the Housing and Utilities Reform Fund. Ten million people have taken advantage of the fund to repair their houses and flats, and 150,000 people will be relocated from slums into new blocks of flats. The fund will continue to work. Its reserves were also spent on landscaping in Russian towns and villages.

As for the other side, the criminal one, we will also operate within the framework of Russian law. Unfortunately, no one recalls that one of the Yukos security chiefs is in jail too. Do you think he acted on his initiative and at his own risk? He had no actual interest. He was not the company's main shareholder. It's obvious that he acted in the interests and under the directives of his bosses. How he acted is a separate matter. At least five murders have been proven. They wanted to include a tea shop building into their office in Moscow. The owner of this small business enterprise, a woman, was requested to give them her business. She refused to do that, and they hired a hitman who shot her just near her apartment, before her husband's eyes. The Mayor of Nefteyugansk demanded that Yukos pay taxes, and what happened to him? He was killed. The people, a married couple, who were hired by Yukos' security service to organise contract killings, tried to blackmail the company to get a share in the business, and they were also killed. All of these crimes are proven, we should not forget about that.

3 December 2009 Special TV programme "Conversation with Vladimir Putin: To Be Continued"

Question: Why don't all able-bodied people work in this country? It is necessary to make sure that salaries and wages for all professions should not differ from one another by more than five times."

Vladimir Putin: I am in complete agreement with this. There is an enormous gap between those people who earn high incomes, and those on the minimum wage. It is one of the key economic and social problems. We must bridge that gap. We have a special programme on combating poverty. The crisis has shaken it a little, but we will definitely implement it fully in the future. That is something we'll work on.

3 December 2009 Special TV programme "Conversation with Vladimir Putin: To Be Continued"

The planned economy showed its inability to become competitive. But it was not always like this. In 1929, during the Great Depression in the United States, people died of hunger while the planned economy of the Soviet Union saw good growth rates. There was a completely different situation here. Engineers and experts from the U.S. came to work in the Soviet Union. I know such people personally. Then, as the technological revolution started to develop, the situation changed, and the planned system turned out to be completely unsustainable. It started to fail and showed that it was uncompetitive, and this had economic, social and political consequences. In the GDR [German Democratic Republic], people saw that the standard of living in the FRG [Federal Republic of Germany] was higher and people there felt free, could move freely around the world and took active part in the political life of their country. Unfortunately, there was nothing similar in the socialist system. It was uncompetitive.

8 November 2009 Vladimir Putin gave an interview for NTV Television's documentary "The Wall"

You have made thousands of people hostages to your bloated ambitions, inefficiency and, possibly, greed. It cannot be tolerated. Where is the social responsibility of the business community? We talk about it at every meeting. We never forget it. ...

Do you know what the reaction was when I said that I was going to come here? "Don't! Let me show you another plant, built quite recently." ... Why were they dashing to and fro here, like frightened roaches, just before I arrived? Weren't any competent decision-makers here before, when people could not get their wages for months on end, and the heating was off? ...

4 June 2009 Vladimir Putin conducted a meeting on the situation at the plants in Pikalyovo, Boksitogorsk District, Leningrad Region

A few words about the possible transfer to a progressive income tax rate. We are currently using a flat scale, 13% for individuals. ... At first glance, the situation does not seem fair: Those who receive a large salary pay 13% and those who have a small income also pay 13%. Is this social justice? It appears that this scheme should be changed. But we used a progressive rate before, and what did we have then? Everyone paid from the minimal wage and received the rest "in envelopes," under the table. After we introduced the flat tax, tax revenue increased by twelve times over eight years. Take note of that – twelve times. And today this budget income exceeds that raised in VAT. The results are absolutely clear.

6 April 2009 Prime Minister Vladimir Putin reported to the State Duma on the Russian Government's performance in 2008

Please colleagues, when you discuss the budget, do not to be too harsh on the bankers. Of course you can call them whatever you like, you can offend them: "fat cat" and so on. It is an important sector of the Russian economy.

6 April 2009 Prime Minister Vladimir Putin reported to the State Duma on the Russian Government's performance in 2008

Now about unemployment benefits. ... We should help those who have worked until recently and have faced problems in connection with the crisis, these are the people we should help first. But ... if we grant these benefits to everyone and for life then, pardon me, what incentive will there be to create new jobs?

6 April 2009 Prime Minister Vladimir Putin reported to the State Duma on the Russian Government's performance in 2008

Regarding our gold and currency reserves. Nothing has been lost. We have no losses because, strange though it may sound, they have been placed competently. Over the past three years we have been removing our gold and currency reserves from the riskier instruments (I am disclosing a state secret) consistently and carefully, in order not to bring down the markets. I issued this directive when I was President three and a half years ago.

6 April 2009 Prime Minister Vladimir Putin reported to the State Duma on the Russian Government's performance in 2008

Alexey Kudrin: We joined the forum on financial stability. Incidentally, it was renamed the Financial Stability Board at the G20, with the English abbreviation FSB.

Vladimir Putin: No matter what they do, they always end up with FSB [formerly KGB].

4 April 2009 Prime Minister Vladimir Putin held a working meeting with Deputy Prime Minister and Minister of Finance Alexey Kudrin

The American economy will recover in the short and medium term, there is no doubt about it. Of course, we do not know what will happen later if they continue to pursue the same careless economic policy as in the previous years.

4 March 2009 Prime Minister Vladimir Putin visited members of staff and jobseekers at the Podolsk Employment Centre

Question: People's salaries have dropped, and unemployment is on the rise. Aren't you afraid that your popularity might plummet?

Vladimir Putin: If one just sits there thinking of how everything is plummeting, nothing will ever rise again.

4 December 2008 After the end of the televised question and answer session, Prime Minister Vladimir Putin gave an interview to the press

We are willing to acquire a share in industrial and banking capital if the business itself welcomes it. This is one of the ways to get industrial companies out of the crisis and re-privatise them when the crisis is over, and is in fact what the Swedish Government did when Sweden was experiencing a bad national financial crisis. In fact, all banks were nationalised and then passed back into private hands afterwards. There is nothing "homemade" about it. We will rely on patterns that have been tested in the world.

4 December 2008 After the end of the televised question and answer session, Prime Minister Vladimir Putin gave an interview to the press

Unlike the developed West European countries, we have very many poor people. They have no savings, no financial "fat" accumulated by previous generations. They have no money in their bank accounts. When I worked in St Petersburg and spent a period of internship in a European bank we were taken to a bank and shown the savings of older people. The savings were not great, but they ran into hundreds of thousands. It was a German bank. They simply showed us the savings. Our people do not have much money. So just to freeze wages and let the people shoulder the burden of combating inflation is not an option for us. We will not do it.

29 June 2008 Prime Minister Vladimir Putin met with members of the United Russia Parliamentary Party

The important thing is that globalisation should not make the poor still poorer and the rich still richer.

16 June 2008 Prime Minister Vladimir Putin had a meeting with World Bank President Robert Zoellick

As for Shell, we have settled our problems with them and we hope that no such problems will arise in the future. They should not arise because our partners must know that the colonial method of exploiting Russian resources has no chance.

31 May 2008 Prime Minister Vladimir Putin gave an interview to the French newspaper Le Monde.

We are developing our country according to the principles and criteria that have become established in the world, in the civilised world, and that can be applied to our reality, with due respect for our history, including the political history, the political culture of the Russian Federation, and our traditions. We will continue to act in this manner in the future.

31 May 2008 Prime Minister Vladimir Putin gave an interview to the French newspaper Le Monde

If you don't swindle people you will not come to the attention of the state. ... When people break the law they line their pockets, and tens of millions lose the rather modest savings that they've acquired over a lifetime. It provokes distrust and alienation between the overwhelming majority of the population and a small group of individuals who amassed billions of dollars in 5 or 7 years. That creates a lack of trust and that is the most important issue.

Interview with Time Magazine December 19, 2007 Given December 12, 2007

V. PUTIN (Turning to S. Weinstock): Semyon Mikhailovich, please, the plans of the companies constructing the pipeline system to the Pacific Ocean coast ... I understand that in carrying out this project we are to a significant degree minimizing the ecological risks.

301

S. WEINSTOCK [President, Transneft]: ... In mathematical modeling, the possibility of an accident is considered 100,000 times less likely than with transport by rail. ...

A. TISHANIN [Governor, Irkutsk Oblast]: ...The public, of course, is concerned that the pipeline will be laid 800 metres away [from Lake Baikal]. ... There is concern that the region is fairly seismic...

L. POTAPOV [President, Buryat Republic]: ...Political roosters have been multiplying on account of this matter, we have to stop this and start construction. This is my position.

V. PUTIN: Thank you, Leonid Vasilyevich. Regarding ecological expertise we have, thank goodness, someone to rely on. I would like to ask the vice-president of the Academy of Sciences of the Russian Federation Nikolai Pavlovich Laverov to express his views on this question.

N. LAVEROV: ... among seismologists who work in this region and among some engineering geologists there is the opinion that in the area north of Lake Baikal it would be better to lay the pipeline somewhat further to the north, that is closer to the watershed, because there is a danger that I ask be taken into account, that of the so-called landslide zones, against which we have no defence at the present time. Therefore I thought that, first, we do have to begin construction immediately... But at the same time as the construction we must look in this northern region for the possibilities of engineering-geological surveying...

L. POTAPOV: Excuse me, but this is in any case within the drainage basin, you are speaking incorrectly. This does not in any case go outside the drainage zone. You have to simply board the train, go through and take a look by rail. And you will clearly picture it.

N. LAVEROV: We were there on foot.

L. POTAPOV: But we were also there on foot.

V. PUTIN: Simeon Mikhailovich, is there the technological, the technical, possibility of going to the north as academic Laverov proposes?

S. WEINSTOCK: Vladimir Vladimirovich, in general you have put me in a bind, because to go...

V. PUTIN: Let's agree in this way. I feel that if you were hesitating that means it is possible, because if it wasn't possible, you would have answered without hesitation that it wasn't possible. Let's agree as follows: As academic Laverov has proposed, we need to start work from both ends. And the moment the point or points are reached when it will be necessary to go round Lake Baikal, by that time we will need to have worked out all the documentation and conduct all the necessary surveying in order to continue this work in the Baikal region. Moreover, the pipeline route must go north of that zone indicated by academic Laverov. This is how we will consider this matter settled.

Transcript of a Meeting on Social and Economic Development in the Siberian Federal District April 26, 2006 Tomsk

Steven Forbes: I am extraordinarily happy to meet you because you introduced the flat tax in Russia. I tried to do the same thing in the USA but it did not work out for me.

Vladimir Putin: There is still a good option. You just need to be registered as a resident in Russia. That's all.

Beginning of the Meeting with the Head of Forbes Publishing Company, Stephen Forbes June 13, 2006 Saint Petersburg

In today's world a nation's power is first and foremost defined by its economic strength. And the state of society, social policy, and defense all derive from the economy. They are all derivatives. If there is no possibility or, to put it more simply, if there is no money... What can you do? You can't go to the store, you can't buy anything, neither a gun, nor a missile, nor medicine. For this reason the economy is at the basis of everything.

Meeting with the Representatives of the Russian State Television and Radio Broadcasting Company May 13, 2006 Sochi

Incidentally, I think it would be a good decision to abolish the inheritance tax, because billion-dollar fortunes are all hidden away in off-shore zones anyway and are not handed down here. Meanwhile, people have to pay sums they often cannot even afford here just to inherit some little garden shack.

Annual Address to the Federal Assembly of the Russian Federation April 25, 2005 The Kremlin, Moscow

When privatisation began, when the country was just beginning to move over to the market, we thought that the new owners would be a lot more effective. This is right. Everywhere in the world private owners have proven more effective than the state.

But there is one thing that we must not forget here. Developed economies already have a smoothly functioning administrative system and in these countries, state revenues, which the state uses to meet its social commitments, depend directly on how effectively companies are run. What happened here, though, was that companies began working well, sometimes very well, but there was no real administrative system in place, as a result of which the state did not collect the revenue it needed.

That is why it seems to me, or rather, why I believe that we need to take another road and not end privatisation, but strengthen the state's organisation, reinforce the legislation and improve the way things are administered so as to ensure that the benefits of successful private companies spill over into the economy as a whole and can be felt by each individual.

Excerpts from the President's Live Television and Radio Dialogue with the Nation December 18, 2003 Moscow, the Kremlin

In any Western European country it would be impossible to make billions of dollars in just 5–6 years, but maybe these people did make the money legally. Having made their billions, they spend tens, hundreds of millions of dollars to protect their billions. We know how this money is being spent – to which lawyers, PR campaigns and politicians it is going...

There are always two sides involved in corruption – the side that gives the money and the side that takes it. It is not clear yet who is more guilty. Incidentally, it is Western business that suffers the most in Russia as a result of this corruption because it has the least protection. It does not have representatives in Russia's state power system and organisations. ...

The state should pay special attention to cases when crimes against people, including murder, were committed during the process of dividing up state assets. ...As for the privatisation process, despite all the difficulties and contradictions that accompanied it, we cannot go back over it now because the consequences would be even worse.

Statement for the Press and Answers to Journalists' Questions at a News Conference following the Russia-European Union Summit November 6, 2003 Rome

We want to build a socially-oriented market economy of the same kind that exists in Europe. This means that we recognize that private property and the market economy are much more effective than an administrative economy, a planned economy. This means that a private owner runs his or her own company more effectively, but the state creates an economically effective and socially sound tax system, and receives more resources in state revenues to solve social tasks.

Interview with the ANSA Italian News Agency, Corriere della Sera Newspaper and the RAI Television Company November 3, 2003 The Kremlin, Moscow

We will do all we can to ensure that our economy and society develop in predictable and stable conditions, both economic and political. But this does not mean that we are just going to curl up under a warm blanket of petrodollars.

Answers to Questions from Participants in the World Economic Forum Session in Moscow October 3, 2003 Moscow

All bosses want to have the right to issue licenses and permits, sign papers and receive payment for this under the table. That is a traditional Russian scourge, which became many times worse during the Soviet period because in a planned economy everything was decided by the state, the state was responsible for everything and everybody had come to take it for granted. But in reality this is not a productive way to go about things. And it is the main obstacle to the development of small and medium-sized business.

Excerpts from a Transcript of the Meeting with the Students of Kaliningrad State University June 27, 2003 Kaliningrad

But on the whole, it is obvious to everyone today that it won't be possible to develop the country unless we resolve the ecological problems. I don't just mean city dumps...but issues related to activities of the army and navy. ... In some places we have half-submerged decommissioned atomic submarines with nuclear reactors still aboard. ... Who is going to invest money in this or that region knowing that some sort of time bomb is lying somewhere nearby?

Excerpts from a Transcript of the Meeting with the Students of Kaliningrad State University June 27, 2003 Kaliningrad

You know, I don't really like the word "oligarch" used to describe big business representatives in Russia. In the sense that we usually use this word, an oligarch is a person with stolen money, who continues to plunder the national wealth, using his special access to bodies of power and administration.

I am doing everything to make sure this situation never repeats itself in Russia, and among big business representatives today, I

306

do not see anyone who acts in this way. Perhaps some of them try. Probably everyone involved in business always looks for ways to earn more money, and to do this as effectively and cheaply as possible. Society's task, our common task – because both the state and the media should keep a very close eye on this – is to make sure this situation does not arise in the country.

Press Conference with Russian and Foreign Media   June 20, 2003   The Kremlin, Moscow

Capital as such is not patriotic in itself. Capital always flows to where the best conditions exist for its use, whatever you might say or desire. So our task is above all to create such conditions and not cry about the fact that capital is flowing out.

Press Conference with Russian and Foreign Media   June 20, 2003   The Kremlin, Moscow

Question: How do you account for the brain drain from our country and what specifically is being done to slow it down or stop it?

Vladimir Putin: First of all, if brains leave the country, at least you can say that there are brains to begin with. And that already is good news. Secondly, it means that they are good quality brains because otherwise there wouldn't have been any drain. That is also good news. It shows the high standard of training. Third, if we want to see our economy integrated into the world economy we should welcome free movement of people, capital, labour and so on. The capital and skills will inevitably flow where they find better conditions for their application. This is the law of the market.

Extracts from a Transcript of the Meeting with the Finalists of the Student Essay Competition "My Home, My City, My Country"   June 5, 2003   The Kremlin, Moscow

We have a lopsided economy. In many ways we live off the energy sector. We must develop the processing industries and pay more attention to the "new" economy based on the latest technologies. We have to adjust our legislation and our government apparatus accordingly. We have to carry out an administrative reform, change the laws, mainly in the sphere of taxation, in order to stimulate these sectors of the economy.

Extracts from a Transcript of the Meeting with the Finalists of the Student Essay Competition "My Home, My City, My Country" June 5, 2003 The Kremlin, Moscow

If by free press you mean the freedom of individual oligarchs, as they are called, to buy journalists and dictate their will to them proceeding from their group interests and promote the oligarchic way of the development of Russia, which they have been imposing on the country over the past decade – if press freedom is interpreted in this way, then yes, it is under threat. I don't think we can allow certain individuals to determine the country's strategy at will, stuffing their pockets with illegally-acquired money.

Excerpts from a Talk with German and Russian Media April 7, 2002

In my country if a person steals a bag of potatoes or drinks too much vodka and starts a fight with his neighbour, he is either a troublemaker or a thief. He is put in jail. And if a person steals hundreds of millions of dollars, he is a political figure and he cannot be touched.

Extracts from a Joint News Conference with President Jacques Chirac of France January 15, 2002 Paris

If by oligarchs you mean business leaders, I think the problem of the influence of big business on the state is universal.

Interview with the French Newspaper Le Figaro October 26, 2000

I wouldn't say that the state and the oligarchs are confronting each other dagger in hand. This is more in line with the West European tradition. Rather, what we wield is a big stick, called "palitsa" in Russian, which can clinch an argument with one fell swoop. But we have not used it yet, we have simply taken it in our hands, and that has had a certain effect already. But if we are provoked, we will have to use it.

Interview with the French Newspaper Le Figaro October 26, 2000

Unless we make real efforts soon, then even the indigenous population will in several decades from now be speaking mainly Japanese, Chinese and Korean. So the question of the future development of the Far East and the Trans-Baikal region is very acute, I would say even dramatic.

Introductory Remarks at a Meeting on the Prospects of the Development of the Far East and the Trans-Baikal Region July 21, 2000 Blagoveshchensk

We should give a clear definition of the term "oligarch". If it means big Russian business which is doing spectacularly well through its own efforts – by introducing new goods, new technologies and breaking into new markets, we are all in favour of such business. We are proud of these fellow Russians. They are helping not only themselves but also their colleagues and the country.

But there is a different kind of "businessmen" who sponge on state budget money, enjoy easy-term credits and various exemptions from Russian legislation, in short, they grab state resources. Some of them are trying to use the resources they thus obtain to influence the government and society. We will wage an uncompromising war on such "oligarchs".

Interview with the Newspaper Welt am Sonntag (Germany) June 11, 2000

The ultimate goal is the well-being of the people. But that cannot be achieved by just throwing in all our resources. The well-being of the people can only be based on real growth in the economy.

Interview with the ORT TV Channel February 7, 2000 Moscow

Mikhail Leontyev: One has the impression that ... the IMF is still not giving us loans, that we are being ill-treated.

Vladimir Putin: He who ill-treats us won't last three days. Forget about "ill-treated". ... We are a large and basically self-sufficient country. We shouldn't turn down loans. You know the famous Russian proverb: "If they give you something, take it, if they beat you, run." It is crude but correct. If they offer loans on good terms it would be folly to turn them down.

Interview with the ORT TV Channel February 7, 2000 Moscow

If we do not ensure that the state enforces the rules of the game, we will never create a good investment climate, and then all our numerous multi-billion resources will never be used to full capacity and in a proper way.

Interview with the RTR TV Channel January 23, 2000

Chapter 5

LIFE AND LEADERSHIP

[Journalist]: I would be remiss not to ask you about Yekaterina Tikhonova, who is in charge of an important project at Moscow State University. Our Western colleagues tell us that she is your daughter. Is it true and what do you think about her endeavour?

Vladimir Putin: I have read online publications and other sources about Yekaterina Tikhonova and my other possible relatives and daughters. A short while ago, everybody was saying that my daughters: a) study abroad; and b) live permanently abroad. Fortunately, no one is saying this now. What they are saying now is that they — and that is true — live in Russia and have never left Russia for permanent residence in any other country. They studied only at Russian universities. This does not mean that they do not have contacts with their colleagues. I am proud of them. ... They are making the first steps in their careers, and are doing well. ... I believe that everyone is entitled to their own destiny. My daughters have never been star-struck children. They never craved the limelight. They just live their lives and do so with great integrity.

Vladimir Putin's annual news conference December 17, 2015 Moscow

My family and my relatives as a whole suffered heavy losses during the Second World War. That is true. In my father's family there were five brothers and four of them were killed, I believe. On my mother's side the situation is much the same. In general, Russia suffered heavily.

Interview to American TV channel CBS and PBS September 29, 2015 Novo-Ogaryovo, Moscow Region

I never get personal. Never, because practice and experience show that personal contacts can always come in handy when settling relations between states or in resolving issues that affect millions of people. Therefore, one should leave any personal ambitions to oneself, for safekeeping.

Answers to journalists' questions September 29, 2015 New York

[Question]: I asked my acquaintances: what question would you ask Mr Putin? And all of my aunt's friends said in unison: he is Russia's number one bridegroom! Yes, that's it. A bachelor's life for more than a year. Does Mr Putin have the time for a private life?

Vladimir Putin: Please pass on my heart-felt greetings to the friends of your aunt. Thank them for such attention... Everything is fine, don't worry. (Laughter.) I recently had a conversation with a friend of mine from Europe, who is a big boss there. After all that happened last year, he asked: "Listen, is there love in your life?" And I said: "What do you mean?" He said, "Is there anyone you love?" I said, "Well, sure." "And does someone love you?" I replied "Yes." He must have thought I was neglected. So he said "Thank God," and drank a shot of vodka. So everything is fine, don't worry.

News conference of Vladimir Putin December 18, 2014 Moscow

Vladimir Putin: I also try to keep in touch with my fellow students from university.

Andrei Vandenko: Are they not necessarily billionaires?

Vladimir Putin: Not at all! They are ordinary people. They are mostly people who work in law enforcement, in the Interior Ministry, Prosecutor General's Office, attorney offices and administrative authorities.

Interview to TASS News Agency November 24, 2014

Vladimir Putin: I never take arbitrary decisions, decisions that may entail consequences I can't foresee. And if I can't foresee the consequences, I prefer to take some time. It's like overtaking another car on the road: never try unless you are certain. ...

Andrei Vandenko: And we are not in the opposite lane at the moment, are we?

Vladimir Putin: It's those trying to race us who are in the opposite lane now. We keep driving along in ours at a steady speed.

Interview to TASS News Agency November 24, 2014

We have this very old joke about a pessimist and an optimist: a pessimist drinks his cognac and says, "It smells of bedbugs," while an optimist catches a bedbug, crushes it, then sniffs it and says, "A slight whiff of cognac."

I would rather be the pessimist who drinks cognac than the optimist who sniffs bedbugs. (Laughter)

Meeting of the Valdai International Discussion Club October 24, 2014 Sochi

There is no disputing whatsoever that Russia is my life. That is a fact. Not for a second can I imagine myself without Russia. I've said in the past about how I looked through my family's genealogy in the archives. They all came from not far from Moscow, 120 kilometres away. There is a village where my forebears have lived since the 17th century, going all these long years to one and the same church. In this sense I feel a connection with the Russian soil and Russian people and could never live anywhere but Russia. Russia can of course get by without people like me, though. Russia has no shortage of people.

But since I have come to where I am today and to this office I hold, I consider it my duty to do all I can for Russia's prosperity and development and to protect its interests.

Meeting of the Valdai International Discussion Club October 24, 2014 Sochi

I am the biggest nationalist in Russia. However, the greatest and most appropriate kind of nationalism is when you act and conduct policies that will benefit the people. However, if nationalism means intolerance of other people, chauvinism – this would destroy this country, which was initially formed as a multi-ethnic and multi-confessional state. This would lead us not only into a dead end but also to self-destruction. Russia will do everything possible to make sure it doesn't happen.

Meeting of the Valdai International Discussion Club October 24, 2014 Sochi

It is not possible to work in espionage all your life. You see, I also changed my place of employment for the better. (Laughter.) You know, Henry Kissinger once told me – I respect him very much – he is an interesting, very smart person. We met in St Petersburg in the 1990s. I was meeting him at the airport, and he began to ask me where I worked. I began to list the places, but without actually mentioning the particular institution where I had worked. And he kept asking me: "And before that?" Finally, he "got" me. I said, "I worked in Soviet intelligence." He looked at me and told me: "All decent people start out in intelligence. I did, too."

Russia Calling! Investment Forum October 2, 2014 Moscow

People come to me when an idea is already in a somewhat developed stage. The people who would come to me would be the Chief of the General Staff, or the Defence Minister, if we speak of the defence industry, or Mr Kostyukov if it has to do with your Institute. Also, you may be aware that I have annual meetings with the Defence Ministry leadership and chief designers. We meet in November and spend a week discussing current and prospective issues – every day for a whole week. During the year, I regularly turn to certain issues in one way or another, and once a year we get together to brainstorm the situation to see what has been done and where we need to go from there.

However, when we debate which direction to move in and what is more promising (in your area, in nuclear power or in rocket and missile engineering) and more efficient in terms of 'value for money', this is when I get involved. However, it is up to the industry leaders, heads of facilities and institutes to decide. I do not undertake the authority to cut things or lobby certain ideas.

Meeting with young nuclear scientists September 19, 2014 Sarov

V. Zhirinovsky [Leader of the Liberal Democratic Party]: My general origins (this is not my analysis but one that was done by American specialists) my general origins are Albert Einstein and Napoleon. ...

G. Zyuganov [Chairman of the Communist Party]: Generally speaking, I have a peasant background. ...

V. Putin: Like most people here I do not know my genetic origins, unfortunately. I am not interested in asking American specialists because it is not known what they will ascribe to me, in the best case scenario they will say that my family founder was a bear. But that would be the best case scenario.

Joint meeting of State Council and Council for Implementation of Priority National Projects and Demographic Policy April 21, 2014 The Kremlin, Moscow

The most important thing in any sphere of activity is to feel that you are a professional and to constantly increase your level of expertise and the quality of your work.

Interview to Russian and foreign media January 19, 2014

How to control one's weight? Don't overeat. How to stay in shape? Do sports. There are no magic pills here. I do a bit of sports every day. ... That's nothing special, but I do it regularly. You know the saying: the chicken pecks grain after grain.

Interview to Russian and foreign media January 19, 2014

My personal view is that society should look after its children at least in order for it to be able to reproduce and grow, and not only on account of immigrants, but from its own population base.

Interview to Russian and foreign media January 19, 2014

If you want to know what I personally think about this, a person's sexual orientation actually does not make any difference to me. I know some [homosexuals] and am on absolutely normal, even friendly, terms with them. ... I do meet with those who live here, and talk to them. ... I even present some of them with state decorations for their achievements in their work, not for their sexual orientation.

Interview to Russian and foreign media January 19, 2014

Whatever level of administration a person is at, the most important thing is not to shirk responsibility for exercising your powers. This is definitely the most important thing. The minute the head of a state, or a region, or a municipality begins to dodge responsibility – that is the end of it: everything begins to fall apart. This is a matter of principle. That is the first concept.

The second is that one should never make arbitrary decisions; you should listen to people with differing points of view regarding this or that issue. However, if we fork out, as we tend to say at our meetings, you need to be brave enough to take responsibility for the final decision.

In addition, there is one more thing I would like to draw your attention to. People who for a number of reasons find themselves at such a high level of authority, those who are vested with the trust of their people, should never break away from the life of ordinary citizens of their country. You need to always be aware of the people's everyday concerns and the challenges they face; you have to constantly think, day and night, of how to help them overcome those challenges. Otherwise, your work is of no use.

News conference of Vladimir Putin December 19, 2013 Moscow

There is no hiding behind your teammates in martial arts. Whether in the ring, or on the mat or the tatami, there is only you and the opponent, and it means a lot to take victory in an uncompromising and honest fight.

Greetings to participants and guests of the World Combat Games 2013 October 18, 2013

I think you can say I am a pragmatist with a conservative perspective. It would be hard for me to explain this, but I always take realities of today, and lessons from the distant and recent past into consideration. I try to take these events and this experience and project them into the future, over a medium and long-term perspective. ...

Conservatism does not mean stagnation. Conservatism is based on traditional values, but at the same time it has one essential element, which is the goal of development. I think it is of fundamental value. It is common practice for conservatives in all countries to accumulate resources and provisions for economic growth, and then the revolutionaries come and apportion it all out one way or another. However, representatives of leftist movements or parties and radicals can also be revolutionaries, they apportion everything out and everyone is happy. Then comes the moment of disappointment – as it turns out, everything has been eaten and ruined and it's time to start accumulating again. People realise this and turn to the conservatives again. The latter start working again, accumulate something, but then they are told that it's enough and the time has come to apportion it out again. So this cycle is an integral part of politics.

Interview to Channel One and Associated Press news agency September 4, 2013 Novo-Ogaryovo, Moscow Region

If anyone thinks ... that I have a dismissive attitude to the minority opinion, they are wrong. I try to hear and to take on board as much as possible. When I make decisions, I try to find out all the different points of view on the issue.

News conference of Vladimir Putin December 20, 2012 Moscow

Question: Good afternoon Mr President, there are many jokes going around about you, no doubt your aides have told them to you?

Vladimir Putin: No, they are afraid to tell me. (Laughter.)

Question: The latest one concerns the end of the world, for example: "Putin promises so much that he knows exactly when it will come". ...

Vladimir Putin: Just a second. First of all, I do know when the world will end.

Question: When?

Vladimir Putin: In approximately 4.5 billion years. As far as I remember, this is because of the life cycle of our sun, which is 7 or 14 billion years. We are now in the middle of the cycle. I may be wrong and it may only be around 7 billion years, but around 4.5 billion have passed, and after another 4.5 billion years everything will end, the reactor will simply go out. That will be the end of the world. But before that point something else will happen to the sun: it will become a white dwarf and life will already stop at that time. If you look at the question of the end of the world from this perspective, it will end earlier.

Question: So you are not afraid of this?

Vladimir Putin: Why be afraid if it's inevitable?

News conference of Vladimir Putin December 20, 2012 Moscow

The West views you as a hawk. What do you think about this portrayal of you?

Vladimir Putin: First of all, the hawk is a good bird. ... But I'm against all clichés. We always have and always will carry out a deliberate policy that seeks to facilitate Russia's development.

17 October 2011 Interview with Prime Minister Vladimir Putin

I have been practising the Asian martial arts for my entire life, and I have a philosophy for relating to a partner. No matter who he is, he must be treated with respect. This philosophy is based on both general human considerations and pragmatism. If we think that we are surrounded by some small fry that are not worthy of our attention, we may take some unexpected hits, and very painful ones at that.

17 October 2011 Interview with Prime Minister Vladimir Putin

People usually seek personal gain while dealing with top officials. Unfortunately, this is the truth. Well, not all people. There are some people I know who have very strict rules for themselves and never make any personal requests, but just live their own lives and handle their own problems. But for most, it is highly tempting to ask a big boss for help, which suggests that a big boss should always keep his or her distance.

17 October 2011 Interview with Prime Minister Vladimir Putin

Decisions must be made soberly and coolly, but making them is impossible without any emotion. ... I think about how they will affect the average citizen. ... I remember how my father walked out onto the landing and carefully read the electric meter. You know, our older generation is precise, meticulous... They may have been pennies, but he wrote down every penny, every kilowatt, and always made these payments on time. And it was important for the family. And I remember all of this – how he went up the ladder and read the meter. This is life – the real lives of ordinary families. We must never forget that.

20 March 2011   Prime Minister Vladimir Putin's interview with the Rossiya and Moya Planeta

Oksana: We learned just a short while ago that you can play the piano, and you can sing, too. Is there any other talent you are hiding from the public?

Vladimir Putin: Well, that's an overstatement on your part. I can't really play the piano, but a friend once taught me to hit the keys with two fingers, and I did just that. Every person has a talent, but not everyone gets the chance to reveal it. Self-accomplishment is what I'd like to wish for every one of us. And the state will do what it can to make that happen. (Applause)

16 December 2010 Television channels Rossiya and Rossiya 24 and radio stations Mayak and Vesti FM have started broadcasting the annual Q&A session, "A Conversation with Vladimir Putin, Continued"

I remember being stopped by the Finnish traffic police for speeding. They were very professional and did not even fine me and for that I'm grateful to them. I still remember that incident. I regret breaking the traffic rules then and pledge never to do so in the future.

10 December 2010 Russian Prime Minister Vladimir Putin and Finnish Prime Minister Mari Kiviniemi hold news conference after talks

Question: In your family, your father fought in the war and your mother survived the blockade. Did your parents talk to you about the war when you were a child?

Vladimir Putin: Of course they did, but not very often. In general, it was not a subject we often discussed. I have a feeling that my parents did not like talking about it very much. Nevertheless, it was something we talked about, especially when marking particularly memorable events.

Question: Do you think they were trying to protect you, or was it a painful subject for them?

Vladimir Putin: I think it was painful for them. They avoided the topic. Not least because they lost a child during the war: my brother, whom I never met. It was a tragedy, they were clearly very difficult times. That's why they did not like talking about it.

Question: What about your personal perception of it... Naturally, this is something that changes with age... While in childhood, it is mainly shaped by war movies, etc., with age you come to understand the tragedy of it. How did your understanding of what the war and blockade really were change as you grew up?

Vladimir Putin: You know, with age I came to see those stories they told me as a child in a different light. For example, I knew that my mum visited my father in hospital after he had been wounded. My father had told me that he was with a partisan unit in the beginning of the war, but I later found out that in reality he was with a sabotage group. When I was President, I requested documents from the archives. My father was no longer alive then, he had already passed away. Amazingly, the documents tallied with everything he had told me, right down to the tiniest detail. I did learn that there were 28 of them who were sent across enemy lines to gather intelligence and carry out sabotage operations. Only four of those 28 survived. One thing that my father had never told me, something I learnt from the archives, was that the group was led by a Russian citizen of German descent.

Question: He wasn't interned at the beginning of the war?

Vladimir Putin: I don't know. I don't know anything about that. They only gave me the archival documents, record cards, personal records, and I was surprised to learn that the group was led by an ethnic German. It was probably because he knew German. I do not know why those in charge back then made that decision. But it was new to me, it was something I knew nothing about. After that my father was sent to the front and fought at the Neva Bridgehead. He was wounded there, and my mother told me how she would visit him in hospital. My father shared his hospital food ration with her and would give her provisions. And then he started having fainting fits from starvation, as he was probably giving all his food to my mother. The hospital staff noticed this, and as sad as it may sound now, but this was the thinking back then, they banned her from visiting. They had banned her from visiting him, and this was truly tragic, when he had recovered, he went to visit her at home. He arrived as they were carrying corpses out of the building, and there among those corpses, he saw my mum. It turned out she was still alive. I will not go into all the details here, but they carried her back in and she lived. It was one thing when they told this story when I was very young. Of course I did not really understand the scale of the tragedy the city, its residents, and my relatives experienced during the war. Later, I started to see everything differently and came to understand the true meaning of the blockade, the enormous suffering and the great tragedy it was for millions of people. My understanding has certainly changed with age.

Question: Mr Putin, what are your primary associations with the word blockade?

Vladimir Putin: The first thought that comes to mind is the tragedy of it, that it was a tragedy for a large number of ordinary citizens. The soldiers were at least fed a little better, but there was a period when civilians were on their own. They died from cold and starvation. Therefore, the blockade is above all an enormous tragedy for millions of people. On the other hand, it is also an unprecedented feat of heroism, and endurance. It was a quite remarkable feat: the amazing endurance of such a large number of people, their collective heroism.

9 May 2010 Prime Minister Vladimir Putin's interview with the filmmakers who made the documentary Lessons from History

Vladimir Putin: Why do you think it's more rewarding to give than receive?

Journalist: It is nice to give a present because you think about the person. It is nice to see the emotions when you give presents.

Vladimir Putin: No. Let's be honest. It is gratifying because you feel like a decent person. Your self-esteem improves. "Well done!" you think to yourself. So it is we who should be grateful to those who accept our presents.

29 December 2009 Prime Minister Vladimir Putin talks with journalists about the outcomes of his visit to the Primorye Territory

Certificate of income of Prime Minister Vladimir Putin for the reporting period from January 1, 2008, to December 31, 2008, on properties owned by him, bank deposits, securities and property commitments.

Income from the principal place of employment: 4,622,400 roubles; military pension: 100,600 roubles; real estate: a 77 sq m flat; a land plot of 1,500 sq m, and a garage on a collective parking lot; a share in a garage cooperative giving the right to park one car; vehicles: two GAZ M21 cars, 1960 and 1965 models; 1987 Skiff trailer; securities: 230 shares of St Petersburg Bank, worth 230 roubles at 1997 prices.

Certificate of income of Lyudmila Putin, the wife of Prime Minister Vladimir Putin, for the reporting period from January 1, 2008, to December 31, 2008, on properties owned by her, bank deposits, securities and property commitments.

Over the reporting period from January 1, 2008, to December 31, 2008, Lyudmila Putin, the wife of Prime Minister Vladimir Putin, earned no independent income and owned no properties, including in the form of securities; she had no property commitments.

6 April 2009 Information has been published on the earnings of Prime Minister Vladimir Putin and his wife, Lyudmila Putin

I was a little boy when I started my judo training. And I was seriously attracted to martial arts, their special philosophy, relations with the opponent and the rules of combat. Judo is an exercise both for your body and your spirit. It develops strength, reaction, and fitness. It teaches self-control, the ability to feel the moment, to see the opponent's strengths and weaknesses, to strive for the best results. And most important is constant improvement and self-cultivation. You will agree that such knowledge, skill and experience are essential for a politician.

6 August 2008 Russian Prime Minister Vladimir Putin gave an interview to the Chinese state news agency Xinhua and to the Renmin Ribao newspaper

As President, I never felt it beneath me to listen to the views of specialists and I often adjust my own views under the influence of respected colleagues when I see that what they are saying is correct, constructive and justified.

Transcript of Annual Big Press Conference February 14, 2008 The Kremlin, Moscow

There is only one measure of power and that is people's trust. There is no other measure. All the rest is just an illusion of power, and a very dangerous illusion it is. Trust is the most important component of power and it is something I value immensely. I am very grateful to people for feeling that I really have spent these last eight years working honestly, toiling like a galley slave every day. And I see that there are also people who do not see things in this way, who do not perceive it as I do, but I do not blame them for this, I blame myself for not having managed to reach out properly to these people. This means I did not work hard enough and could have done more. But overall, what I am most grateful for is people's trust.

Interview with Time Magazine December 19, 2007 Given December 12, 2007

Until I went to Germany and lived in that linguistic environment, I didn't speak the language well. ... With regard to English, I only study it from time to time, for 10–15 minutes at a time, but fairly regularly. ... It is not always possible to talk about everything with an interpreter present. ... A foreign language is not just a gateway to communication, it is a gateway to the culture of another people. It is very interesting, it opens up a whole world. In fact, having a second language is like living another life.

Live with President Vladimir Putin - Hot line (excerpts) October 18, 2007 The Kremlin, Moscow

If I always paid attention to different threats or the recommendations of the security services, I would never leave my house.

Joint Press Conference with the Federal Chancellor of Germany, Angela Merkel, on the Results of the Ninth Round of High Level Russian-German Intergovernmental Consultations October 15, 2007 Wiesbaden

Do you change your watch to local time [when traveling]?

Vladimir Putin: No, my watch is always on Moscow time.

Responses to Questions from Russian Journalists September 10, 2007 Abu Dhabi

When I, as someone who grew up on the streets of Leningrad, hear about something elitist, I always find myself immediately feeling suspicious towards it, because I get the feeling that is something beyond the reach of ordinary citizens, something cut off from citizens and from the people.

Excerpts from Transcript of Meeting with Participants in the National Russian Conference of Humanities and Social Sciences Teachers June 21, 2007 Novo-Ogaryovo

Russia has always been a very pious country, a very religious country. My father's family lived close to Moscow, I think about 120 or 130 kilometres away from Moscow. And colleagues looked in the archives and traced this family's history back to 1680, I think, sometime at the end of the 17th century. And do you know how they calculated this? Through church records and mainly through so-called records of confession. When people come to confession every week. Imagine, a family lived for more than 300 years in one village and went to church every week. I have never really reflected on this before, on how sedentary and yet how stable society was at that time and in Russia in particular. For 300 years and in one village they went to one church.

Moreover, do you know what I found most interesting. The notes on these confession sheets. The priest made a schedule by hand of who was at confession and further on listed their surnames. Still further on were lists of who was absent from confession. (Laughter). Honestly, yes, it is surprising. But it was the next list that amazed me most: 'The reasons for absence from confession'. (Laughter). Can you imagine? It is simply surprising. And what did confession consist of, in those days, especially for peasants? They had to come in at the end of every week to confess to the priest, to give him an honest account of what they had done, of the sins they had committed. So during the week it was necessary to think twice about what you were doing because on Sunday you had to go to the priest and report on this. And this is a small society. Everything takes place in one small village, everyone knows one another.

Transcript of Meeting with Participants in the Third Meeting of the Valdai Discussion Club September 9, 2006 Novo-Ogaryovo

Sometimes Koni leaves the room where journalists are with a very happy face and cookie crumbs on her muzzle. For that reason I would like to say once again to everyone who comes to my house, and this time over the internet: please, do not feed my dog.

Answers to Questions Asked During the President of Russia's Interactive Webcast held 6 July 2006 July 13, 2006

My father was a worker at one of Leningrad's industrial enterprises and my mother was also a worker. We lived in a communal apartment... This is an apartment shared by several families. We had one room of just over 20 square metres and with virtually no conveniences. But this was not what mattered the most. What was most important was that I always felt the love, attention and care of my parents and the people who surrounded me, and so I do not recall this time as a difficult time and do not have bad memories of it. We had the basic minimum and really, people do not need such a lot to be happy.

Interview with Television Channel Nederland 1 and Newspaper NRC Handelsblad October 31, 2005

And are you able to talk to Vladimir Vladimirovich when you catch him?

Lyudmila Putin: We don't catch him. He simply doesn't get home until 11:30 or 12 midnight. This is the time when we can talk a little and ask about how the day went.

Interview with Lyudmila Putin June 1, 2005 Milan, Italy

Putin: Both my father and mother were ordinary citizens. We lived three of us in a small room, in a so-called communal apartment, without any conveniences. We did not even have a bath or a shower, and they worked a lot. I was actually left to myself and spent a good deal of time with other teenagers in the street...

Wallace: Is it true that you once chased rats with a stick?

Putin: Yes, I did do that once. And drew a very curious conclusion for myself: if a rat is driven into a corner, it turns back and attacks you, and does so very aggressively, and pursues the fleeing opponent. That taught me a lot.

Interview to CBS anchor Mike Wallace May 9, 2005

Question: Mr President, your brother died during the siege of Leningrad. Did you hate the Germans for this?

Vladimir Putin: I know that this caused my parents much suffering and they never forgot it, but there was never hatred towards the Germans in my family for this, strange as it may sound. My parents always said that it was not the people who were guilty, not the ordinary soldiers sent to war by the regime in power. It is not the people who carry the blame, but the ideology, in this terrible case, the ideology of national socialism.

My mother told me a story about my grandfather, who fought during the First World War. Troops on the opposing sides took up positions in trenches within sight of each other. Austrian soldiers had taken up position on the other side of the section where my grandfather was. My grandfather shot one of the Austrians and badly wounded him. The Austrian was lying there in a pool of his own blood and no one was making any moves to come and help him. My grandfather then climbed up out of the trench, went over to him and bandaged his wound. They embraced each other before parting.

Question: What did your parents tell you about their personal experience during World War II? How did your family greet the end of the war?

Vladimir Putin: My parents were reluctant to talk about those years. They were very difficult memories for them. They usually talked about the war only when friends and acquaintances came to our home. I was born in 1952. My parents never told me about how they greeted the end of the war, about May 8 and May 9, 1945. For them at that time it marked the end of an unimaginably difficult period in their lives. My father was wounded and was in hospital in Leningrad when the city was still besieged by the Nazi forces. At one point he came home to look for my mother and arrived right at the moment when the so-called "burial teams" were about to put her with the corpses and take her to the cemetery. But she was still alive and my father had to pull her out from under this mountain of corpses. She survived only because he gave her the rations that he was entitled to as someone who was wounded and recovering in hospital.

Joint Interview with Federal Chancellor of Germany Gerhard Schroeder for Bild Newspaper May 7, 2005

It is indeed here, on this patch, that my father fought... It is a small patch of land that is only 3 kilometres wide and 1.5 kilometres long. This place was the "key" to besieged Leningrad and played a very important role in the defence of the city and in breaking the blockade. Here my father really did fight, was seriously injured and then, in hospital in Leningrad, this seemingly tragic circumstance saved the life of my mother, as she was then also in the Leningrad blockade, and as they said, he fed her from his hospital rations. But they could not save their son who fell ill and died in the Leningrad blockade. This was my brother, whom I never saw. Every Leningrad family has such a loss on account of the war.

Visit to the Nevsky Patch Memorial January 27, 2004 Kirovsk, Leningrad Region

I think one should most be guided in one's activities, not by the opinion of other people, but rather by one's own conscience.

Interview Granted to Bulgarian National Television and the Newspaper Trud February 28, 2003

Why does Vladimir Putin wear his wrist watch on his right hand? Are you left-handed?

Vladimir Putin: It's just a habit. No, I am not left-handed. I like my watch to dangle around my wrist. And the winder, if it is on the left hand always rubs against my hand, which hurts. That is the whole secret, as simple as that, nothing unusual about it.

Excerpts from a Transcript of a TV and Radio Broadcast (Hotline with the President of Russia) December 19, 2002 The Kremlin, Moscow

I lived almost 30 years in a communal apartment in Leningrad, even after becoming a KGB officer. And I know very well and feel how an ordinary Russian citizen lives. It is a big advantage when making decisions, it helps. Feedback from the people is very important, you must not lose it, but it is hard to keep because technological life is such that it leads, as everyone knows, to isolation.

Transcript of the News Conference for Russian and Foreign Journalists June 24, 2002 The Kremlin, Moscow

One should never be dismissive of criticism. It is always possible and necessary to identify the elements of the criticism that can help you to adjust your own actions, your own position and policy. ... Some people tend to criticise you no matter what you do. We don't mind that. On the whole, it may even be a good thing.

Excerpts from a Talk with German and Russian Media April 7, 2002

I would recall Roosevelt who led the country in a period of grave crisis. I think it was not by chance that he broadcast his 'fireside chats', talking at length to the country's people. I think his genius, like that of de Gaulle and Erhard, was that they felt what needed to be done, they felt the mood of their people and tried to be on the same wavelength as the people, and they did it very well.

You know what the most important thing is? The most important thing is the people's confidence in the country's political leadership. Only then can economic reforms and transformations in the economic and political spheres be carried out. If we go back to the early period of the activities of President Roosevelt, when he assumed leadership of the country, the economy and society were in turmoil, people had to trust him so that he could effectively carry out his plans.

Interview with the Wall Street Journal February 11, 2002

When did you earn your first money and how did you spend it?

Vladimir Putin: ... I first earned money when I was a member of a student construction team. We went to the Komi Republic where we cut down trees for a power transmission line to be made, and we built and repaired houses. I earned about a thousand roubles, a fantastic amount at the time. A car cost around 4000 then, I think. I must confess that I made very poor use of that money. I won't tell you how.

Live with President Vladimir Putin - Hot Line (excerpts) December 24, 2001 Moscow

I find it strange that you say I had a difficult childhood. It may appear so to people who lived in affluence and who enjoyed all the benefits of modern civilization. I did not have such opportunities, but I never felt disadvantaged or miserable. Basically I had the same kind of childhood as millions of Soviet – now Russian – citizens, perhaps even a better childhood in some ways. The main thing was not the material everyday conditions in which I lived, the main thing was the moral conditions. And what mattered was that everybody had affection for me. My parents were very fond of me, I have always felt that, and I am very grateful to them for that.

Interview with the American Broadcasting Company ABC November 7, 2001

The person at the top of the power pyramid should never forget that he should act in such a way as to be able tomorrow to live in this country, look people honestly in the eye and recall fondly the times when he was taking decisions on which the fates of millions of people depended.

Interview with the German Magazine Focus September 19, 2001 Sochi

In order to work with people effectively you have to be able to establish a dialogue and bring out the best in your partner. If you want to achieve results you have to respect your partner. And to respect means to recognise that he is in some way better than you are. You should make that person an ally, make him feel that there is something that unites you, that you have some common goals.

Conversation with Heads of Local Bureaus of Leading US Media Outlets June 18, 2001 Moscow

I know that some leaders in other countries, even US presidents, once worked in intelligence. I served my country and I did it honestly and I have nothing to repent about. And I must say that, strange though it may sound, I have never broken the laws of other countries.

From an Interview with the Canadian CBC and CTV Channels, the Globe and Mail Newspaper and the Russian RTR Television December 14, 2000

My mother was a believer. In the former Soviet Union it was not just unfashionable, as it is now, but it was even dangerous. And she had me baptised in church, not secretly, but without publicising the matter. ... I am proud to be associated with the Russian Orthodox Church. I think it is a great honour. It links me to my people, its culture, and it gives me inner calm and moral fortitude. I think it is very good.

Interview with the French Newspaper Le Figaro October 26, 2000

Larry King [asking about the Kursk submarine tragedy]: In retrospect, Mr. President, is there anything you would have done differently knowing what you know now?

Vladimir Putin: ... There were some suggestions and recommendations made to do something different. To go immediately to the location of the tragedy, to go down in the rescue vessel to the submarine and so on. You are smiling yourself, but that's true...

Larry King: I don't think security would have let you do that.

Vladimir Putin: In such situations I don't ask permission from security. Security exists for me, not I for them.

Interview with CNN's Larry King Live September 8, 2000 New York

I enjoy reading Russian classics, especially Dostoevsky and Tolstoy. I am fond of Hemingway. I used to really love Saint-Exupery. I memorised "The Little Prince" by heart.

Interview with the French Weekly Paris-Match July 6, 2000

I am absolutely certain that for someone involved in politics willpower is the most important quality. People who have no willpower are just experts. They may be good experts or bad experts, but they are specialists who can only give advice. Without willpower you cannot make decisions.

Excerpts from Transcript of a Meeting with Students at the Irkutsk State University February 18, 2000 Irkutsk

Question: A terrorist organization has declared open season on you. ...

Putin: ...There is a popular opinion that if you are afraid of a dog, it will bite you some day, but if you behave as its owner, it will wag its tail. This is how we should behave in dealing with criminals.

Excerpts from Interview to Baltika Radio Station February 24, 2000 St. Petersburg

If you behave in a disorganised and lax fashion, this spreads down the chain of command. It sends the wrong signal to the whole government. So you have to be tough and demanding.

Interview with the ORT TV Channel February 7, 2000 Moscow

Mr Yeltsin invited me to come and see him and said that he wanted to offer me the prime minister's job. ... Incidentally, he never used the word 'successor' in his conversation with me then, but spoke of becoming 'prime minister with prospects', and said that if all went well, he thought this could be possible. ... I thought then, if I can get through a year that will already be a good start. If I can do something to help save Russia from falling apart then this would be something to be proud of.

Vladimir Putin Personal Website en.putin.kremlin.ru

INDEX

INDEX

INDEX

INDEX

INDEX

INDEX